城市动员 CITY MOBILI-ZATION

BYOB

BRING YOUR OWN BIENNALE

"09香港·深圳城市\建築雙城雙年展"

"2009 Hong Kong & Shenzhen Bi-City Biennale of Urbanism\Architecture"

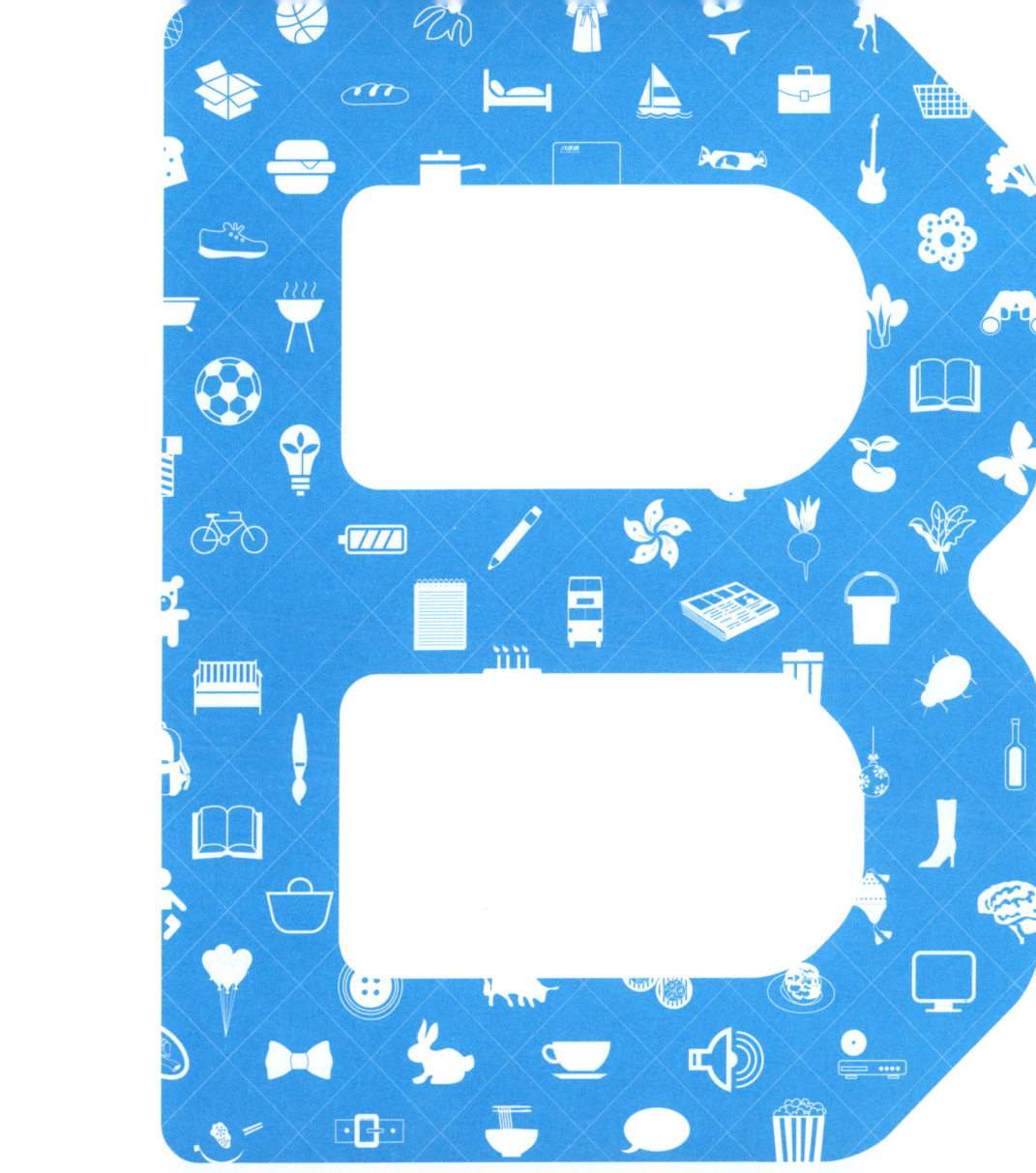

instant
culture

architecture and
urbanism as a
collective process

Edited by Eric Schuldenfrei and Marisa Yiu

mccm creations

Notes from the Editors

Eric Schuldenfrei and Marisa Yiu // editors

Hong Kong's rapid transformation has produced a culture of the "instant," where desires, market forces, global-local exchanges, technologies, and a need for immediate gratification dominate our cultural landscape and social behaviors. This book brings together a multitude of voices from the design, architecture, planning, and arts community to examine this situation as a general provocation and a cross-over of documentation, statements, essays, and thoughts. What kinds of contemporary conditions unique to this region can elevate new ways of addressing social sustainability in its various forms?

Throughout this book a panoply of activities, interactions, and exhibitions are documented from the Hong Kong component of the Hong Kong & Shenzhen Bi-City Biennale of Architecture\Urbanism, which took place at the West Kowloon Cultural District site and along its waterfront. We have invited responses from individuals to answer a series of questions, tailored to the person's expertise, to further our mode of interaction and experimentation that thrived throughout the Biennale. With the book we seek to continue the crucial role as cultural provocateurs by questioning regional values, cultural consumption, architecture and the environment, as well as global pressures that all cities currently face.

Instant Culture reflects our experience as curators in a constant race against time and resources. With a limited budget and unsuitable buildings on the West Kowloon site in which to house the Biennale, the challenges were large and wide. Yet, with optimism, we saw this as an advantage. It is like a cup of instant noodles, an opportunity for nourishment in a time of need, but not necessarily something one should maintain as a consistent diet for long. Instead of an ad hoc approach conceived on pure speed, we wonder if there are more efficient structures in which to implement this event? Is the concept of a Biennale really to attain short-term goals, or should it provide the opportunity to rethink culture within our city? Could these events be far more probing, proactively addressing timely issues of how to tackle environmental demands and social problems by strengthening our urban strategies? By featuring architectural and art projects that are committed to cultural, creative, and economic enhancement, we believe in the considerable substance temporary installations offer by questioning the normative conditions.

During this process-driven Biennale, and the countless conversations around the book, we started to build a new type of audience – not as spectators, but as an audience of authors and contributors. *Instant Culture* illuminates and inspires a reassessment of our collective values by building productive dialogues across the disciplines. From outlining educational initiatives to debates that encourage greater exchanges of ideas, this study reformulates a critical reframing of the role of architecture and urbanism as tools and processes for cultural advocacy within Hong Kong and China.

Naturally, this publication would not have been possible without the many voices, friends, artists, architects, community members, public intellectuals, statisticians, volunteers, and the behind the scene humble administrators. Additionally, we would like to thank the dedicated curatorial team consisting of Claude Wong, Solomon Fong, Wang Ho, Amber Young, Chow Kayan, Sze Pui Ki, Janice Ho, Nick Gu, Jiaxin Chum, and Sam Yu; our fellow curators Alan Lo and Frank Yu; and our publisher MCCM Creations. Most importantly, we thank our families for their encouragement and support for our continuing challenge. Our modest book, at a cursory glance, may seem a little too pictorial and fragmentary; yet, it hopes to raise questions that are still unanswered, questions that require a collective rethinking of celebrating the differences and nuances in order to produce a socially sustainable future.

How I See the Hong Kong & Shenzhen Bi-City Biennale of Urbanism\Architecture

Raymond Fung // foreword

I feel privileged to be a member of the Steering Committee that launched the first and second "Hong Kong & Shenzhen Bi-City Biennale of Urbanism \ Architecture" in 2007 and 2009. The Biennale is a project extending beyond the economic ties of the two cities, reaching out to new dimensions in the exchange and discourse of architecture and urbanism – leading to deeper reflections and aspirations in the pursuit of both sustainable and quality living.

With different curatorial directions every two years, site selection is a crucial factor in setting the major theme for the Hong Kong component of the Biennale. The first Biennale was located within the heritage site of the Former Central Police Station Compound and was conducive to the theme "Refabricating City," inviting in different social strata to examine the issue of the regeneration of heritage buildings. The second Biennale featured the theme "City Mobilization," which uniquely and dynamically addressed the versatility of Hong Kong's largest open venue in the cultural arts domain – the site of the West Kowloon Cultural District.

The expansive forty-hectare site of the future West Kowloon Cultural District not only provides a green open space for art, culture and leisure, but also creates a paradigm shift towards a new urban strategy for Hong Kong, possibly becoming a model city by emphasizing low-density planning with a low-carbon footprint.

Before this first ever international scale Biennale, the temporary West Kowloon Waterfront Park area pioneered a small scale, artistic and participatory approach in its design. Seventy Hong Kong artists were invited to become involved with the design of the waterfront park by painting the light columns, while the general public was encouraged to engage in hand-printed graffiti as a public art participation exercise. This small opportunity was one step to opening up to a larger audience. The staging of this Biennale, with its multiple events, activities, and interactive projects, created an extravaganza that cemented the arrival of a new era in creative culture.

Leading the curatorial team with the concept of public participation via the slogan "Bring Your Own Biennale (BYOB)," Marisa, Eric, Alan and Frank initiated an echoing of the ideology of the West Kowloon Cultural District: to spread art and culture to all walks of life throughout the city. They believed the Biennale should take different sectors of the society into consideration and the content should evolve from environmental protection in its many interpretations. There were large-scale events such as experimental farms, outdoor bench designs, outdoor architectural installations, art education projects, local guided-tours in the Yau Tsim Mong area and outdoor musical performances. The most festive of all was a grand scale outdoor banquet which gathered thousands of the elderly to enjoy the feast, appreciate the arts, and experience our respect for the ageing of Hong Kong. This highlighted the important curatorial axiom of "City Mobilization."

The second Biennale in 2009 was exceptional as its scale and boundaries hugely surpassed those of the art events previously launched in the city. Among the many exciting activities and artworks, the highlight was the grand pavilion in paper tubes designed by the renowned Japanese architect, Mr. Shigeru Ban, who has been so generous to donate his idea for the formation of an iconic yet modest architecture for this successful event. Although we had failed to keep the pavilion for future use, I was grateful to have heard Eric's comments: "The effort that the Hong Kong Government has put into this cultural event is perhaps more promising than the effort made in many other cities, in terms of finance, collaboration and kindness."

Despite the exhaustion everyone experienced during the process, such an event would not have been possible without the collective effort and wisdom of the Curators, in addition to the financial support from the Home Affairs Bureau, as well as the collaboration of the Steering Committee members in extending their invaluable experience to resolve the countless hurdles.

social sustainability

contents

cultural education

participatory protocols

cultural
advocacy

Bring Your Own Biennale
City Mobilization

Marisa Yiu   Chief Curator Hong Kong

Bring Your Own Biennale (BYOB) is a catchphrase, framework, and approach envisioned to stimulate our collective role in the creation of an innovative Bi-City Biennale between Hong Kong and Shenzhen. It calls for individual participation and networked collaboration – working within and outside boundaries to generate unexpected results. BYOB makes the process of cultural production transparent, an approach that relies on the citizens and the city's infrastructure for our Bi-City engagement. It is at once contextual but also reflective, a unique opportunity to speculate on what our impact on the metropolis could be.

Our Biennale's central location in the future West Kowloon Cultural District provides an open platform for dialogue. By inviting inventive practices onto the site, we build upon people's interest and their participation to formulate this Biennale. Our Biennale is not a frozen, definitive statement comprised of vacant representations of architecture – but alive with debate, events, and activities inspired from decidedly "performative" (experimental and self-reflexive) practices.

The Hong Kong component of the Bi-City Biennale is about creating fresh tools and new ways of working, about designing intelligence, and appropriating mechanisms that deal with direct feedback to engage the public. This concept of public is diverse, and we embrace this diversity in the ownership of space, where public good, public space, and the public domain can be reconceptualized. Diversity within cities and the creation of cultural capital is complex, as exemplified by Sharon Zukin's critique on the "representations of culture in public space" in parks, art museums, and city streets. Thus BYOB asks: how is public culture defined? Who has the right to experience, conceptualize, and control culture? In essence, we are publishing a real-time "Users Manual" for this diversity, where the West Kowloon promenade site becomes a backdrop for creative speculation and dynamic ingenuity. We learn from people, from nature, and from our daily interactions. We are inspired by everyday practices, appreciate the informality and spontaneity that rubs up against the rigid, the formal, and the planned. Here we create

ephemera and use weblogs as social levellers to share and exchange information in order to generate new models and paradigms that fully embrace the creative cultural practice of architecture, art and urbanism.

We seek to examine the issue of sustainability not only from a material vantage point but also from a social one. Respecting sensitive ecologies, we not only look toward the organic farm, the wind farm, the solar farm, and the compost heap, but we intend to utilize our modest gains appropriately by generating socially sustainable practices of working.

Onsite mobility is supplied by way of an organic lunch for the energy source and a bicycle to provide a slight mechanical advantage. Once we have generated modest amounts of electricity, we utilize energy-saving LED lights to power the art and illuminate the paths. Interdisciplinary design competitions seek out enduring self-sufficient systems, which develop architectural prototypes as instruments to drive further engagement with a renewed focus on socially progressive models. By dynamically engaging the public, we learn directly from our own community, discover conscientious models of design, and showcase the collection of exemplars.

We ask you to help envision a new model metropolis that uses social and intellectual capital as the main driving force. While celebrating the 60th National Anniversary of the 30th Anniversary of Shenzhen as a Special Economic Zone, we seek more interaction. We believe the Pearl River Delta is a potential "model," always testing and speculating on its future. Hong Kong operates with efficiency, mediates, connects; it is at once global and local. Yet, we provoke and question our past to aspire for a unique, perhaps singular future. How can Hong Kong develop further as a model city? What is the "next" Hong Kong after 2046? What happens when the Frontier Closed Area border reopens? How will the relationship between Hong Kong and Shenzhen alter the entire region? Will Hong Kong's uniqueness accelerate further and be redefined once more? What visions can we produce that embrace the individual and the greater metropolis?

Our mode of operation is to condense information instead of simply dispersing it. We want YOU to bring the qualities of Hong Kong and Shenzhen onto the site, to highlight the power of creative activism. We want YOU to contribute, speak-out, and make your future cultural metropolis Hong Kong and Shenzhen *what you want it to be*. This form of speculation uses chatter, online "tweeting," and exchange and dialogue of unseen and unheard kinds to bring more to the site and more to the contemporary discourse of architecture, art, and urbanism in the making of our cultural and social landscape. Most significant is the critical role of the individual; that is, our individual voice and our independent judgment as designers, curators, pedagogues, and creative or productive citizens. This Biennale is about observing the subtle details in our urban environment: rediscovering the harbor's edge, redesigning the park, encouraging more street activity, recalling the significance of the sidewalk and the growth of grass. How does the individual and the collective relate to each other? How can we debate the social and cultural value of the "city," the "urban plan," "architecture," "artefacts," and "products" in this complex negotiation? How can architecture and the making of cities highlight the nuances of elitism and populism? Can low and high culture be used proactively? Architecture must communicate openness, transparency, and perform as active social registers, if not enlightened apparatuses.

This Biennale aspires to celebrate ownership and make oneself accountable in the design of your very own Biennale. We believe that a sincere process creates stronger provocations. On behalf of my fellow curators Alan, Frank, and Eric, we warmly invite everyone to make an imprint on the public cultural landscape of Hong Kong.

2009   **2010**

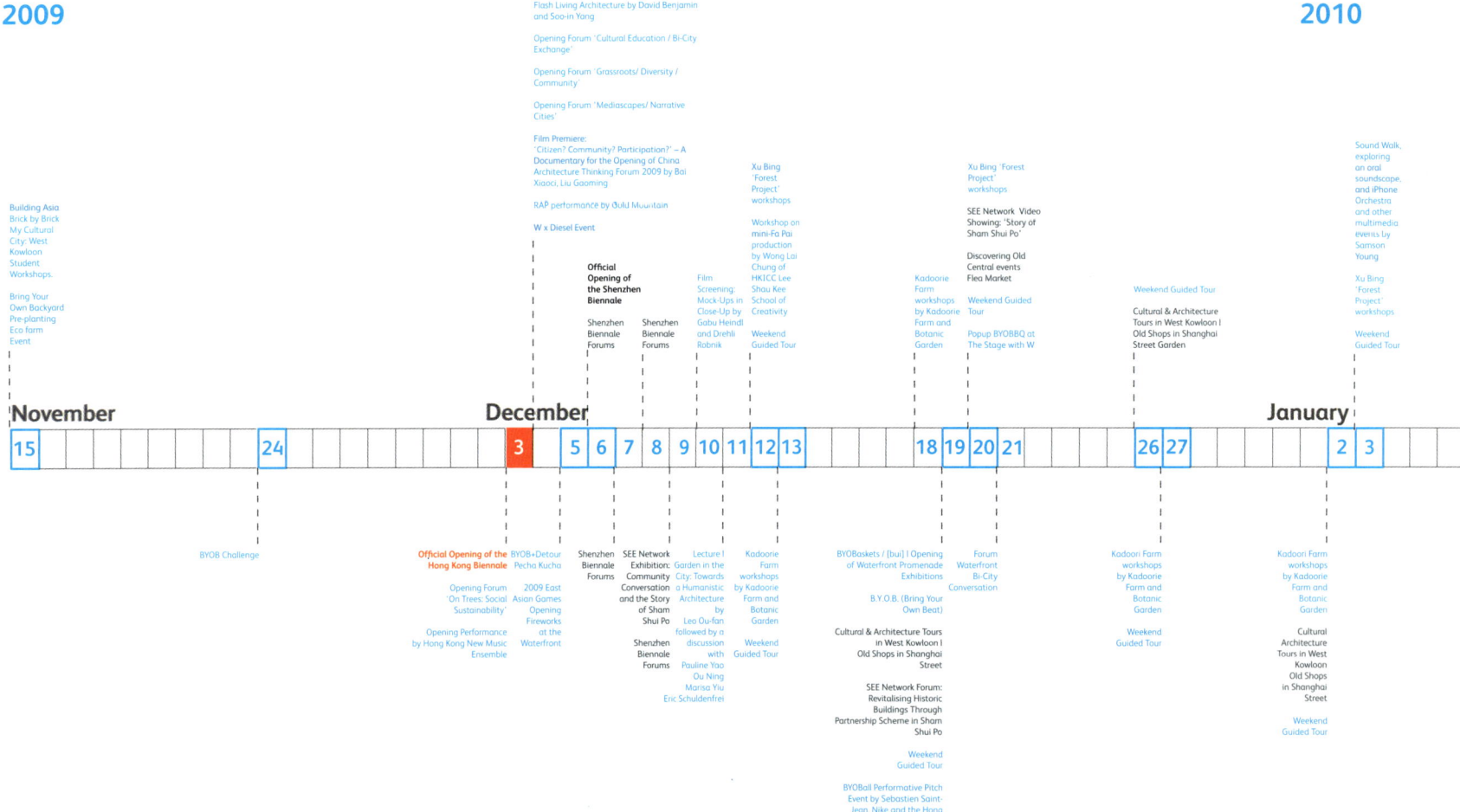

Flash Living Architecture by David Benjamin and Soo-in Yang

Opening Forum 'Cultural Education / Bi-City Exchange'

Opening Forum 'Grassroots/ Diversity / Community'

Opening Forum 'Mediascapes/ Narrative Cities'

Film Premiere: 'Citizen? Community? Participation?' – A Documentary for the Opening of China Architecture Thinking Forum 2009 by Bai Xiaoci, Liu Gaoming

RAP performance by Gold Mountain

W x Diesel Event

Building Asia Brick by Brick My Cultural City: West Kowloon Student Workshops.

Bring Your Own Backyard Pre-planting Eco farm Event

Official Opening of the Shenzhen Biennale

Shenzhen Biennale Forums

Shenzhen Biennale Forums

Film Screening: Mock-Ups in Close-Up by Gabu Heindl and Drehli Robnik

Xu Bing 'Forest Project' workshops

Workshop on mini-Fa Pai production by Wong Lai Chung of HKICC Lee Shau Kee School of Creativity

Weekend Guided Tour

Xu Bing 'Forest Project' workshops

SEE Network Video Showing: 'Story of Sham Shui Po'

Discovering Old Central events Flea Market

Kadoorie Farm workshops by Kadoorie Farm and Botanic Garden

Weekend Guided Tour

Popup BYOBBQ at The Stage with W

Weekend Guided Tour

Cultural & Architecture Tours in West Kowloon I Old Shops in Shanghai Street Garden

Sound Walk, exploring an oral soundscape, and iPhone Orchestra and other multimedia events by Samson Young

Xu Bing 'Forest Project' workshops

Weekend Guided Tour

November   **December**   **January**

| 15 | | | | | | | | 24 | | | | | | | | | 3 | | 5 | 6 | 7 | 8 | 9 | 10 | 11 | 12 | 13 | | | | | 18 | 19 | 20 | 21 | | | | | 26 | 27 | | | | | | 2 | 3 | | | |

BYOB Challenge

Official Opening of the Hong Kong Biennale

Opening Forum 'On Trees: Social Sustainability'

Opening Performance by Hong Kong New Music Ensemble

BYOB+Detour Pecha Kucha

2009 East Asian Games Opening Fireworks at the Waterfront

Shenzhen Biennale Forums

Shenzhen Biennale Forums

SEE Network Exhibition: Community Conversation and the Story of Sham Shui Po

Lecture I Garden in the City: Towards a Humanistic Architecture by Leo Ou-fan followed by a discussion with Pauline Yao Ou Ning Marisa Yiu Eric Schuldenfrei

Kadoorie Farm workshops by Kadoorie Farm and Botanic Garden

Weekend Guided Tour

BYOBaskets + [bui] I Opening of Waterfront Promenade Exhibitions

B.Y.O.B. (Bring Your Own Beat)

Cultural & Architecture Tours in West Kowloon I Old Shops in Shanghai Street

SEE Network Forum: Revitalising Historic Buildings Through Partnership Scheme in Sham Shui Po

Weekend Guided Tour

BYOBall Performative Pitch Event by Sebastien Saint-Jean, Nike and the Hong Kong Curatorial Team

Forum Waterfront Bi-City Conversation

Kadoorie Farm workshops by Kadoorie Farm and Botanic Garden

Weekend Guided Tour

Kadoori Farm workshops by Kadoorie Farm and Botanic Garden

Cultural Architecture Tours in West Kowloon Old Shops in Shanghai Street

Weekend Guided Tour

Events Bulletin Board

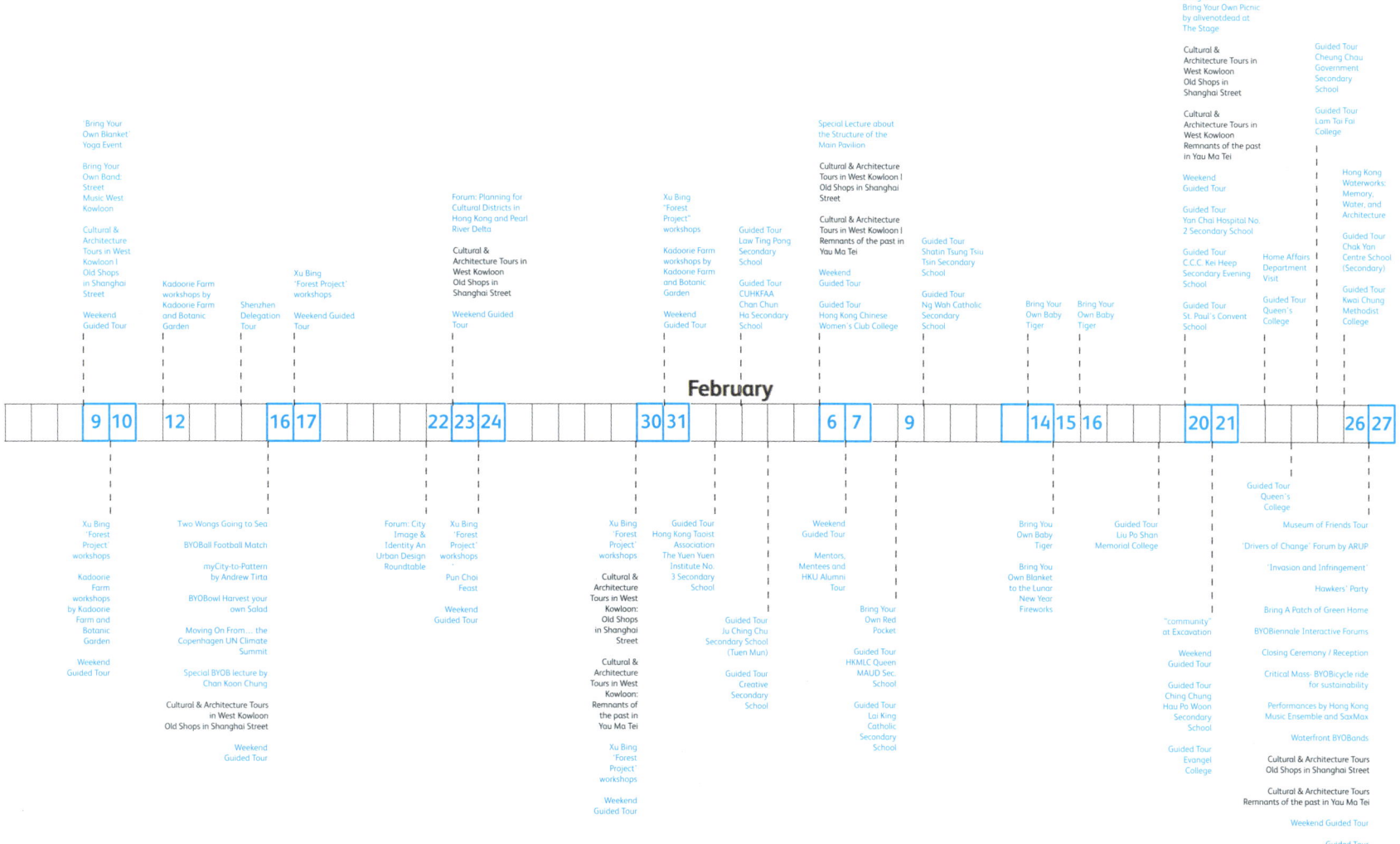

February

9 10 12 16 17 22 23 24 30 31 | 6 7 9 14 15 16 20 21 26 27

'Bring Your Own Blanket' Yoga Event

Bring Your Own Band: Street Music West Kowloon

Cultural & Architecture Tours in West Kowloon I Old Shops in Shanghai Street

Weekend Guided Tour

Xu Bing 'Forest Project' workshops

Kadoorie Farm workshops by Kadoorie Farm and Botanic Garden

Weekend Guided Tour

Kadoorie Farm workshops by Kadoorie Farm and Botanic Garden

Shenzhen Delegation Tour

Two Wongs Going to Sea

BYOBall Football Match

myCity-to-Pattern by Andrew Tirta

BYOBowl Harvest your own Salad

Moving On From.... the Copenhagen UN Climate Summit

Special BYOB lecture by Chan Koon Chung

Cultural & Architecture Tours in West Kowloon Old Shops in Shanghai Street

Weekend Guided Tour

Xu Bing 'Forest Project' workshops

Weekend Guided Tour

Forum: City Image & Identity An Urban Design Roundtable

Forum: Planning for Cultural Districts in Hong Kong and Pearl River Delta

Cultural & Architecture Tours in West Kowloon Old Shops in Shanghai Street

Weekend Guided Tour

Xu Bing 'Forest Project' workshops

Pun Choi Feast

Weekend Guided Tour

Xu Bing 'Forest Project' workshops

Cultural & Architecture Tours in West Kowloon: Old Shops in Shanghai Street

Cultural & Architecture Tours in West Kowloon: Remnants of the past in You Ma Tei

Xu Bing 'Forest Project' workshops

Weekend Guided Tour

Xu Bing "Forest Project" workshops

Kadoorie Farm workshops by Kadoorie Farm and Botanic Garden

Weekend Guided Tour

Guided Tour Hong Kong Taoist Association The Yuen Yuen Institute No. 3 Secondary School

Guided Tour Law Ting Pong Secondary School

Guided Tour CUHKFAA Chan Chun Ha Secondary School

Guided Tour Ju Ching Chu Secondary School (Tuen Mun)

Guided Tour Creative Secondary School

Special Lecture about the Structure of the Main Pavilion

Cultural & Architecture Tours in West Kowloon I Old Shops in Shanghai Street

Cultural & Architecture Tours in West Kowloon I Remnants of the past in Yau Ma Tei

Weekend Guided Tour

Guided Tour Hong Kong Chinese Women's Club College

Weekend Guided Tour

Mentors, Mentees and HKU Alumni Tour

Bring Your Own Red Pocket

Guided Tour HKMLC Queen MAUD Sec. School

Guided Tour Lai King Catholic Secondary School

Guided Tour Shatin Tsung Tsiu Tsin Secondary School

Guided Tour Ng Wah Catholic Secondary School

Bring Your Own Baby Tiger

Bring You Own Baby Tiger

Bring You Own Blanket to the Lunar New Year Fireworks

Bring Your Own Baby Tiger

Guided Tour Liu Po Shan Memorial College

Bring Your Own Picnic
Bring Your Own Picnic by alivenotdead at The Stage

Cultural & Architecture Tours in West Kowloon Old Shops in Shanghai Street

Cultural & Architecture Tours in West Kowloon Remnants of the past in Yau Ma Tei

Weekend Guided Tour

Guided Tour Yan Chai Hospital No. 2 Secondary School

Guided Tour C.C.C. Kei Heep Secondary Evening School

Guided Tour St. Paul's Convent School

"community" at Excavation

Weekend Guided Tour

Guided Tour Ching Chung Hau Po Woon Secondary School

Guided Tour Evangel College

Home Affairs Department Visit

Guided Tour Queen's College

Guided Tour Queen's College

Guided Tour Cheung Chau Government Secondary School

Guided Tour Lam Tai Fai College

Hong Kong Waterworks: Memory, Water, and Architecture

Guided Tour Chak Yan Centre School (Secondary)

Guided Tour Kwai Chung Methodist College

Museum of Friends Tour

'Drivers of Change' Forum by ARUP

'Invasion and Infringement'

Hawkers' Party

Bring A Patch of Green Home

BYOBiennale Interactive Forums

Closing Ceremony / Reception

Critical Mass- BYOBicycle ride for sustainability

Performances by Hong Kong Music Ensemble and SaxMax

Waterfront BYOBands

Cultural & Architecture Tours Old Shops in Shanghai Street

Cultural & Architecture Tours Remnants of the past in Yau Ma Tei

Weekend Guided Tour

Guided Tour St. Margaret's Co-educational English Secondary and Primary School

Instant Culture Pledge by Marisa Yiu, Alan Lo, Eric Schuldenfrei, Frank Yu: Instant Culture is cultural transparency, celebrating ownership, understanding social ecologies, believing that nature is culture, culture is nature, collective respect, building cross disciplinary platforms, long lasting social sustainability, producing constructive dialogues, building with innocence and inquiry, prioritizing our local communities, educational experimentation, refusing conclusive statements, celebrating craft and rethinking luxury.

Instant Culture Pledge Instant Culture is Cultural transparency, Celebrating ownership, Understanding social ecologies, Believing that nature is culture, culture is nature, Collective respect, Building cross disciplinary platforms, Long lasting social sustainability, Producing constructive dialogues, Building with innocence and inquiry, Prioritizing our local communities, Educational experimentation, Refusing conclusive statements, Celebrating craft and rethinking luxury. Instant Culture Pledge Instant Culture is Cultural transparency, Celebrating ownership, Understanding social ecologies, Believing that nature is culture, culture is nature, Collective respect, Building cross disciplinary platforms, Long lasting social sustainability, Producing constructive dialogues, Building with innocence and inquiry, Prioritizing our local communities, Educational experimentation, Refusing conclusive statements, Celebrating craft and rethinking luxury. Instant Culture Pledge Instant Culture is Cultural transparency, Celebrating ownership, Understanding social ecologies, Believing that nature is culture, culture is nature, Collective respect, Building cross disciplinary platforms, Long lasting social sustainability, Producing constructive dialogues, Building with innocence and inquiry, Prioritizing our local communities, Educational experimentation, Refusing conclusive statements, Celebrating craft and rethinking luxury. Instant Culture Pledge Instant Culture is Cultural transparency, Celebrating ownership, Understanding social ecologies, Believing that nature is culture, culture is nature, Collective respect, Building cross disciplinary platforms, Long lasting social sustainability, Producing constructive dialogues, Building with innocence and inquiry, Prioritizing our local communities, Educational experimentation, Refusing conclusive statements, Celebrating craft and rethinking luxury. Instant Culture Pledge Instant Culture is Cultural transparency, Celebrating ownership, Understanding social ecologies, Believing that nature is culture, culture is nature, Collective respect, Building cross disciplinary platforms, Long lasting social sustainability, Producing constructive dialogues, Building with innocence and inquiry, Prioritizing our local communities, Educational experimentation, Refusing conclusive statements, Celebrating craft and rethinking luxury.

Mutual Adjustment

Preservation of Instant Culture within the Pearl River Delta

Rem Koolhaas | David Gianotten // essay

Hong Kong, Shenzhen, and the rest of the cities in the Pearl River Delta (PRD) are an economic unity, yet they exist as totally different individual worlds. The development of the region "happened" when China opened up in the late 1970s, now thirty years ago; since then, a strong development of a new city life in the region has become increasingly evident. New economic connections between the PRD cities and the rest of the world started an unintentional and uncontrolled development of unprecedented scale both in terms of area and magnitude of change. Sharing a new global function, cities in one region were confronted with each other and forced to relate to one another, while remaining determined to develop their own unique life and culture.

Many of the cities in the PRD have a long history, yet none of them were able to respond to the new development of the region instantaneously or in a planned and controlled manner. Each city underwent its own unique transformation. In the 1980s, Hong Kong, the classical gateway of the West into China, was preparing for the handover, with its new identity waiting to be discovered and shaped. In less than two decades since China's economic reform, Shenzhen, driven by a new labor force that came from the rural areas of China, grew from a village into an economic powerhouse. Other cities within the PRD had to adjust their inherent historical regional strengths in order to find a new regional position with an international outlook. Not only did luxury goods for trading with the West need to be produced, new relationships and city cultures also had to be invented, initiated and produced at a pace never displayed anywhere else in the world. An instant new city culture had to be created, while no prediction of its outcome could be foreseen.

At the moment, Hong Kong, Shenzhen and the other cities in the PRD (such as Guangzhou, Dongguan, Zhuhai and Macau) have respectively seen their new city cultures and regional functions go through their first phase of development. The first conclusion of the development can be drawn and the first prediction of its potential can be made. A new social order of the region has been established and its social and cultural values can be analyzed. The unintentional and unplanned development that the cities experienced in the past decades created a melting pot of new city cultures that provides a strong base for a future of the PRD that can be intentionally planned. The period of instant "happening" made way for the new phase of mutual adjustments with a deep emphasis on cultural differences that bring benefits to the PRD as a unity. The identity of the whole region is established and can be intentionally strengthened, while the cultural uniqueness of each city, which is undoubtedly evident, cannot only be retained but also magnified to establish a strong identity for each city within the overall cultural and social structure of the PRD.

Under the new dynamics of the PRD, the development of the cities can be intentionally shaped and the social dimension of the cities can be mutually adjusted. Contrary to the random state of the past three decades, the region's social, political and economic structure of is now established, laying the groundwork for strategic planning to play a significant role. Within this mutually planned adjustment, it will be important that the current unplanned social dimension and the current unique interaction between the inhabitants are preserved on both the city and regional scales. The existence of the melting pot of city cultures, which has been growing rapidly, is the key to the development of the PRD. Not only is the development or preservation of the physical environment important, the development and preservation of this social interaction that will determine the overall future of the PRD is critical.

Preservation is often perceived as the preservation of the historical physical past, which is under the constant threat of erasure by aggressive economic development. But in fact, preservation should have a much stronger social and cultural dimension rooted in the communication between people, between cities and between countries; it is about connecting the dots differences and similarities. Within the PRD, it is therefore important that mutual adjustments be made between the different cities to bring about coherence, while at the same time ensuring that the distinct, optimistic, unintentional, socially ingenious, culturally vital, and unique realms are maintained. The future development of the relationship between Hong Kong, Shenzhen, and the other cities of the PRD will be determined by the exploration of not only the infrastructural connections between the cities but also the social, ecological, and cultural connections between the cities' inhabitants.

Rem Koolhaas founded OMA in 1975 together with Elia and Zoe Zenghelis and Madelon Vriesendorp. He graduated from the Architectural Association in London, and in 1978 published *Delirious New York: A Retroactive Manifesto for Manhattan*. He heads both OMA and the research branch AMO, operating in areas beyond the realm of architecture such as media, politics, renewable energy and fashion. Koolhaas has won several international awards including the Pritzker Architecture Prize in 2000 and the Golden Lion for Lifetime Achievement at the 2010 Venice Biennale. Koolhaas is a Professor at Harvard University where he conducts the Project on the City.

David Gianotten joined OMA in 2008 and became partner in charge of OMA Asia in 2010, overseeing OMA Hong Kong and Beijing. Projects currently under his supervision include the Shenzhen Stock Exchange, the Taipei Performing Arts Centre, Chu Hai College in Hong Kong, and the end stages of the construction of the Beijing CCTV headquarters. In 2010 he delivered the OMA conceptual masterplan for the West Kowloon Cultural District. Born in 1974 in the Netherlands, he studied Architecture and Construction Technology at the Eindhoven University of Technology. Before joining OMA, he was the managing director – Architect of SeARCH.

Diagram by Michael Chen and Jason Lee

Express Creativity

Innovating Industries

Victor Lo // essay

Over the last few decades, Hong Kong's design-related industries have grown with the rise of manufacturing in China, particularly along the eastern seaboard and Guangdong Province. With China's manufacturing industries entering a new phase, design is increasingly important, as diverse sectors from commercial to non-profit organizations seek to create unique identities that challenge the norms of cultural and creative production.

Design is a multi-faceted discipline that addresses urgent issues such as sustainability, efficiency, service deployment, system management, and brand building, and has penetrated every sector of society and our lives, ranging from urban planning, architecture, fashion, lifestyle, science and technology to arts, crafts, and culture. Design is the intrinsic binding element that enables innovation, and, as we all know, is fundamentally about innovation and change. It is a tool to drive value creation.

Contributing about four percent to the city's annual GDP, Hong Kong's creative industries over the past decade have grown alongside its economic development and are playing an increasingly greater role in the economy, when compared to tourism or manufacturing. Hong Kong as a metropolitan city may be hardly visible on the world map geographically, but its creative scene is exceptionally vibrant and vital, boasting more than 32,000 establishments of all sizes involved in a wide spectrum of industries ranging from jewelry and fashion design to architecture, brand building, and new media.

On the mainland, design is similarly emerging as a new economic direction with government policy aimed to help the manufacturing and service industries to advance, especially with the formation of the design corridor from a cluster of manufacturing based cities in the Pearl River Delta such as Shunde, Jiangmen, and Zhongshan. With Hong Kong's even closer economic integration into PRD's development on all fronts, the city will have a leading role to play in furthering collaboration with numerous mainland cities. The Biennale has definitely provided a platform connecting creative talents and design professionals from Hong Kong, the mainland, and Asia, encouraging exchanges of new insights and ideas, and helping in a concerted effort to build a culturally enriched environment for the sustainable development of our creative industries across Asia.

Victor Lo, GBS, JP is Chairman and Chief Executive of the Hong Kong-listed Gold Peak Industries (Holdings) Ltd. He currently serves as the Chairman of the Board of Directors of the Hong Kong Design Centre and the CreateSmart Initiative Vetting Committee of Hong Kong SAR. He is also a member of the Board of the West Kowloon Cultural District Authority and the Chairman of its Museum Committee. He received the Young Industrialist Award of Hong Kong in 1989, and the Industrialist of the Year Award in 2005. Lo graduated from the Institute of Design of the Illinois Institute of Technology, US with a Bachelor of Science degree in Product Design.

Naked Sunbeam 2017: Cantonese Opera Is Not North Point's Collective Memory

George Cheuk Hin Wong // exhibit

The term collective memory has become a political catchphrase to denote the prevailing public sentiment attached to a specific locale, but how "collective" is it really? The Sunbeam Theatre in North Point has been portrayed as the sanctuary of Cantonese opera which must be preserved, whereas closer scrutiny reveals that the theatre was purposely built as a political, educational and congregational venue – it was a product of a direct response to the leftist's defeat in the riots of '67. This work goes beyond the clichés of nostalgic aesthetics, unveiling the past only to create new possibilities for the future.

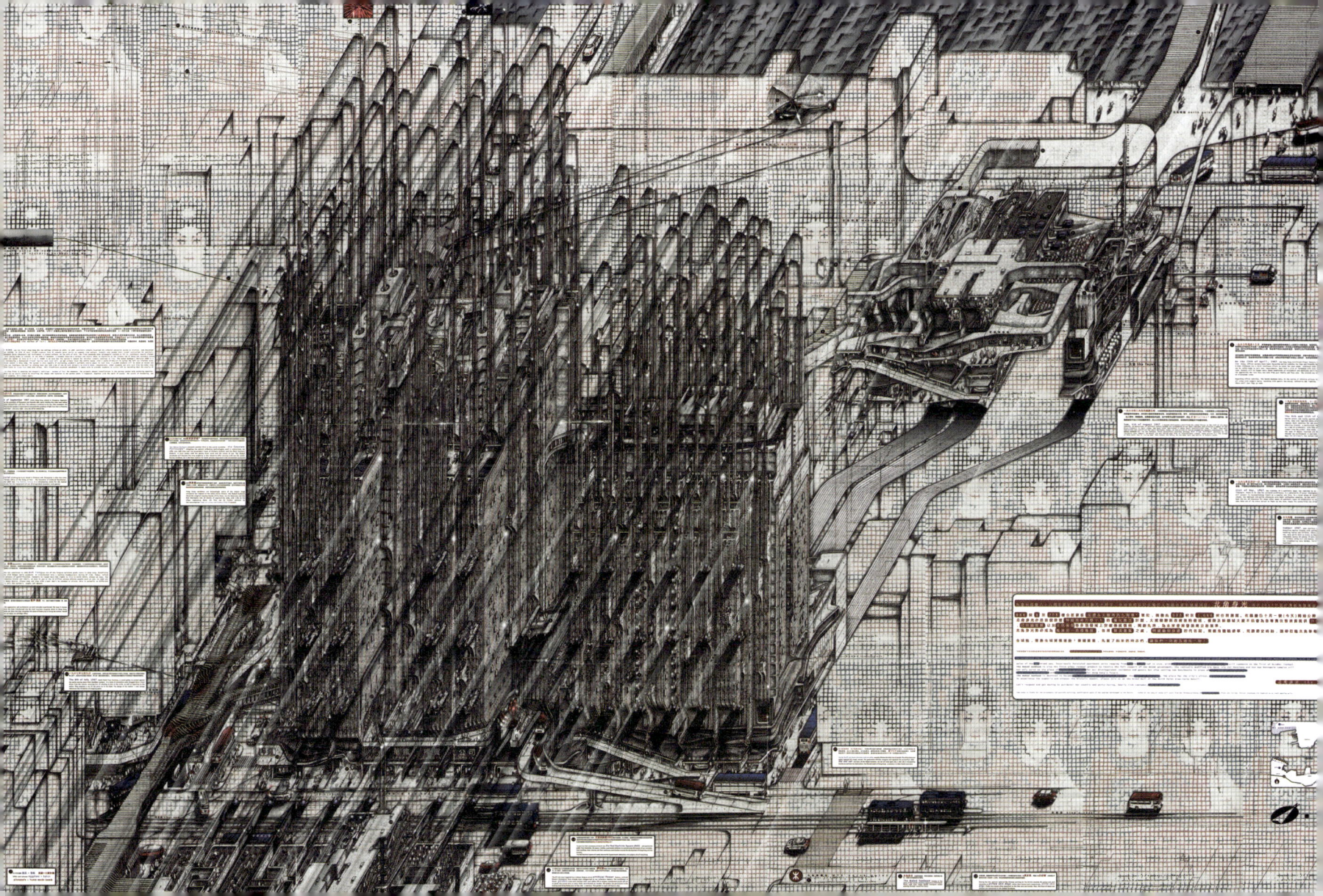

West Kowloon Walled City

Douglas Young // exhibit

What is the indigenous architecture of Hong Kong? Which buildings best represent local culture? The answer lies in the legendary Kowloon Walled City, home of Hong Kong's untouchables and social outcasts until it was demolished in 1993. It was Hong Kong's "forbidden city," built not by royalty but by the city's underclass. Yet people were still able to survive and thrive. It is the story of Hong Kong itself encapsulated in architecture, a place that has succeeded despite the odds.

The Bi-City Biennale

A Catalyst for Change?

Tao Zhu // essay

In a speech to his colleagues in the media, Ching Cheong, the prominent Hong Kong journalist, discussed Hong Kong's "core values" and the catalytic influence they could exert over mainland China. According to Cheong, three components constitute Hong Kong's central principles: the rule of law within the common-law tradition that presumes innocence; the freedom of thought, speech, and expression that allows individuals to think independently and speak critically; and, the respect for human rights that expresses itself in the strong public pressure for greater transparency and a fair trial, which helps prevent arbitrary actions by those in power.

Cheong urged his peers to consciously protect these core values and prevent their gradual erosion: to not take them for granted and only learn to treasure them when they are lost; to not submit to the various forms of bribery and intimidation; to be dictated by nothing but one's own conscience; to think in terms of the big picture — by defending Hong Kong's core values one is actually promoting positive changes in China; and to protect these core values on the basis of professionalism. If all this can be done then "tiny Hong Kong" can continue to exert a "disproportionately big influence" on China.[1]

What would it be like if we transposed these issues addressed in Hong Kong's media to its architectural discipline? One might regrettably say that Hong Kong's architectural community has not taken the responsibility that it should have taken and has not exerted its full potential to claim a higher purpose for its activities beyond "making money."

Morally, while fully enjoying the freedom of speech, Hong Kong's architectural community appears timid. While Hong Kong's media was busy exposing the acute problems related to the construction quality of the collapsed school buildings in China's earthquake zone, most Hong Kong architects and engineers remained silent. When requested by the media to make a technical examination of the damage to the collapsed schools, some of the architectural and engineering consultants on the one hand claimed in the media to be "senior experts," but on the other "would like to remain anonymous," essentially divesting themselves of any responsibility.

In terms of professional practice, although with a vast array of global cultural resources at hand, Hong Kong architects resemble, upon closer inspection, tiny gear wheels embedded within the machinery of a gigantic real-estate operation. Ever since China's reform and opening up in the 80s, Hong Kong architects have brought to the mainland their excellence in efficiency and calculation, rather than their cultural sensitivity and spatial imagination.

With respect to publishing, compared to Hong Kong's brilliant achievement in promulgating vast information about China's history, society, and politics that had an enormous and positive influence on mainland readers, Hong Kong's architectural publishing can only be described as overwhelmingly bleak.

How is it that such a dynamic metropolis, with both a rich spatial cultural tradition and constant exposure to international influences, has, in general, an architectural culture that is so pitiful, its architects' attitudes so passive, and its architectural development so divorced from its vibrant local cultural development?

My hope is that the Hong Kong-Shenzhen Bi-City Biennale may serve as a catalyst to trigger a series of changes to breach such an impasse. I also hope that through the mechanism of the Bi-City Biennale we can generate positive interactions between the architectural communities of Hong Kong and mainland China.

Tao Zhu is Assistant Professor in the Department of Architecture, the University of Hong Kong, a PhD candidate in Architecture History and Theory at Columbia University, and a co-founder of the design firm ZL Architecture. He received his Bachelor of Engineering in Architecture at Chongqing Architecture and Engineering Institute in 1990, Master of Architecture at Columbia University in 2001 and Master of Philosophy in Architecture History and Theory at Columbia University in 2007. While actively practicing in China, he writes extensively on contemporary Chinese architecture and urbanism.

On Policy

Reflections on Why Policy Matters

Desmond Hui // essay

Hong Kong is one of the few places on earth that prides itself on not having a cultural policy, or more specifically, a "prescriptive" cultural policy. Supporters of this position often draw on the United States as a model, a country that has never set up a Ministry of Culture. But they forget that while there is no specific department in charge of culture in the United States, culture and cultural life abounds and flourishes everywhere because of a strong and vibrant non-profit sector – philanthropy, foundations, corporate giving, universities, and endowments – made possible by both the state and the market. In Hong Kong, we seem to have only the state and the market. Our in-between non-profit sector, if there is one, is so weak and insignificant that it can never sustain culture or cultural life as in the American model. And, it is precisely this reason why we need a government cultural policy so badly to support events such as an art or architecture biennial.

Here are five suggestions:

• The government should seriously reconsider categorizing culture within its portfolio division now that there is a statutory body, the West Kowloon Cultural District Authority.

• To help foster the non-profit culture in Hong Kong, the government should consider establishing an art and cultural trust, as suggested by Rafael Hui when he was the Chief Secretary.

• As development in art and culture relies to a large extent on industries, again to borrow the American model, our creative industries' policies must not be separated from the arts and cultural policies. At the moment in Hong Kong there is minimal coordination between the Home Affairs Bureau and the Commerce and Economic Development Bureau regarding the creative, arts, and cultural policies.

• As a city we should devote both manpower and monetary resources specifically to the organization of the art and architecture biennials on a regular basis, continuing on from and in acknowledgement of the success of Hong Kong's participation in the Venice Biennale for the last decade and the budding efforts of our own biennale.

• Finally, our policy must consider Hong Kong from a regional perspective and therefore involve Shenzhen, Guangdong, and Taiwan as our close neighbors and partners in arts and culture.

Desmond Hui is Professor and Director of the Centre for Culture and Development, Head of the Division of Cultural Studies in the Department of Cultural and Religious Studies, Associate Director of the Research Institute of Humanities, and Associate Dean of the Arts Faculty at the Chinese University of Hong Kong. He obtained a Bachelor of Architecture from Cornell University, a Master and a Doctor of Philosophy from the University of Cambridge, and was Director of the Centre for Cultural Policy Research at the University of Hong Kong.

On Archive

Archive and Forgettory

Li Shiqiao // essay

Although all cities remember, keep, and forget in different ways, Hong Kong discards its spatial past with an almost pathological determination. Memory is essential to biological life forms, and it is also critical to cultures. As we attempt to build culture in Hong Kong we must first understand how memory works. Collective memory can be sustained and some form of historicity (hence notions of space and time in the Hegelian sense) can be achieved through the construction of archives. The high value of the archive is visible in many cities through the *gravitas* of the architecture of the archival institutions (museums, libraries, public record offices), as well as through strict and influential conservation laws. The word archive is derived from the Greek word for town hall (*arkheion*). This high respect for the archive also induces a tremendous anxiety over the loss of the archive. Walter Benjamin's characterization of the modern condition of homelessness – memories and meanings in search of authentic locations – can perhaps be understood as an attempt to live with the impending loss of the archive in the late nineteenth century context, when mechanical reproduction threatened to remove authenticity from objects.

Jacques Derrida problematized this deep anxiety over the loss of the archive as a Freudian "death drive," an "archive fever": an act of archiving that erases as much as it imprints, and which produces as much as it records. The forgettory – a space for the lost archive – indicates a state of complete intellectual void.

Hong Kong's ability to sustain a spatial archive is severely weakened by two fundamental forces. The first is the Chinese cultural tradition of placing memories in literary sources instead of spatial ones. This traditional memory strategy often meant a form of poetic records, a memory without location. It has its strong powers as well as its disabling influences, as it has been keenly commented on by people as wide-ranging as Matteo Ricci and Liang Qichao. Matteo Ricci considered the absence of the critical link between memory and location in China a chance for him to introduce a spatially grounded "memory methods of western countries," while Liang Qichao saw the establishment of historical facts – similar to the documents in archives – as one of the key tasks of a rebirth of Chinese civilization. The second is the domination of money. Money has an archive, but it operates without its influence. It is a form of perpetual present. Money has no interest in the archive since it is an obstacle to endless accumulation and circulation which is the fundamental logic of capital. This is particularly apparent in the world of real-estate speculation, which deeply impacts the spatial archive of Hong Kong. The vivid episodes of the demolition, relocation, and reconstitution of the Central Pier in the recent past highlight the dim concept of the archive. Today, many districts in Hong Kong face an unfortunate future of becoming sites for fake antiques – indeed, a forgettory in the image of an archive – like the former Marine Police Headquarters. It is time for all to ponder over the meaning of the archive.

Li Shiqiao's research is concerned with understanding emergent conditions in Chinese cities by contextualizing them in traditional discourses of modernity and architecture in their Western and Asian manifestations. Li Shiqiao obtained his BA from Tsinghua University in Beijing, and PhD from the AA School of Architecture and Birkbeck College, the University of London. He practiced in Hong Kong from 1995 to 2000, and was co-founder and consultant of BHSL Design from 2002 to 2007. He taught at the AA School of Architecture and the National University of Singapore, and has been at The Chinese University of Hong Kong since 2006.

On Legacy

The City is Built on Its Past and Future

Puay Peng Ho // essay

More than thirteen years after the handover to Chinese sovereignty, Hong Kong continues to struggle to find its identity while witnessing the rise of avant-garde culture and architecture in China. The number of construction projects in Hong Kong has been reduced to a trickle, with most innovative mainland projects given to foreign architects and young Chinese designers. Where, then, is the stage for showcasing Hong Kong architects and building Hong Kong's identity for the future?

The answer, interesting enough, may have to come from the past, through the conservation of heritage. The growing movement to conserve local historic buildings that has gathered steam in the last three years sparked by the public campaigns to save the Star Ferry Terminal and the Queen's Pier. Aided by sizable government and NGO initiatives of similar concerns, the local community has turned toward the preservation and conservation of monumental or common heritage buildings, and natural or urban landscapes in its search for Hong Kong's identity.

The 2007-2008 edition of the Biennale focused the attention of the city on the conservation of the Central Police Headquarters Compound. The 2009-2010 Biennale challenged the direction of the West Kowloon Cultural District as well as the semi-natural habitat that had sprung up in the vacant site. In the meantime, efforts were also directed at several keystone projects such as the Married Police Quarters and the Central Market that had involved government agencies, professionals, and the public at different levels of engagement.

While I am excited by the possibilities of a vibrant future supported by new cultural facilities and other infrastructural projects, I would argue that keeping the urban fabric, such as some neighborhoods that might be endangered by piecemeal developments, is just as critical, if not more so. I am referring to clusters around Graham Street, Wing Lee Street, or those in Wanchai and Tai Hang. To some extent, the ambitious initiative announced in 2009 to preserve structures in the city under the umbrella of "Conserving Central" aims to address the issues through preserving some of the best of our architectural legacy into the near and distant future. Whether it is a new hotel development taking the existing government offices at Murray Building, or a creative industry hub at the Married Police Quarters, Hong Kong is now on the verge of conjuring a confident self-image through embracing the past with an eye on the future.

Puay Peng Ho is Director of the School of Architecture at the CUHK, and was the Chairman of the Department at the CUHK since 2007. He is also directing the Centre for Architectural Heritage Research (CAHR) in academic and research work including conservation and consultancy services for historic buildings in various districts in Hong Kong. He is a locally and internationally renowned researcher in the area of Chinese architectural history, Buddhist art and architecture, Dunhuang study and vernacular Chinese architecture.

A People's Biennale of Architecture and Urbanism

West Kowloon as a Permanent Site for Public Cultural Exchange

// forum

---

date: 27 February 2010

participants: Augustine Ng, Christine Bruckner, Christopher Law, David Gianotten, Kai Yin Lo, Patrick Lau, Peter Cookson Smith, Rocco Yim, William Yiu

moderators: Laurence Liauw, Marisa Yiu

There is no mystery that the future West Kowloon Cultural District is an exciting endeavor for Hong Kong's progress in the fields of art, architecture, performing arts, and many other disciplines; however, is and should the Biennale be restricted to its site and context? How does one integrate a contextual approach to shape of the Biennale? Can West Kowloon be a permanent home for the Biennale?

Marisa Yiu: We wish to treat this as a positive and productive discussion. We do not want to just criticize; we are here to really make things work.

Laurence Liauw: Hong Kong bashing is like an echo chamber. We've been sitting here, complaining for twenty years. We should not dwell on only the problems of today, but think about the future as well. Biennales are about speculation, and that is the first rule. What are the odds of producing anarchy or chaos versus risk taking, which is productive? How can we use the Biennale to improve the desperate situations that we have identified and are discussing here?

Patrick Lau: We can improve things, in part, through communication and by sharing our thoughts. And, through these exchanges, we will be able to develop concrete planning decisions. There are three distinct Hong Kong characteristics. One is that we have an existing pattern. Hong Kong is a high-density city, but it works because we have an amazing transportation system. Secondly, we are rich in culture. We have influences from both the East and the West. We are foreign educated and yet we have kept our traditions. These traditions are passed on from generation to generation. Thirdly, "time" is very important — it is important to reflect, to "take time." I think now is a crucial time for us to look into a museum of architecture for Hong Kong.

Augustine Ng: When the West Kowloon Cultural District Authority (WKCDA) was established, the question was asked why we should not have exhibitions outside of this particular site, say in Tuen Mun or Tsuen Wan. WKCDA's work in promoting art and culture should not be confined to West Kowloon site itself. Why not collaborates with other institutions to organize a biennale either here in West Kowloon or elsewhere, for example?

During the first stage of the public engagement program for the West Kowloon Cultural District's future development, we had some 6,000 questionnaires returned to us, compared to the similar exercise for the same site in 2006, when only about 3,000 questionnaires were returned. From this increase alone, I believe that the people are concerned about the West Kowloon Cultural District development. So, how can we sustain and elevate that to an even higher level of community concern? I think this particular Biennale on this particular site is quite important. I believe that public engagement should not end at the planning stage; it should be a continuous process throughout the life of the project.

Christopher Law: This future West Kowloon Cultural District looks like another high quality, glassy complex which forbids graffiti. Where is the risk? Where are the dangerous alleyways that every city needs? My only hope is that the Cultural District will not have complete coverage of the entire site. At least leave a good portion of the land for diverse events like the Biennale, so, different things can happen, buildings can be converted, altered, and changed by the Biennale every two years.

Laurence Liauw: How can an institution lead the way? I am really, really curious. If we are going to build all the things that we are proposing for the West Kowloon Cultural District, what is the role of the institution?

Kai Yin Lo: I think the idea of Bring Your Own Biennale means exactly the opposite of the institutional approach — it reaches out directly to the people. It is participatory. It also involves people from the inside of the institution or organization, of course, but favors the people on the outside. A museum with walls is such a nineteenth century idea.

The public is really confused about the WKCD; all these consultations, such tremendous costs. We are not truly inclusive in that respect; but neither are we truly exclusive. There are just too many people involved in the project development committee. All you need is ten people whom you know you can trust.

The problem in Hong Kong is that we have no space; we have no physical space, and, as a result,

> I think the idea of Bring Your Own Biennale means exactly the opposite of the institutional approach — it reaches out directly to the people. It is participatory.
>
> — Kai Yin Lo

there is no mental space. I think the Biennale is very successful this time around. By including Shenzhen, it focused on the nature of building and the environment, encompassing the entire South China region. In Hong Kong we presented creativity as a form of expression. The Biennale has created a kind of ecology for creativity. This environment for creativity needs to grow in the city, and we have to educate people to be more flexible about design. We have to promote creative entrepreneurship because without it we will be nowhere.

William Yiu: Two years ago, The Hong Kong Jockey Club Charities Trust was the sole funder for the first Biennale. We were most thrilled to find out this time that the government is interested in funding the Biennale. However, when you think about it, you are working with a site with no infrastructure, with ten times more space, and with the same exact amount of funding we had for the first Biennale. How can you do that? The numbers just do not add up! The curators probably spent more time on fundraising than on curating.

Laurence Liauw: Most funding for a program is a one-off situation. But the Biennale is not a program; it is an institution, like the Venice Biennale. When the institution is strong, you do not need to always search for extra funding.

William Yiu: It is not going to happen if you ask a commercial institution to fund these cultural activities. That is why the government needs to step up and get involved.

Rocco Yim: Maybe I will start with an expression of my own feelings toward the Biennale. The purpose of the Venice Biennale is to make the entire profession aware of the architectural debates and dialogues that are occurring worldwide. The main goal in Hong Kong is to engage the public with whatever the Biennale is about. Right now, they do not engage much. The government officials do not pay attention; the public does, but not to any great degree; and the profession, for the most part, stays away!

So, the purpose of the Biennale, and especially the most urgent goal of this Biennale, is to promote architecture by observing what is happening around the region. This is for Hong Kong itself. But eventually, perhaps, it will gradually expand its scope and be an influence for the region, if not the world. Therefore, the West Kowloon Cultural District Authority is the natural organization to promote the Biennale, short of creating an independent institution to insure a long-term, sustainable biennale.

Laurence Liauw: In the Shenzhen Marathon interview held by the Biennale organizers, we talked about the public intellectual, about how the Biennale could act as a public forum. What do you think about the role of architecture in this?

David Gianotten: What we are trying to do here is to build a foundation for the Biennale. It all starts with being able to do research. What we realized in both Hong Kong and Shenzhen is that there is simply no time for research. Therefore, it cannot be comparable to any of the other biennales in the world.

> It all starts with being able to do research. What we realized in both Hong Kong and Shenzhen is that there is simply no time for research.
>
> — David Gianotten

Christine Bruckner: Having the WKCD site activated and bringing the public here has been a great exercise. The concept of a free community classroom with workshops, events,

changing exhibitions, interactions, installations, and waterfront activities is one which could be successfully extended into the future to bring in new ways of teaching with public integration. Ideally, we must encourage a venue where all can explore the value, potential, and future of Hong Kong's architecture.

Peter Cookson Smith: This Biennale is about improvisation but also incubation. Looking ahead, we need to follow an experimental program for the cultural district. It has to be an urban design of inventiveness in which innovation and inherent flexibility is built in, since we do not quite know where the design trajectories are going to lead us.

Bring Your Own Crowd

The Architecture of Audience

Brett Steele // essay

The history of modern art is also the history of the progressive loss of art's audience. Art has increasingly become the concern of the artist and the bafflement of the public.

– Paul Gaugin

The future will be found in a crowd.

– Don Delillo

Architecture and urbanism, worldwide, suffers from a serious, staggering, and inescapable audience problem today; as in the kinds of popular, large-scale groups of intelligent people able or interested to engage, to push, query, and demand more from architects and other makers of buildings, spaces, and cities.

Changing this situation will be one of the defining and urgent projects of early twenty-first century architectural culture – most especially for a rising generation of architectural experimentalists coming of age in an era in which architecture seems to exist as if in a vacuum, largely silent during a time when, in fact, some of its greatest forms of productive intelligence or means to alter the status quo are most needed on an earth too crowded, too hot, too close to collapse, and altogether too unstable to discern a clear way forward.

Architecture's contemporary lack of audience is the defining reality that allows most architects to spend most of their days thinking only in relation to other architects, or architectures: perhaps the least interesting architectural context one might ever imagine. It is time for architects to begin to see the concept of audience anew, for the real and formative architectural force it can be; a crowd-like, collective aggregation of minds through which ideas of any kind are received, conveyed, and stored awaiting future realization or provocation – the reactivation of the architectural archive as the driving force for new and better worlds.

A paradox of contemporary cosmopolitan life is its shocking lack of international, cultural, or real public discussion regarding the future of cities. One of the great challenges facing cultures worldwide, including architectural culture, is the imagination and not only the creation of new forums; the kinds of events, spaces, or interfaces allowing more open, collaborative forms of public exchange about the way people should live, work, and organize themselves today.

In their own small way, a notable recent rise of architectural biennales worldwide – a phenomenon within which Hong Kong and Shenzen now sit comfortably and equally with many other world cities – certainly can help create new audiences, and not simply by catering to the presumed or expected participants (the professional cadre) or the usual suspects/voyeurs (the worldwide archi-tourist). It is this presumed audience – the already initiated – whose ideas and experiences deserve greater acknowledgement in the one kind of architectural form that matters above all else today: the forum of the architectural audience as discourse. There is a need to engage, challenge, and provoke architects everywhere, to rise to the global challenge – a situation suggesting that the sense that it is "too late" is, after all, "too soon"; that is, that there is time, once again, to "save the world."

Brett Steele is Director of the Architectural Association School of Architecture and AA Publications. The AA is the United Kingdom's oldest and only private school of architecture, and has for decades been recognized as an influential world-wide leader in architectural education. Brett is the founder and the former Director of the AADRL Design Research Lab and is a partner of DAL, desArchLab, an architectural office in London, and has taught and lectured at schools throughout the world. His interests include contemporary architecture and cities, architectural culture, and the impact of new media and today's network-based distributed design and communication systems on architectural education.

Building Philanthropy
A Story of Generational Giving

Andrew Lee King Fun // essay

If philanthropy, the act of giving and respecting humanity, is a means to build community aspirations, then an architect should be a true facilitator to support this culture of altruism. As a professional, an architect should be a humble person that gives to people, helps to build society and support the under-served by ensuring the exchange is positive while building capacity for the city's population.

Architecture is not about fame, it is about serving the community. We need to design for the end users, we need to accommodate people's needs and we need to do it by shaping space. Hong Kong's architecture and urbanization accelerated during the 1980s, and undeniably the process of development has given rise to our living conditions. Architecture shapes space, mentality and lifestyles. Our development of the elemental scissors-stair structure in Hong Kong has solved tight urban housing problems while giving rise to efficient tower buildings to house the people. Building codes developed since the 1960s, such as the one encouraging bay windows, have allowed maximum sunlight penetration for smaller spaces while giving

rise to the identity of the city. However, what is most interesting is the cleverness of the three-dimensional quality and volumetric spaces within the metropolis. Hong Kong's land ownership system and China's relationship with Hong Kong is symptomatic of the forces of exchange, adding to the complexity of building and designing intelligent infrastructural systems that serve everyone across society.

I became an architect not by desire, but more by accident with an original interest for a career in medicine. However, with some trial and error, studying at the University of Hong Kong (HKU), Melbourne University, and then working abroad in Australia and Malaysia, I became very much engaged with the support and contributions that an individual can make in society. I opened my office in 1962, and since have designed over 700 buildings of all categories in Hong Kong, Macau, Vietnam, and China.

Earlier in 1961, I was one of the first HKU graduates to return to Hong Kong from overseas

as an Authorized Architect, joined the Hong Kong Institute of Architects (HKIA) as the Honorary Secretary in 1963 and have been participating in the affairs of the Institute ever since. Appointed by HKU as an Honorary Lecturer in 1976, I shared my experience as a practicing architect with the students. I initiated the Andrew Lee Travelling Scholarship in 1975 for students to travel overseas for annual exchanges. Wong Wah Sung, currently an Associate Professor at HKU, was the first recipient, and he went to Singapore for one month to study public housing. A number of students as well as teachers made use of the scholarship to travel overseas and China in the following years. In 1978 Professor Eric Lye and I led Wong Wah Sung and Joanlin Au to receive the UIA International Students Competition Top Award in Mexico City, which led to subsequent international recognition for Hong Kong students' work. Bernard Lim, currently a Professor at the Chinese University of Hong Kong, and Joseph Tang won awards in other UIA competitions over the years.

An architect should participate and contribute

towards humanistic projects. Architects should build trust and give. Architects should, through their professional knowledge and work, contribute towards the betterment of the communal living environment. We should have a broad mind, as everything is connected from human behavior to technological advancement. I am happy that I became an architect rather than a doctor, as I can contribute even more to a larger group of people in society, both as a professional and through my honorary work as a lecturer or advisor for universities. For this Biennale in particular, supporting the first traditional Chinese Pun Choi feast at the West Kowloon waterfront site was exhilarating. I value the perspective of understanding the role of an architect not only as a designer of physical spaces, but as a philanthropist – one who fosters positive growth and the community's well-being in society.

Andrew Lee is the principal partner of Andrew Lee King Fun & Associates Architects. He was the president of HKIA from 1975 to 1976. He is a Fellow of the Hong Kong Institute of Architects, a member of University Court, the Council and the Standing Committee of Convocation and a Director of the University of Hong Kong Foundation for Educational Development and Research.

social
sustainability

The Six Faces of a Socially Responsible Architect

Koon Chung Chan // essay

Architects as Urbanists

While more than half of the world's population now lives in heavily urbanized areas, and high-density living is the common fate for an increasing number of people, the irony is that only with reasonably high-density urban living can humankind still hope to preserve agricultural land and the real countryside. In this sense, Hong Kong may have a lesson or two from which the world could learn, along with our fair share of mistakes to avoid. Therefore, in Hong Kong local architects need to aspire to achieve decent high-density living for all members of society, not simply the wealthy, while providing high-quality public space that, in turn, ameliorates the density required of the modern city, creating a sense of place and civility. Thus, I put forward the notion that an architect in Hong Kong must first and foremost be an urbanist; one who cares for the city as opposed to singular buildings.

Architects as Communitarians

Architecture and public spaces are the anchors of communities. Architects should be builders of convivial communities, not their spoilers. Architects should build to encourage inclusiveness, not segregation. In other words, architects should be communitarians at heart.

Architects as Environmentalists

At the most basic level, an environmentalist-architect conserves energy, keeping the house warm in winter and cool in summer. This is the elemental datum for the conscious practice. They help us to leave the smallest carbon footprint in the world, as we found it. This is the foundation for architectural ethics.

Therefore, we should stop blindly adoring big-name architects, for example Frank Gehry, whose Disney Concert Hall in Los Angeles, which sits under the often blazing Southern California sun, was wrapped in twenty-two million pounds of steel and thus is heating up surrounding buildings by as much as fifteen degrees. Also, dear architects, you cannot leave environmental inputs to the structural engineers or building contractors, or to the developers who, even if they wanted to bother, do not know how to measure or implement such things. It is you, architects, who must insist. Therefore, I implore you, architects, to be environmentalists and to insist on building environmentally friendly architecture.

Architects as Contextualists

In the late nineteenth century and early twentieth century a few intelligent Austrian architect-urbanists, such as Camillo Sitte and Otto Wagner, advocated "contextualism" – a point of view that stated that architectural design in urban areas should take into consideration its neighboring buildings, as well as the pedestrian experience *at the street level*. Their ideas inspired many architects to build some of the most beautiful European cities such as Vienna and Amsterdam. Architecture does not stand alone. Architecture is not an installation art. It has externalities. Knowing how compact Hong Kong is, we cannot afford the beggar-thy-neighbor mentality of some developments. Please do not build anything that is pedestrian unfriendly and do not design any building that damages the neighborhood. As much as you can, be a contextualist.

Architects as Occasional Whistle Blowers

In the mid-nineteenth century, several high-minded critics of Victorian, industrial-age Britain, from Sir Henry Wotton to John Ruskin, largely agreed that successful buildings have three main properties – that is, commodity, firmness, and delight. In their view, commodity was the suitability to purpose (for example, the proper envelope for the activity that will take place within it), firmness was the ability to stand up and endure (without cracks, stains, or pieces falling off, and parts fitting together solidly), and delight was quite simply the pleasure of appearance or experience within and/or without.

I think to most people these criteria still stand, partly because many buildings in our age may not even pass these nineteenth-century tests of basic "utility" plus "aesthetic value." Bad buildings are everywhere – the dysfunctional, the shoddy, and the ugly. Why? Who made them? For every such building is there a dysfunctional, shoddy, or ugly architect? Well, maybe it is the developer's greed or the contractor's negligence or the government supervisor's incompetence that makes a building bad, and the architect had no choice. The bad guys cheat the consumers and deliver an inferior product. But it takes an architect who looks the other way, who does not care about the end product, for that to happen. In my younger days, there was a common view in Hong Kong that the three professions people really looked up to were physicians, lawyers, and accountants at times, or physicians, lawyers, and architects at other times. Among other reasons, it shows local citizenry's trust in these professions. I do not know whether local architects as a discipline have ethical codes as physicians, a Hippocratic Oath of architects. If not, peer-pressure and self-discipline are all you have, and I can understand keeping the profession's integrity could be an uphill battle, even in Hong Kong. Still, I ask all local architects to live up to the best of your discipline and not to betray the trust of the local citizenry, and occasionally when all corrective efforts fail and something pricks your conscience, blow the whistle on the perpetrators (no matter how high and mighty).

Architects as Archivists

I could have used the word historicists, but historicism may have had a bad name for a few brief decades of the last century among coteries of high modernism and I am sure it still puts some architects among us today into a defensive posture simply upon mention. I am not dictating a style or a form to you. All I am saying is, on my home ground and for my home town, Hong Kong, I would ask all architects to know your history, to do your "home" work. Respect what has come before you. Be innovative, but conserve our tangible and intangible past and preserve our diversity before you leave your signature or simply carry out the wishes of your employers. Be like an archivist. In short, handle Hong Kong with care.

Koon Chung Chan is a writer, critic, and media practitioner. He is co-founder of City Magazine, the most influential cultural magazine in the 1970s and 1980s in Hong Kong. He now lives in Beijing and shuttles between mainland China, Hong Kong, and Taiwan.

Bring Your Own Beacon

Po Yiu Tam // essay

John Ruskin, an art critic of the nineteenth century, wrote about the Seven Lamps of Architecture. They are the "lamps" of Power, Life, Memory, Truth, Beauty, Sacrifice, and Obedience. While architecture was viewed in the light of the conventional English Decorated Early Gothic, where the power and beauty of architecture was dedicated to God, his views do contrast with values in modern aesthetics of functionality in the industrial and post-industrial eras. Nevertheless, he did believe in the honest display of materials and nature and was confident in the natural instinct for rightness and beauty in the average person. The "lamps" of Life and Memory illuminated that buildings should be made by human hands, with expressive freedom given to the builders, and that buildings should respect the culture from which they have developed.

Today, should not we pause for a moment amidst the hustle and bustle to ponder the cityscape we are creating and wonder at the various and repetitive processes shaping our environment? Have our natural human instincts for rightness and beauty been overwhelmed, and the collective memories of the city been lost under such mega-forces?

In fact, the seven "lamps" of urban planning have now taken on new dimensions above and beyond the seven lamps of architecture: Power – decision-making is shared with stakeholders through envisioning; Life – greater participation in safeguarding the environment; Memory – collective memories are cherished, leading to greater emphasis on heritage conservation; Truth – the planning system is more open and accountable; Beauty – a greater protection of the natural environment so that we can continue to enjoy its beauty; Sacrifice – citizens' appreciation of their responsibility towards matters of public interest; Obedience – universal values of fairness, and trust in a fair legal system.

The beacons of knowledge and wisdom are illuminated in Hong Kong and Shenzhen. Come, enjoy, display and share, under the beams of the beacons and the seven lamps.

Po Yiu Tam was born in 1950. He joined the civil service in 1973 and has more than thirty-seven years of experience planning new towns, territorial and sub-regional planning strategies, statutory planning, planning enforcement, urban renewal, information technology, as well as urban design. He became Assistant Director in the Planning Department of the Hong Kong Government in December 2000, until his retirement in 2011. He was a vice president of HKIP in 2007-2009 and the president of the HKIP in 2009-2011. He is currently an External Examiner of the Department of Urban Planning and Design, HKU.

ecological
urban infrastructure

Eco Farm - Green Pixel

Meta4 Design Forum | The Organic Farm // exhibit

Meta4 believes that green architecture is not just a dream, and the more we take part, the more we can change the world. The Eco Farm project creates an interactive and enjoyable process by asking participants to plant seeds in recycled egg crates that other participants had previously made. People can choose their own crops to sow and bring them home at the end of the Biennale. Meta4 wants to remind urban dwellers, through planting and "potlatch," of their respect for and responsibility to the natural environment.

The Organic Farm emphasizes teamwork with participants planting seedlings in recyclable papier-mâché pots made from biodegradable and water soluble paper. Everybody is welcome to take the pot home; as long as they themselves make a papier-mâché pot for a future participant.

Eco Farm Recipe

Pad Pui Kwan Chu // essay

Hong Kong has evolved rapidly from a quaint farming and fishing port community into a towering capital of global finance within the span of a hundred years. Yet it is pathetic, if not absurd, that most residents have no idea, nor care, where their food comes from.

Organic farming practices demonstrate that we need a healthy environment before we can have wholesome home-grown foods (wild or otherwise) – it is a simple case of mutually determined realities. Yet, as we convert more land into real estate, deplete the soil, and pollute the air, we, in turn, require food to be brought from ever greater distances at ever greater prices. Furthermore, local production is important, not only for the freshness, the taste, and the nutrients of the produce; but also because it helps to conserve energy and reduce carbon emission, all of which are essential to the sustainable development of Hong Kong and its long-term prosperity.

There are many ways that we, as activist-citizens, might engage in the actual versus technical greening of our city. It is easy to learn to grow one's own food and become a farmer or gardener, at home or at a neighboring community garden. What is truly necessary is a refined *long-term vision*, one which is paradoxically related to the not-so-ancient agrarian origins of Hong Kong.

In growing food, people learn much more about the rhythms of nature and the interconnections between the soil, atmosphere, and plant life as they learn the ecology of natural systems. Rather than simply buying produce in the marketplace, the introduction of seasonality is critical, as local foods are tied to the cycle of the season, of *what* can be grown *when*. Organic gardening is a simple but radical gesture and platform for increased communication among friends and families, and particularly – in this day and age – an insurrectional activity if introduced to children. Gardening is therapeutic, personally and socially, but most especially in the modern metropolis.

Pad Pui Kwan Chu returned to Hong Kong in the 1980s and is among the pioneers in the organic movement in Hong Kong – being both the director of The Organic Farm and Simply Organic. Both operations are closely associated with international non-profit making organisations as well as growers, suppliers, and manufacturers within the organic business worldwide. Being a long-time veteran of design, Chu has always been a patron of all forms of the arts and performances locally and internationally.

BYOBackyard
BYOBowl
BYOPatch of
Green Home //event

Our Bring Your Own Backyard event marked the first of
many exciting events with the gathering of a hundred
enthusiastic volunteers to plant their first organic seeds
to help create our Eco Farm, just a few minutes away
from the center of the city.

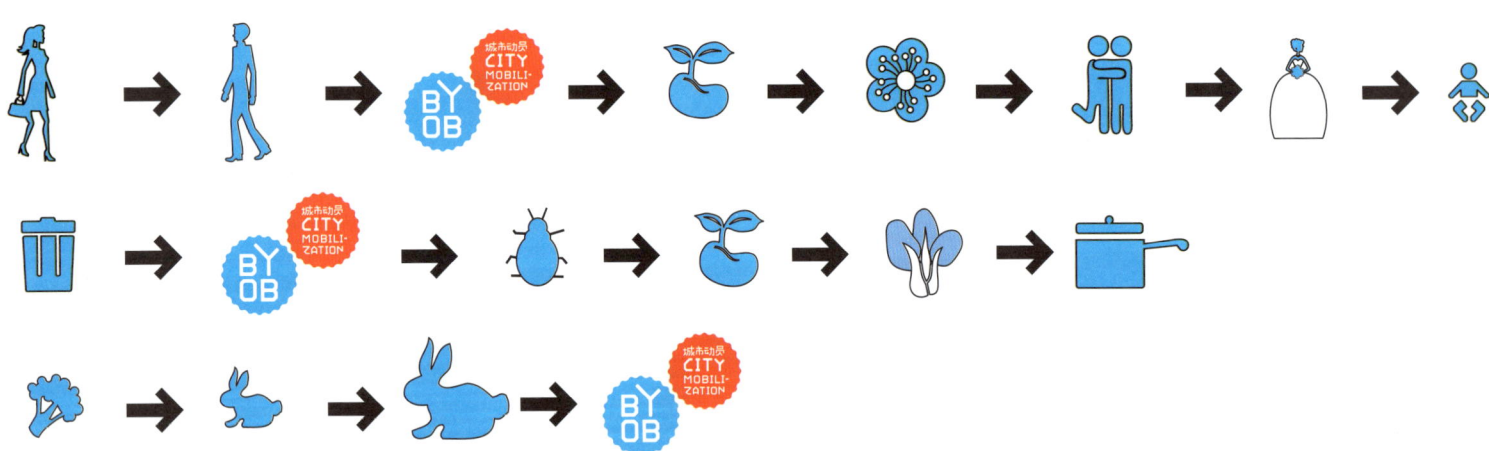

Garden in the City
A Dream and a Provocation

Leo Ou Fan Lee // essay

The density and hubbub of cities is a hallmark of all Asian cities today. Does it have to remain so?

Early modern cities in China also had dense populations, but in cities like Suzhou and Hangzhou there were gardens and canals to ease the tension of life and impart a rustic air and an aesthetic sense of leisure.

Gardens are reincarnations of ancient ideals in both China and the West. The old Suzhou gardens were built to reproduce landscapes in Chinese paintings: the precise placement of rocks and streams were crucial components used to attain the ideal vision of rural aestheticism. The person who embodied such idyllic aesthetics was called *wenren* (文人).

But somehow the tradition is lost in the current rush to build super-modern global metropolises. I am certain architects have been debating such issues, and a few experiments of urban design such as the campus of the New Academy of Art in Hangzhou by Wang Shu, which intentionally uses old materials to create a rustic atmosphere, are undertaken in order to bring the countryside back into the cities. In their contribution to the Hong Kong pavilion at the Venice Biennale in 2008, Eric Schuldenfrei and Marisa Yiu created a model of "hanging gardens," which evinces a similar spirit.

Now that we are all urban dwellers, perhaps the time has come to reinvent this old *wenren* ideal of the Ming Dynasty by placing human lives at the center of buildings in a "leisurely" fashion surrounded by real or imagined gardens. Is it possible? Yes, but to many it is perhaps too naïve and utopian in an over-crowded city like Hong Kong.

How can we bring the past into the present and use it to create new forms of architecture? Can we inscribe our collective memories onto our new skyscrapers? Can Le Corbusier be harnessed by Asian aesthetics? Can we wage an urban guerilla war on behalf of ourselves (as Tadao Ando does in Japan)?

I love to dream the impossible – to throw seemingly impossible dreams at city planners in order to encourage a more humanistic vision of architecture.

Leo Ou Fan Lee is the Wei Lun Professor of Humanities at the Chinese University of Hong Kong, having taught at Harvard University and a number of other universities. Though a literary scholar by profession, he has recently developed a keen interest in architecture. His writings are extensively published in Chinese and English.

BYOBotanist: GREENACTIVITIES

Edith Pui Yee Li | Bob Chin Wah Pang   // exhibit right

Applying the mantra "form follows function," the modern city famously values everything by functionality, and so we build our cities in the most rational, utilitarian, and non-contextual ways as a result. Regulated by systematic thinking, we are unconscious about the spirituality of every being. GREENACTIVITIES brings back the spiritual and interactive relationships between the human and natural worlds by exploring the configuration of the green wall. By creating an undulating wall that not only resembles the organic form of nature but also remains highly adaptive to a wide range of postures, GREENACTIVITIES seeks to alter the everyday relationship of the urban dweller to the natural environment by allowing the public to lie down, sit, or lean on the structure. Creating a new "ground," the green wall becomes an interface between two worlds in our inevitably ever-expanding urban context.

Green Panel System and Eco-Turf System

Strongly International Limited // exhibit left

Green Panel System is an innovative solution to vertical planting, suitable for various sites and designs. Offering a high level of protection to the plants, the structure enables installation at almost all locations. For horizontal or slightly inclined planting, the Eco-Turf System provides a lightweight solution for placing vegetation on rooftops. Its oil-free and highly absorptive components result in thinner and lighter breeding, properties which allow for much broader applications that are suitable for both extensive and intensive green roofs.

Green Tapestry

Hay Fung Ip | Kit Wang Choi | Kwan Ho Li | Sing Lam Ng   // exhibit right

Green Tapestry is a device that seals off the noise of traffic from the surrounding environment. It is not just a noise barrier, but a visual, physical, and psychological barrier. Conveying a sense of placelessness, the generic tunnel-like traffic corridor effectively seals off noise, but also obscures views to the outside. Developed in Tai Po, Green Tapestry questions whether it is possible to transcend a typical noise barrier in the urban setting by creating a center of focus for the community while improving the experience of commuting.

On Trees: Social Sustainability

date:	3 December 2009
participants:	Claude Wong, Elizabeth Diller, Gabu Heindl, Katharina Mischer, Kathy Ng, Sada Lam, Thomas Traxier, William Lim
moderators:	Eric Schuldenfrei, Marisa Yiu
respondent:	Sujata Govada

Both natural and manmade ecosystems create vitality within a city. Responding to the concept of the tree in relationship to building society and the urban landscape of a city, speakers differentiated approaches towards designing, with perspectives coming from New York, Vienna, and China. How does architecture affect cultural sustainability? How does it relate to the community, magnifying the potential for creating new ecologies?

Elizabeth Diller: The High Line has a really interesting history, as it was originally built for the shipping containers that were taken off from ships and distributed into the Meatpacking District by rail. The train was colliding with pedestrians as the city grew, so the elevated High Line was built. It survived for about fifty years, until it started to become a ruin, and in 2001 Rudy Giuliani, the mayor of New York, decided to rip it down, for it was felt that the High Line was devaluing land, and property owners around the Meatpacking District wanted it removed.

Friends of the High Line, which was a citizen activist group, hired a photographer to take photos on the High Line and these were published in the New Yorker. The political power of photography really worked because for the first time the public was able to imagine opening this bit of railway and repurposing it.

One of the great things is that this line meanders through and between buildings and into sun-drenched and wind-swept areas, and, depending on where it is, different things, different plants, took root. For this reason, the High Line was considered to be an eyesore, while now, it has become a catalyst for growth in the city, with movie stars, branding, the High Line Festival, condos emerging all over the place with a lot of celebrity architects, and a first wedding – many unforeseen things that we really did not imagine in terms of the public and what the public means. People seem to be now posing in front of the High Line and flashing in front of the High Line, something that we never anticipated and actually do not want to control. It has produced

a different kind of activity and sport – and things are happening all the time, unforeseen things. We planned for a certain kind of emergence of growth there but we did not realize what kind of urban growth would happen.

We originally thought of ourselves as the architects of the High Line, but later saw ourselves as the architects that prevented and preserved the High Line, defending it from architecture. We could never have predicted this kind of urban growth and now we welcome it along with a new kind of urban biodiversity. The High Line will be charged with all sorts of things that we could have never foreseen: that is what we call public.

Kathy Ng: When we talk about trees and social sustainability, we talk about several things, for trees have always been a source of life because a tree gives us oxygen, fuel, food, building material, magazines, and all sorts of other items. We cannot live without trees, we need them. But we have to remember that the trees do not need us, they are very happy without human beings. That is something very important to understand and appreciate; they are life-givers. An American poet once said, "We have to treat them with good manners." This is a very humble request, but it is also very difficult. Exploitation of the natural world has effectively disconnected us from trees and nature; we tend to concentrate on development. How can we change the approach into a more socially sustainable concept?

Thomas Traxler: *The Idea of a Tree* project we are exhibiting will produce one singular,

documentary object every day. The main intention of this project is to bring together machines and the natural world. A tree grows according to external influences and stores this information internally. If you take a core sample of a tree, you can read in it the whole life of the tree. Our machine produces one object a day and records the difference of the sun's intensity in the documentary object; the solar panel both provides power and connects the machine with its environment. By connecting the machine and its surrounding, you get locality built into the object since it reflects the natural surroundings of the production location.

> The main intention of this project is to bring together machines and the natural world. A tree grows according to external influences and stores this information internally. If you take a core sample of a tree, you can read in it the whole life of the tree.
>
> — Thomas Traxler

We originally thought of ourselves as
the architects of the High Line
but later saw ourselves as the architects
that prevented and preserved the High
Line, defending it from architecture.

— Elizabeth Diller

Katharina Mischer: *The Idea of a Tree* is an ongoing project and it has an archival side. Every time we find an inspirational statement or a poem about trees, we add it to the project. For example, during the building of Oxford University a whole forest was planted next to it, so that new beams could be cut after hundreds of years to be used in the periodic renovation of the buildings. In terms of ethics and our relationship to natural resources, I think we should all start thinking again in the long term.

William Lim: The first thing in the curatorial statement that caught my attention was the term creative activism. Three words, then, come to mind – environment, nature, and culture. But what is an environment? Consider Graham Street in Hong Kong. The environment is really the place where people live. You can dream about the environment being the green environment, but to me it is the place where people live, and nature is just our habits or our way of life; how we eat, sleep, go to the toilet, do whatever it is we do. So to me, nature might not mean trees at all, especially in a dense urban environment. I really do not know where you would plant more trees, yet green nature really does satisfy certain needs.

Regarding culture, there is North Point in Hong Kong. The interesting thing is that you see a tram in the middle of the street, and whenever the tram passes by the people will clear the tram path, but after the tram passes by, then everyone will go back into the street. To me it is a very natural way of living in a very dense city like Hong Kong. It is a typical way of Hong Kong living. We do not do things at one level, we do things at multiple levels, we really maximize whatever piece of land we have.

> It is a typical way of Hong Kong living. We do not do things at one level, we do things at multiple levels, we really maximize whatever piece of land we have.
>
> — William Lim

Elizabeth Diller: The High Line, as I mentioned before, was selected for demolition because nobody really understood the potential except for architects and architectural students. But it was the most improbable notion, saving it, and then transforming it into public space.

Yet, very fortunate things happened, we had a change of government in New York, where there were a lot of really interesting and new, very cultivated people that came into the government with the Bloomberg administration. All of the sudden there was an enlightened consciousness about public space, which there had never been before.

Eric Schuldenfrei: Many of the projects featured in the biennale seem to actually grab and hold onto this idea of what is found. In the case of the High Line, it was already an existing structure.

And in the *Idea of a Tree* project, it is examining a concept borrowed directly from nature. So I want to return to this concept, perhaps to the *Idea of a Tree*, for many of the projects that you have worked on seem to respond directly to something, rather than come solely out of your own imagination.

Katharina Mischer: We like looking around and being inspired by what we see – by what already exists. Curiously, very small, tiny things can be really inspiring and by tying things together, suddenly many things make sense in a larger system or order.

It is really important that things make sense in the end, that you have the whole story. For example, a table will get lot of money in auctions because it is "limited" – that is, unique or having been made just once. Its value soars. Yet concepts of biodiversity contradict this model. Limitations are not especially useful in reality, yet they seem to be permissible in art. In one case they create value; in the other they destroy it.

Kathy Ng: This is the first time that I have been to West Kowloon. It is a very dynamic site, and, as all of us are trying to envisage what we are going to witness here in the years to come, I believe now is the time to think hard about what's going on and who we are, what we are expecting for the generations to come. I think this event is the turning point for us, to really think what we would like to do, because the world is actually exploding with people and this Biennale could trigger something that really makes a difference, so that thirty years from now, when we look back, this moment may be seen as a point of departure.

Sada Lam: There is a funny thing about regulations. I do not know who actually had the genius to invent this thing called a clubhouse, and the building regulation that goes along with it, but apparently developers can build GFA-free clubhouses and then, of course, offer memberships to these totally anti-social and anti-urban facilities to whoever can afford them. So we are actually building fortresses, or gated communities, with swimming pools and elite services. In my estimation, in the very near future, we will see this big fortress of clubhouses here in West Kowloon. Let's face it, this waterfront site will become a fortress of privilege, one way or another. So everything circles back to the question of transience and ownership and how we might reclaim our rights to the city?

Let's face it, this water-front site will become a fortress of privilege, one way or another. So everything circles back to the question of transience and ownership and how we might reclaim our rights to the city?

— Sada Lam

Sujata Govada: I think this is a great venue to hold the Biennale. I hope it remains like this for some time so we can enjoy the space. Architecture has an obvious impact on the city, but at the same time when people are designing buildings, they do not always think of how they relate to the surrounding context. I think that's why thinking more about city scale and how people enjoy the city is a critical part of urban culture. One thing that is very important to Hong Kong is the disappearing urban grid, because of our bigger and bigger block developments. As a result of it we are doing two things: one is erasing the grid of the city and the other is the destruction of public space. I think a city with great public open space offers a choice for people and is actually a city that can celebrate urban life versus merely tolerate it. I think Hong Kong can do better. I think we should make it incumbent upon people to be more sensitive to why this occurs, whether it is because of building regulations or other forms of governance.

Sada Lam: In our Sanlitun village project, we are trying to open up the city's plot versus close it up through building a shopping mall. Instead, we are building eighteen blocks which communicate to one another, forming a fabric of streets which mirror the footprints of the original buildings. We can, in such instances, build open cities without losing profitability.

Claude Wong: The most important thing as the architect for the Biennale is perseverance. I think without that it is nearly impossible to break the system and to get any innovative structures built in Hong Kong. Even though we had a very good team in place to help Shigeru Ban, to get the paper tube pavilion built in Hong Kong is not an easy task because it has to go through the local regulations, it has to meet the budget, and also the timing is critical. We had only about three months to put this structure up and at that time I was not confident of getting it built on time. But anyway, we did not give up, the team did not give up and luckily we had some help from the Buildings Department and Fire Services Department insofar as they expedited the process for us. Today at 1:55 p.m., just two hours before the event opened, I received the Occupation Permit; so it was that tight!

Gabu Heindl: I wrote down this line from Liz Diller: "We wanted to save the High Line from architecture." I think what is common to everyone here is the search for a new culture for design and the construction of urban culture. I was worried that this discussion would focus on the topic of sustainability, the term nobody wants to mention, and which everybody is tired of hearing about. And that is why I really like all your statements, where you can sense there is a highly differentiated approach to the metaphor or concept of a tree. I would say that the High Line is as much a tree to the city as an actual tree is, and to save the High Line from architecture is an example of the creating of this culture of taking serious what is there, and how we work with what already exists, as a measure of sustainability – that is, social sustainability, but also cultural sustainability.

William Lim: It is very limited as to what an architect can actually do today in Hong Kong, and, as a result, a lot of us find ourselves working in greater China. I think the common responsibility of architects is to build a better city; to get together and change the situation. Just doing this Biennale, here in West Kowloon, and the issues that you faced is unbelievable. How can you erect this fantastic pavilion without negotiating all of the excessive building regulations? Given all of these overlapping constraints, it is almost impossible to do anything here without problems. As architects, I really think that we need to get together and do something about this cultural problem.

Marisa Yiu: Shigeru Ban worked very hard with our team to build this pavilion we are sitting in, for this is Hong Kong's first major paper-tube structure. So, it is hopefully something with which we can challenge the building codes and eventually paper tubes will be formally part of the building codes, so everyone can actually build their own.

Elizabeth Diller: I do want to congratulate the curators for this great initiative. It is great to see something occurring on this piece of land that is kind of unofficial. I guess if I were sitting in the audience and I did not know who was here on this panel, I could possibly hear nostalgia in the air, for it sounds like anti-progress, like let us get back to the real stuff, real materials, old-fashioned values, but it is really a borderline condition and I think that we are in a very funny place; we are talking about things that our ancestors discussed. It is a reaction to green; maybe it is a reaction to rapid development that is kind of uncensored and uncritical. We do have a responsibility to think broadly about what is for the public good. At the same time we need to think progressively, generatively, about new materials and new technologies.

The High Line

Diller Scofidio + Renfro | Field Operations
// exhibit

The High Line is a new one and a half mile public park built on an abandoned elevated railroad stretching from the Meatpacking District to the Hudson Rail Yards in Manhattan. Inspired by the melancholic, unruly beauty of this post-industrial ruin, where nature has reclaimed a once vital piece of urban infrastructure, the new park interprets its inheritance. The High Line is a work of agri-tecture – that is, part agriculture, part architecture – employing a paving system of individual pre-cast concrete planks with open joints to encourage emergent growth like wild grass through cracks in the sidewalk. The park accommodates the wild and cultivated, intimate and social.

Idea of a Tree

mischer'traxler // exhibit

Inspired by a fascination for machines and nature, Idea of a Tree reinterprets the "recording" capacities of a tree. Driven by solar energy, the machine starts producing its written record when the sun rises and stops when the sun sets. After sunset, the finished object can be harvested. As the machine reacts to various light intensities and records it in the artefact, each outcome represents its day and place of production. This object of "industrialized locality" is not so much about local culture, craftsmanship, or resources, but instead addresses the climatic and environmental factors of the surroundings and the act of recording those conditions.

farmScape

UMAMI-UTILITIES | CL3 // exhibit

farmScape is an eventscape, an interactive pavilion that requires the visitor's help to reimagine the traditional pavilion as a prosthetic landscape that simultaneously hijacks and implants itself within a local ecosystem. A device of both nature and synthesis, and a platform for the community, it takes its cues from the temporal nature of the biennale and the rapidly changing landscape of Hong Kong as a whole. Visitors are allowed to utilize individual plots within the diagonally-gridded field and are encouraged to plant seeds of their own choice from a catalogue of local crops.

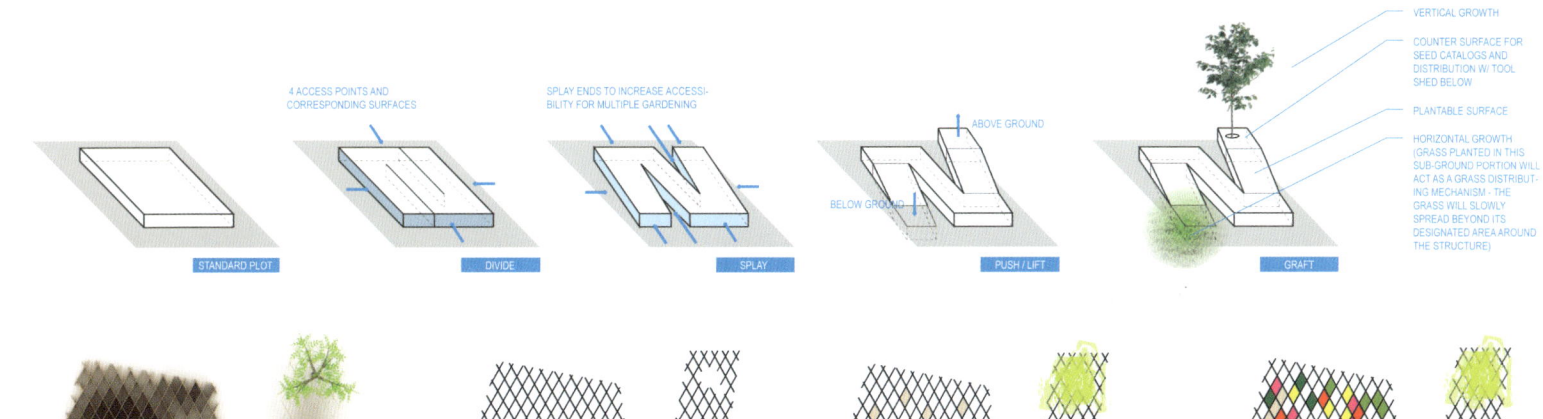

4 ACCESS POINTS AND CORRESPONDING SURFACES

SPLAY ENDS TO INCREASE ACCESSIBILITY FOR MULTIPLE GARDENING

ABOVE GROUND

BELOW GROUND

VERTICAL GROWTH

COUNTER SURFACE FOR SEED CATALOGS AND DISTRIBUTION W/ TOOL SHED BELOW

PLANTABLE SURFACE

HORIZONTAL GROWTH (GRASS PLANTED IN THIS SUB-GROUND PORTION WILL ACT AS A GRASS DISTRIBUTING MECHANISM - THE GRASS WILL SLOWLY SPREAD BEYOND ITS DESIGNATED AREA AROUND THE STRUCTURE)

STANDARD PLOT

DIVIDE

SPLAY

PUSH / LIFT

GRAFT

DIA-GRID FRAME WORK

DIA-GRID FRAME WORK

+ GRASS
+ TREE
+ SOIL INFILL

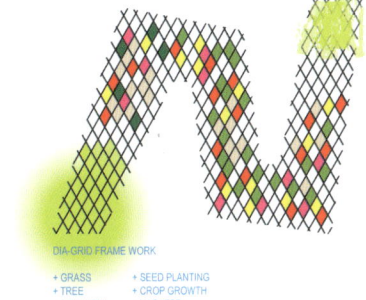

DIA-GRID FRAME WORK

+ GRASS
+ TREE
+ SOIL INFILL
+ SEED PLANTING
+ CROP GROWTH
+ HARVEST

LOCAL VEGETABLES	Name	Mature Length	Soil Depth	Seed Spacing	Method
	Hairy Gourd	10-12"	1/4"	5-6"	Vine
	Lettuce	6-8" Diameter	1/4"	6-8"	Soil
	Water Cress	6-8"	N/A	1-2"	Water bed
	Yard-long Bean	30-36"	1/4"	6-8"	Vine
	Bitter Cucumber	10-12"	1/4"	5-6"	Vine
	Chinese White Cabbage	12-18"	1/4"	6-10"	Soil

World Organization of Transients

Oval Partnership // exhibit

Economic stratification, urban fragmentation, and social polarization have turned Hong Kong into a city of extremes. Saturated with propaganda but deprived of real opportunities, individuals aspiring to dreams that can never materialize are withdrawn from reality and the social fabric. The World Organization of Transients is a model for a socially, economically, and environmentally sustainable development where individuals are free to explore, express, and improvise, once again, germinating cultural diversity and reintegrating individuals into society. Hopefully, the institutional urban infrastructure can be reconceived to regain individual identities and dreams and reduce the polarization of society.

IN 1972 THE GOVERNMENT
INITIATED A COUNTRY PARK
PROGRAM AND BY 1979
40% OF HONG KONG WAS
PROTECTED NATURE

Catching Up with Nature
Tracking the Activist-Academic

Christopher DeWolf // essay

Jim Chi-yung normally walks with a steady, deliberate pace, but on the grey afternoon of February 4th, he broke into an uncharacteristic sprint, running from his office at the University of Hong Kong to a friend's waiting car. He was heading to Maryknoll Convent School in Kowloon Tong, where the future of a tree was at stake.

Last year, Maryknoll decided to chop down a twenty-metre-tall Norfolk Island Pine that leaned to the north and seeped resin from its trunk, giving the eerie impression that it was crying. The school girls called it the Ghost Pine. Since it was planted in the late 1930s, it had become an emblem of Maryknoll, which is one of Hong Kong's most prestigious private girls' schools. The decision to fell the tree was met with a furious response from the school's network of well-connected alumni, who called Jim for help. He helped publicize the case and after a flurry of media attention, the school rescinded their decision.

But in January, a crew of contractors dug a trench around the pine and severed most of its roots. The school declared that the tree could not be saved. Its felling was scheduled for February 5th. When he arrived on the afternoon of the 4th, he asked to look at the tree, but the school's administrators refused. He looked worried. "Like a doctor who will use every effort trying to save a patient, immediate stabilization work can be imposed on the trunk instead of cutting the tree," he told reporters.

Jim is the "Tree Professor," Hong Kong's foremost expert on urban nature. He has spent a lifetime at the University of Hong Kong, where he was tenured shortly after joining the Department of Geography in 1981. His early career was spent buried in books, content in his research – classic ivory tower. After he began studying Hong Kong's oldest and most impressive trees in the 1990s, however, Jim began to realize the extent to which they were threatened by abuse and mismanagement. His focus turned outwards. He became as much an activist as an academic.

It has not been an easy path. "Knowledge has been compartmentalized excessively," says Jim. Academia does not always encourage broad-mindedness. His interdisciplinary studies on urban nature – everything from the economic value of trees to the latest innovations in rooftop greening – are often viewed askance by specialist journals. Though he sits on a number of important advisory committees, Jim's advice to government often falls victim to the same rigid thinking, which sees nature as something well removed from urban development.

But Jim is an optimist. He has seen Hong Kong's attitudes towards trees and urban nature evolve from total disregard to grudging respect. Even if he is bitter about cases like the Maryknoll Ghost Pine, he is hopeful that the cases like that are relics from a past era. "Hong Kong is lagging behind, but it is trying to catch up. We are going in the right direction," he says.

Christopher DeWolf is a writer and photographer based in Hong Kong. His work focuses mainly on urban life, culture and art, as well as social issues, politics, media, history and heritage.

living
environment

Painting by God

anothermountainman // exhibit

Seeing the light,
I believe in divinity.
Seeing the land,
I believe in time:
the past, present, and future.
Seeing the wind move,
I believe in the breath and life.
Seeing tears of sadness and of gladness,
I believe in the communication of the soul.
Believing that life is beautiful,
I see the light ahead.
I see, therefore I believe.
I believe, and so I see.

Live Nature

Ida Sze | Billy Chan // exhibit

We have a desire to live by nature.

We use this pavilion to create a setting
to taste the joy of living under a tree.

Sections of home lives are abstracted
to sculpt this pavilion, a tree crown replaces a
concrete roof to provide a shelter for sleeping,
dining, and conversing among the soothing
sunlight, singing birds, and swaying shadows.

The Projecting Window

Sophia Cheuk Lam Ip | Edith Pui Yee Li | Haynie Wing Yee Sze | Eva Yiu Wah Chan
// exhibit

The Projecting Window is designed as a commentary on the current conditions regarding residential property development and the construction industry. Comprised of a group of precast bay window panels, the installation on the external grassland near the waterline of the West Kowloon Promenade creates a novel spatial experience for the viewers. It functions not only as a simple landscape installation but also as an introspective representation of a prominent urban phenomenon, projecting a view of the future of generic architecture and urbanism while serving as a provocative reflection on the conventional perception of the built environment of the city.

Bay Window Boom

Sophia Cheuk Lam Ip | **Edith Pui Yee Li** |
Haynie Wing Yee Sze | **Eva Yiu Wah Chan**
// essay

The Projecting Window is a sardonic commentary on the development of the cross-border residential property market, and the related construction industries over the past decade. Executed in the form of a landscape installation art project, it consists of eight prefabricated bay windows arranged and erected on the external grassland near the waterfront of the West Kowloon Promenade in order to provide optimal "views" of Hong Kong.

The precast bay window, deployed here as a stand-alone sculptural object, is a metaphor for a type of surplus value attached to residential property developments in Hong Kong. Over the past decade it has become an indispensable architectural element in most private residential developments, representing or symbolizing a "bonus" in the "home-sweet-home" fantasy of many homeowners – and strangely reminiscent of the iconic "picture window" in 1950s American suburban developments.

The notion of the projecting window was first introduced in the late 1970s to provide shading to residential units, but bay windows were not widely adopted in residential buildings in Hong Kong until March 1980, when a new practice note was issued by the Buildings Department (PNAP 68/ APP-19) as a concession to developers. In the 1980s the city underwent a dramatic increase in population with the attendant high demand for housing.[1] The lack of skilled labor demanded a more expeditious means of construction, and precast concrete elements started to play a larger role in the construction of all public housing sponsored by the Housing Authority. Since bay windows are mass-produced in off-site factories using reusable formwork and transported to the construction site for installation, they provided a faster and cleaner manner to construct buildings with the added advantages of uniformity, predictability, and other issues of quality control.

The real boom in bay window design, however, started in the 1990s when the prefabrication technique matured. The government encouraged green and innovative designs for bay windows in private residential developments by stipulating requirements for obtaining certain exemptions within the gross floor area calculations; that is, a "subsidy by exemption."[2] The precast bay window design was believed not only to save construction time and cost, but also used to reduce wet trades on site and thus present more environmentally viable solutions to the building industry. As a result, the bay window started to appear on the façade of almost every private residential tower and resulted in what today can only be called a mass-produced "urban aesthetic."

Shenzhen, as the primary production base for inexpensive prefabricated façade panels, contributes the physical matter. Yet, in the dialectical relations between production and consumption, the Shenzhen-Hong Kong system of trade is uneven, and, as a side product, the bay window and its privileged views suggest this elemental and productive dialogue is in fact reversed, where Hong Kong regulations and subsidies by exemption become the principal "value-producers."

The Projecting Window is an introspective representation of this prominent urban phenomenon – the two-way gaze to and from Hong Kong. By misplacing the bay window panel from the external wall of a high-rise residential unit to a stand-alone position on the West Kowloon Biennale grounds, the viewer is given a chance to observe from a different perspective what has, in fact, become naturalized within Shenzhen-Hong Kong relations. Situated on the ground, the panel is reconceived as an object of contemplation, a simple product of mass production and a value-constructing industry (the real estate market), with the additional sculptural effect enhanced by the stark contrast of the finely finished surface and the raw concrete and underlying steel reinforcement bars. The glass pane of the bay window frames the most promising view along the West Kowloon waterfront, gazing out to the Central skyline while simultaneously projecting a speculative view toward the future of generic architecture and urbanism within the metropolis.

Sophia Ip, Haynie Sze, Edith Li, and Eva Chan are practicing architects who graduated from the Chinese University of Hong Kong. They have participated in many local art projects, exhibitions, and community projects, including the *Whistling Aloft* outdoor sculpture in the Hong Kong Science Museum (Sophia Ip & Haynie Sze) and *Smiling Up High*, a shortlisted sculpture for the Sai Kung District Council Public Art Project (Sophia Ip, Edith Li & Haynie Sze).

85% OF THE APARTMENTS
IN HONG KONG ARE
UNDER 650 SQUARE FEET
AS OF 2008

THE NET ADDITION TO THE PRIVATE HOUSING STOCK DROPPED FROM 34,870 IN 1999 TO 7,360 IN 2008

AVERAGE RESIDENTIAL PRICES ON HONG KONG ISLAND ARE HK$25,600 PER SQUARE FOOT IN THE 1ST QUARTER OF 2011

MORE THAN 28 %
OF HONG KONG'S
DOMESTIC HOUSEHOLDS
IN 2009 EARN LESS THAN
HK$10,000 A MONTH

Paddling Home

Kacey Wong // exhibit

Paddling Home is a four-foot by four-foot apartment floating on the sea. The concept of this project was inspired by the extremely expensive living condition in Hong Kong, where people can only afford a tiny apartment and have to spend their lifetime repaying the mortgage. The image of a helpless little house paddling away in a vast dangerous ocean towards the infinite shoreline is similar to using twenty to thirty years to repay a huge mortgage loan; it is dangerous and creates a feeling of helplessness. Paddling Home is about mobility and compact living, freedom and the search for a better place.

Distant Waters

Eric Schuldenfrei // essay

We are never too far away from the water's edge but are often physically separated from it by a variety of factors. The tragedy is that we typically view the harbor from a car on a highway or from afar within a building; we rarely experience it up close. Although over a third of Hong Kong's developed land is reclaimed from the sea, we do not often inhabit the edge of the harbor.[1] As layer upon layer of additional land is added to the existing coastline, the water seems to recede further and become more distant than ever. This last stratum is frequently reserved for infrastructure: the airport, container ports, utility power stations, industrial spaces, and highways – the very spaces within a city that lack life and inhabitants.[2] Recreational waterfront spaces exist in Hong Kong, but they are usually in the form of immense parks that represent yet another obstacle disconnecting the public from the water, resulting in a harbor that remains a place of utility and not a naturally integrated component of everyday life.

However, a linear park of variable width could exist between the city edge and the waterfront. An interconnected contiguous strip of land with various venues bringing a range of activities to the waterfront would create a park system close to everyone instead of merely being a large land segment serving only localized communities. This design configuration would promote the waterfront as an urban coastline stitching Hong Kong's most dense areas together.

Victoria Harbor is a public body of water and a grand resource with which every person has the right to engage, although this is only true if people can easily access it. Only in a few locations in Hong Kong does it actually feel like it belongs in the public sphere. The entire urban waterfront has the potential to become a unified linear region, opening up new possibilities by functioning as a laboratory for design ideas, as well as a space to develop prototypes and concepts across the city. Crucially, it is not enough to provide just waterfront space. The government needs individuals to activate it. Urban curators are essential to serve as a catalyst for change.

Waterfront parks cultivate civilization by enticing people to come to them, reaching out to the audience through festivals, concerts, outdoor film screenings, dance, and theatre events. An intelligent relaxation of regulations within this zone would be beneficial for Hong Kong. For example, an easing of the public noise regulations for activities that face the sea, so new spaces can be created for performance venues. Flexible multifunctional spaces within a linear park would generate exceptional opportunities: a place where bicycle paths might connect different districts together, with slopes on the grass providing areas for impromptu audiences, open air orchestras, and recitals. Inexpensive marinas for mooring sailboats within walking distance to all residential areas would create convenient access points to the harbor, offering a means to instantly escape the city density. A culture of outdoor cafés away from traffic, noise, and pollution would allow the population to emerge from under the shadows of the skyscrapers, providing an opportunity to see the horizon again.

Waterfronts are spaces of constant evolution, requiring a long-term vision, continuous involvement, and a process of slow refinement. Inviting the public to see how they choose to transform the park daily, yearly, and over the decades encourages greater interaction among the population. This collaboration generates alliances which in turn enable even more creative exchange. Architecture and urbanism should function as facilitators for greater social engagement, where the intelligent design of spaces generates a wider range of activities. Hong Kong needs to encourage the collective ownership of public space, to believe that participation by all is essential for society. Highly scripted spaces are not necessary; rather, we need spaces that allow for the freedom to spontaneously organize events. The quality of life should not solely be measurable by per capita income, but by the range of opportunities afforded to the public. Historically in Hong Kong pure profit comes from the water, as government policy utilizes the land reclamation projects as a revenue source. However, as we look forward, activating the public space close to the residential areas is crucial for a city that is responsive, equitable, and inclusive for all.

public
open spaces

Heaven on Earth

anothermountainman // exhibit

mirage in his eyes
oasis from your angle
for me ... it is heaven on earth

Two Wongs Going To Sea

Kacey Wong | **Stanley Wong** // event

Two installations took to the water of Victoria Harbor as part of a series of events that question how public culture is defined. Stanley Wong's Heaven on Earth united a traditional Chinese sampan with an idyllic and sublimely pruned Chinese penjing tree, summoning the image of a tranquil pastoral scene. A hallucinating calmness for viewers, the lone tree creates a supple contrast to the urban forest of towers that form the skyline of Hong Kong and the hectic pace of the inhabitants within. Kacey Wong's Paddling Home, a floating four by four-foot cube, commented on the overheated real estate market that attaches shameless price tags to luxury apartments with any sort of harbor view. Clad in pink tiles with exterior plumbing typical of Hong Kong's housing blocks, the boat doubled as a tiny apartment that, once in the water, has a priceless 360-degree view of the harbor. Rising periodically to the rooftop to golf or go fishing, Kacey waved to spectators on the shoreline, some of whom undoubtedly waited for the entire vessel to capsize. Miraculously, he stayed afloat.

Second Skin

Academy of Visual Arts // exhibit

One only understands the things that one tames.

– Antoine de Saint- Exupéry

Although it may be a natural habitat to various animals and vegetation, the Biennale site is situated on a piece of urban wilderness that can cause discomfort to those who do not often venture into such an untamed environment.

Second Skin aims to domesticate this wilderness using simple and abstract symbols that reiterate the history of the land in contrast with its past and its future as a cultural district. Enticed to walk through and between the various clusters that make up the installation, visitors are unconsciously drawn into a more intimate interaction with nature. The juxtaposition of the symbols in the natural environment, and the visual tension between the trees and the skyline, turns the site into a sculpture that changes with time and weather.

123

Dressing Nature

Peter Benz // essay

There is, at the heart of Hong Kong, in the middle of the most densely populated place on earth, a piece of wilderness with all kinds of insects, dirt roads, and even areas with sketchy mobile phone reception. How can it be integrated into the city, appropriated for its citizens? Why not directly address the trees?

Dressing nature would allow people to see something familiar in the unfamiliar, and make it easier for them to build a connection with nature, maybe even encourage some direct, physical interaction. Admittedly a simplistic idea, yet in opposition to almost everyone's subsequent presumption, each dress created for Second Skin was tailor-made for one specific tree. Initially, on the West Kowloon site, the team spent several afternoons measuring trees ("Waist?", "Hem?") and deciding on suitable styles for each of them, depending on the tree size, stem length, perimeter, shape, position, foliage color, kind of undergrowth, setting within the site, and neighboring trees. Each tree was marked with a number, located on a map, and communicated to the site management as well as the curatorial team.

Nevertheless, it did not really help, as unanticipated appropriations occurred, trees changed, the site changed, and at one point a whole grove of trees vanished overnight. In the end, there had to be compromises. For example, it had been a subversive side-intention of the project to smuggle our skirts into all the photographs possibly taken on the site, thus appropriating not only the physical site, but also its virtual representation. That idea had to be given up. However, after setting up on the evening of the Biennale opening, we found one spot on site – and one spot only – from which all the skirt clusters could be seen at the same time.

Instead of hiring contractors to do the actual production work, we set up a temporary student workshop on campus, in which all the tree skirts were produced from scratch. This included pattern-making and pattern-cutting for the seventy individual skirts; sewing all the parts and pieces (despite the fact that only one of the participants had any previous sewing experience); spraying all the skirts with a toxic fire-resistant solution; drying and cleaning the skirts; packing them for transportation; threading in the draw-strings and bamboo-hoops. Throughout the process the integrity of each skirt – the right size, right color, and correct design – was maintained, too, for this decidedly polemical and mischievous enterprise.

In the end, each skirt had a story – a tiny and unimportant story, but a story nonetheless. It may seem a rather romantic idea, but we even liked to believe that the stories gave character to each of the skirts. This allowed the project team to develop ownership of the skirts before handing them over to the public.

After the opening, Second Skin began a life of its own, for over time we discovered that the original bright magenta color of our skirts started fading, depending on the skirts exposure to sunlight and weather. Surprisingly, the skirts turned out to be almost a kind of photo-sensitive surface, able to represent the large individual branches of trees looming overhead. This photogram quality, in combination with bird droppings, insect carcasses, all sorts of mucus and tree secretions, and other natural evidential materials, turned the skirts into documentary art pieces of sorts – action paintings, as it were.

It also implied that over the exhibition time, the skirts – intentionally sticking out in the beginning – started to blend in, to become part of the milieu until a balance was reached between the "natural wilderness" and "artificial intruder" that allowed the two to coexist. In the end, "appropriation" turned out to be the underlying theme of the project in a variety of forms: appropriation of the objects, the site, and nature, through nature.

Peter Benz is Assistant Professor for Spatial Design at the Academy of Visual Arts at the Hong Kong Baptist University. His personal research interests lie in everyday design, in particular, everyday products. Peter is an avid collector of spoons and in "un-designed" marginal spaces. Beyond that Peter is also interested in the medialisation of cities, and is currently working to establish Experience Design as a subject of academic discourse.

Hole in the Wall

Jody Marie Bielun | Pablo Leppe // exhibit

In Hong Kong and Shenzhen, where space is at a premium, where do we find a place for the public? Hole in the Wall cuts a ribbon of space into a vertical wall. Inspired by the flourishing Frontier Closed Area that separates the two cities, a strip of no-man's land reclaimed by nature, we want to reclaim a strip of space as a niche for the city's inhabitants. This bench is a public space in which people can lie down, sit, take a break, or even take a nap. The seat is made of renewable bamboo poles and grass areas. Businesses sponsor the space above the bench, creating a billboard for art which allow for a sign of culture to appear in the bustling urban streets. For the Biennale, Dom a local street artist of Start From Zero created the graphics.

Discovering possibilities

Revealing potential

Tetraphobia

RAD // exhibit

Looking to discover urban clues and logic that contribute to the living fabric of the city, "the missing floor number" phenomenon has always been intriguing. Rather than seeing this merely as a result of superstition in the East Asian culture, is there the possibility to turn this trend into an urban opportunity? Can we save endangered numbers like four and forty-four from disappearing in our numerical ecosystem? Can we create a new urban catalyst? We begin our journey to the new urban tetraphobia.

We surveyed various buildings in Kennedy Town & West Kowloon and record the floor numbers that were skipped in some of them.

我們在堅尼地城及西九龍區內的建築物作調查並紀錄當中某些樓宇省略去的層數

WEST KOWLOON 西九龍
SURVEY 調查

KENNEDY TOWN 堅尼地城
SURVEY 調查

BUILDING A
6 SKIPPED FLOORS BUILT
2005

BUILDING B
3 SKIPPED FLOORS BUILT
2003

BUILDING C
4 SKIPPED FLOORS BUILT
2000

BUILDING A
7 SKIPPED FLOORS BUILT
2003

BUILDING B
8 SKIPPED FLOORS BUILT
2003

BUILDING C
18 SKIPPED FLOORS BUILT
2005

BUILDING D
25 SKIPPED FLOORS BUILT
2007

BUILDING E
19 SKIPPED FLOORS BUILT
2008

PROGRAM PROPOSAL 項目方案

We propose that, instead of skipping these floors, we offer them to the public.

我們提議將被省略去的層回饋大眾作公共空間使用

These programs are:

項目包括:

VIP HOMELESS SHELTER

直線露營區

ORGANIC FARM

WANCHAI BUNGEE JUMPING

單車徑

WEDDING CHAPEL

鬼佬公園

ROLLER SKATE SKY COURT

滾軸溜冰場

永樂崎壁

BICYCLE TRAIL

鰂仔區笨豬跳

堅尼地城地鐵站D出口

營地

INFANT PARADISE (TRAFFIC ACCIDENT FREE)

SWIMMING POOL

ZOO

KENNEDY TOWN MTR EXIT D

CAMPING SITE

四樓俱樂部

不收費幼稚園

WANCHAI BUNGEE JUMPING

外傭會所

結婚禮堂

4TH FLOOR CLUBHOUSE

PET SOCIETY

幼兒樂園(無交通意外)

動物園

馬尼拉瞭望台

FREE KINDER-GARTEN

PHILIPPINO WORKERS' CLUB

MANILA LOOKOUT

LINEAR CAMPING

露宿者之家

GWEILO PARK

寵物社區

港島徑第9段

WING LOK CRAG

露天展覽館

有機農莊

HONG KONG TRAIL STAGE 9

游泳池

OPEN AIR MUSEUM

4
Tetraphobia!

ANDREA

Mathieu Lehanneur | David Edwards // exhibit

Andrea naturally purifies air via a fan, propelling air through the leaves and root system of a plant, through water and soil filtration units, and back into the room. Since the late 1980s, scientists have sought to utilize the efficiency of living plants to naturally clean the air of harmful pollutants. Andrea passes polluted air through living surfaces, eliminating pollution.

energy
innovation

too much light

Leopold Fiala | Stijn Deferm | Karta Healy

// exhibit right

In the installation, too much light, we bring together two aspects of a creative workflow, working without knowing where it is leading, and unexpected enlightenment. Everybody relates to the situation where we work, work and work, without knowing what we are working for and where it is going to lead us. Then, all of a sudden it hits us like a flash from above. When the light hits us, we experience gratification and release, after feeling lost and disoriented during the process.

We would like to invite everyone to this enlightening experience.

SL-Tree Prototype 00

SLHO & Associates | Motorwave Group

// exhibit left

A tree planted today is a reflection of our long-term social commitment, as the tree is an amazing life form and metaphor, transforming solar energy and mineral resources into the basic architecture of organic life.

Energy is omnipresent, intangible, invisible, and it governs all forms of life, sustaining the very foundations of our civilization. Can this free and abundant energy be captured, transformed, and utilized in better and more efficient ways?

To capture the intangible through the wind, turning it into light, and transforming the state of water by creating a sea of mist suggests the nurturing of our surroundings as an elemental garden.

If one is willing to look at nature from an empirical level, in terms of its protean abundance, the possibilities are limited only by one's own imagination.

Wind Tree Lamp Tree

Lucien Gambarota // essay

The idea of the Wind Tree is to mix art, nature, and energy, while proving that the modern world can adapt. In nature a tree will collect carbon and transform it into wood, which will then be used as an energy source. The same way a robot is a very distant copy of a human being, a lamp tree is a copy of a tree that generates clean power and helps cool the environment. In the same way that a tree can resist high winds through flexibility, the lamp tree is made from highly flexible components to provide the same adaptability to stresses. The lamp tree can move and bend under high wind and, as bamboo reverts to its original position, so does a lamp tree. Along the trunk, several nozzles spray a water mist that absorbs the sun's energy to provide a cooling area and, unlike a real tree, mounted lights provide visibility at night.

We can make lamp trees in different sizes and colors. A lamp tree has a trunk with several branches, at the end of each branch there is a wind turbine designed to spin with very low wind speed. Each wind turbine can rotate dynamically to face the wind direction. The faster the wind speed, the faster the turbines spin, and the more energy is generated. A lamp tree with ten branches can generate a hundred Watts for twenty-two hours a day, enough to watch forty television sets for one hour.

In Hong Kong more awareness needs to be generated to address pollution issues. In the West, conserving energy and limiting pollution started in early 1970s after the first oil crisis. This explains the reason Europe is one of the lowest carbon and pollution emitters among the industrialized nations. In Hong Kong and China, measures will only be taken by responsible bodies when citizens' lives are endangered. Since it takes many years for pollution to show its corrosive effects, we cannot expect action anytime soon.

Hong Kong's current economic regime leaves little room for financial incentives to affect promoting a healthier environment. People spending nearly half of their income on rent or mortgage payments are simply too busy to worry about the long-term viability of the city. So, how do we bring these issues to the public and policy level? How can we work with the government to generate more incentives within the city for renewable energy systems?

Corporations or individuals will only adopt energy-saving and renewable-energy generation equipment if there is a financial incentive. They may want a better life, but they also want to save money. Instead of spending twenty billion Hong Kong dollars for other new developments, we could decrease the pollution in the city by half within five years by modifying buildings that are energy inefficient, by building large renewable energy farms, and by building a clean transportation industry across Hong Kong.

Lucien Gambarota, who was born in 1957 in Italy, studied physics and chemistry in a French university. He worked as an international buyer for four years for the world's second largest retailer. He moved to Hong Kong in 1987, and opened a watch factory. He has been doing private research in many fields for more than fifteen years and has designed many consumer products. He invented and developed Motorwave and Motorwind technology. He also developed the California Fitness concept of harvesting human energy during workouts.

xDesign

Natalie Jeremijenko // exhibit

xDesign explores opportunities presented by new technologies for non-violent social change through examining structures of participation in the production of knowledge and information, inclusive of the political and social possibilities of information and emerging technologies. In this vein, xDesign spans a range of media from statistical indices, such as the Despondency Index project which linked the Dow Jones to the suicide rate at San Francisco's Golden Gate Bridge; to biological substrates, such as the installation of cloned trees in pairs in various urban micro-climates; to robotics, such as the development of feral robotic dog packs to investigate environmental hazards.

PLANCH™
& The Grand Resource

AUSTIN + MERGOLD // exhibit

PLANCH™ is a planter-bench that combines potentially toxic chemical products from urban construction waste with a plant, for phytoremediation is one way to deal with the toxins we produce daily. In front of PLANCH™ is the Grand Resource, an installation that rethinks the future of large-scale urban infrastructure by integrating renewable energy systems within the existing urban fabric to simultaneously generate clean power for the city, provide programs and spaces for social activity within the community, and attract tourists from other parts of the city, the country, and abroad.

Draw Your Future with Light and Shadow

Spectrum Design & Associates | Frank Leung | Pak King Lam // exhibit

The walking path is illuminated with poetic blue light, leading people to the exhibition Draw Your Future with Light and Shadow. Adding to the reflective or meditative visual journey, there are two totems transformed into a canvas for people to map out their thoughts and desires of their ideal neighborhood for the future. A trace of their own character and feelings toward Hong Kong are recorded under light and shadow, projecting different experiences between day and night.

Black Tee

Michael Yuen // exhibit

An intervention for the official Biennale shirt, fifty black shirts have been specially produced for the biennale staff with a single blue LED on the back. Stitching electronic circuitry into the fabric using conductive silver threads and conductive silver Velcro, it comes with a detachable power pack. It affects both the wearer and those around them.

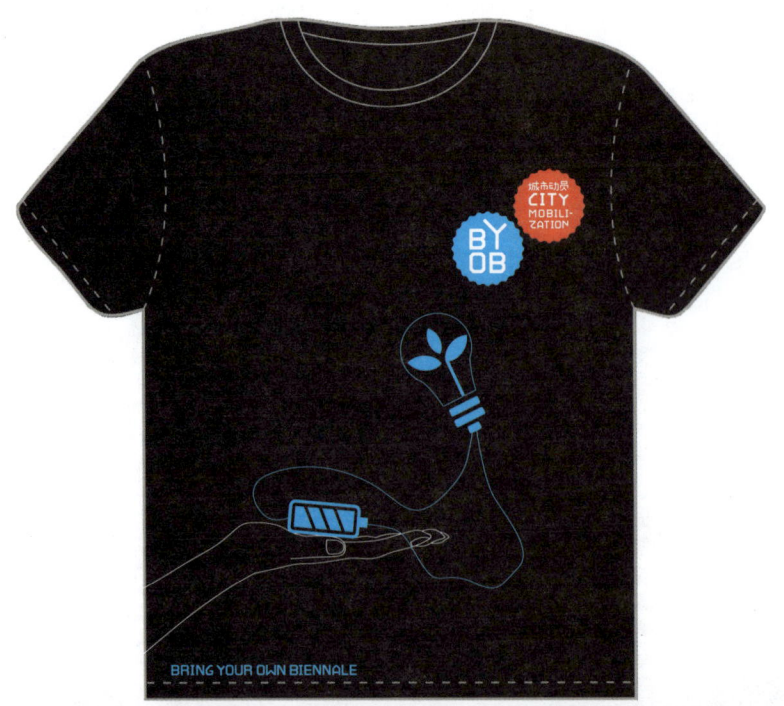

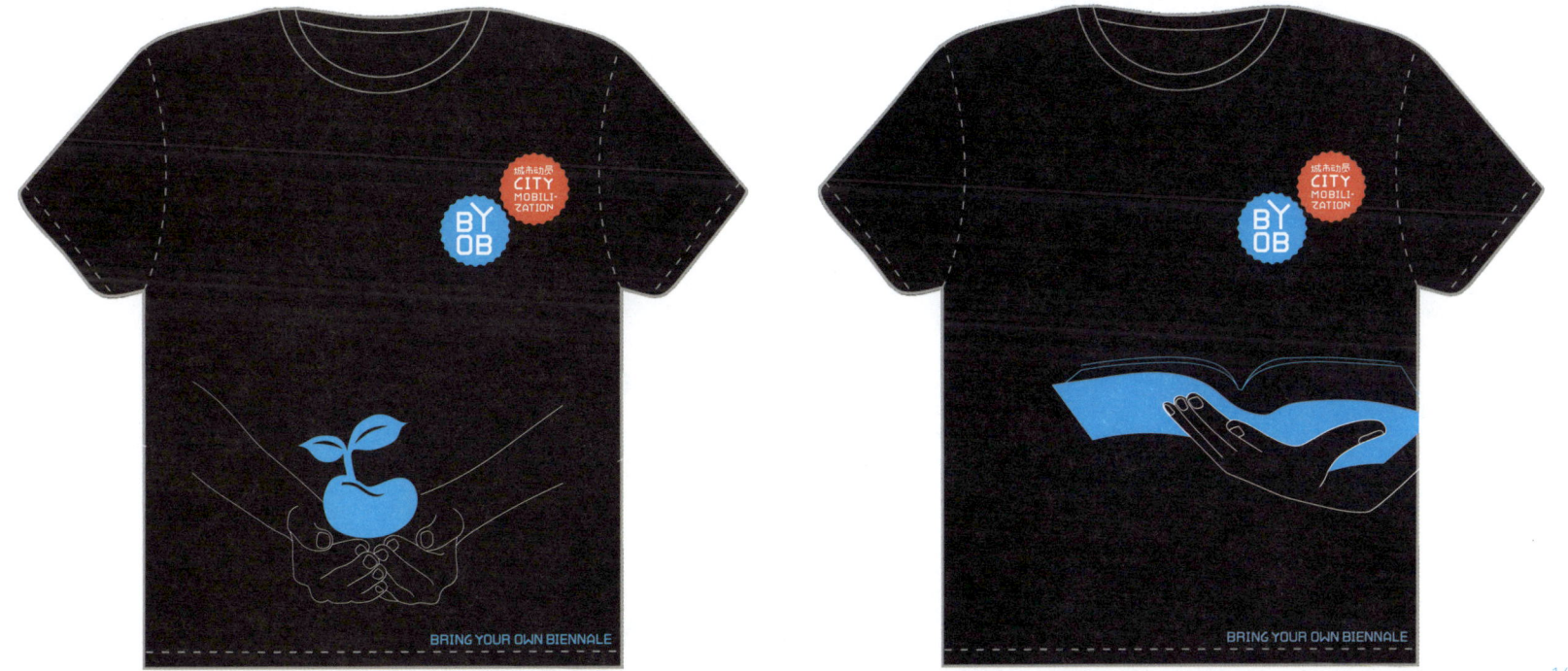

BRING YOUR OWN BIENNALE

BRING YOUR OWN BIENNALE

Moving on from Copenhagen UN Climate Conference

// forum

---

date: 16 January 2010

participants: Debra Lam, Edward Ng, Fontane Lau, Lam Chiu Ying, Raymond Cole, Ryan Ng, Trevor Ng, William Yu

moderators: KS Wong, Vincent Cheng

Much has been discussed at the United Nations Climate Summit held in Copenhagen. But what does it really mean for Hong Kong, the Pearl River Delta, and greater China? A diverse panel of experts, building practitioners, concerned groups, and members of the general public offered a variety of insights. Firsthand accounts by youth representatives, expert meteorologists, and professors returning from the UN Climate Summit debated the way forward.

Fontane Lau: What I have learned from the UN meeting is the limits of having this kind of international negotiation. What we need to do is work at the grassroots level. In Hong Kong, we have little risk, but we are contributing to the climate change problem by our way of living here. Therefore, it shows we need an educational vehicle in Hong Kong to drive change at the most fundamental level.

Ryan Ng: Climate justice is an important question because the most affected countries, the most vulnerable countries are not the countries that are actually emitting the most carbon dioxide. What I brought back are not really answers but more questions on the matter of climate justice.

Edward Ng: Hong Kong has high per capita carbon dioxide emissions and we cannot afford to carry on like that. The reason why we are unaware of the problem is that we are insulated. This needs to change.

Trevor Ng: Intervention measures will be needed in many sectors in order for Hong Kong to achieve its emissions reduction target. One scenario will see us retrofitting 50% of our 41,000 buildings over the next ten years with energy efficient systems, increasing the proportion of electricity generated by natural gas to 50%, adopting low carbon transportation, and dealing with our waste stream in a less carbon intensive manner.

Debra Lam: It is a collision of forces. When we position it as us versus the government or us versus the business society, that means nothing is going to happen. It is always going to be a battle.

Mr. Lam Chiu Ying
Chartered Meteorologist

Ms. Fontane Lau
WWF Hong Kong

Raymond Cole: David Suzuki once argued that humans have flourished and become the dominant species because they have the ability to anticipate danger and take the necessary evasive action. We no longer have to rely solely on human instinct to understand the current and potential threats. We have accumulated knowledge and have enormous computer capability and other means at our disposal, assisting us in making assessments and guiding our actions. This research has provided us with a considerable amount of evidence on how human activity is causing climate change and of the potentially catastrophic consequences of failing to significantly reduce greenhouse gas emissions. We are ignoring this enhanced ability of foresight at our peril.

Given the wealth of scientific evidence, we clearly cannot claim ignorance regarding the damaging effects of current human activity.

— Raymond Cole

Given the wealth of scientific evidence, we clearly cannot claim ignorance regarding the damaging effects of current human activity and patterns of consumption on the biological health of the planet. The notion of criminal negligence typically applies when in either doing nothing, or omitting to do anything, shows wanton and reckless disregard for the lives and safety of others. With more than 300,000 people currently dying each year as a direct or indirect result of climate change, those governments stalling, ignoring or failing to act decisively on addressing global warming are effectively acting in a morally and criminally negligent manner.

William Yu: If temperatures rise above two degrees there is a possibility that 30% of all species will face extinction. Climate change will alter patterns of water availability by intensifying the water cycle. Further deterioration of water quality will continue through changes in rainfall distribution, glacier ice, and snow melt. Hong Kong has the second largest per capita seafood consumption in Asia. Nearly 25% of marine creatures rely on coral reefs for shelter and food. Coral bleaching will eventually affect our food supply by affecting our fish population.

Jovita Ho: One of the great innovations in urban design is the green roof, which is probably applicable in Hong Kong in some ways, and I think it illustrates that even with all the differences between cities worldwide it is still possible to implement ideas from regions after certain modifications are made.

CY Lam: As a rigorous scientist, I accept that there is a small chance that the data might be wrong. But that very small chance does not justify doing nothing. The skeptics cite the recent cold spell here or there. We should not flip-flop between positions based on the occurrence of individual events in a single winter. To turn knowledge into action is quite a transformation and I think that needs a revolution. And revolutions are not initiated by governments. Revolutions are initiated by people.

ELECTRICITY CONSUMED BY BUILDINGS CONTRIBUTES TO ABOUT 60% OF HONG KONG'S GREENHOUSE GAS EMISSIONS

Bring Your Own Green Building

KS Wong // essay

There are signs of promising and positive changes for Hong Kong and China. Recently, in mainland China, the 12th Five-Year Plan has set new energy and climate goals. In Hong Kong, the government launched the consultation document on "Hong Kong's Climate Change Strategy and Action Agenda." The proposed strategy and agenda outlines various means of combating climate change, including enhancing energy efficiency, promoting green transport, turning waste into energy, and revamping the fuel mix. In addition to these mitigation measures, it also highlights vulnerable areas in light of the growing impact of climate change. This is a critical milestone to chart Hong Kong's way forward as it develops into a low-carbon city. In the consultation document Hong Kong set a 2020 target for bringing down carbon intensity by fifty to sixty percent. Carbon intensity is defined as the amount of greenhouse gas or carbon emissions per unit of gross domestic product. This seeks to measure the effectiveness of efforts taken to reduce emissions which are highly associated with economic activities.

Looking ahead, we need to solidly formulate the corresponding action plans from both the supply and demand sides. In Hong Kong, managing building energy efficiency from the demand side should be the key challenge, since 90% of our electricity is consumed in buildings. Regarding the public's engagement with addressing climate change, considerable work needs to be done for the building user groups of residential and commercial buildings to engage the major players of these user groups: the government and public sector, developers, listed companies, property management companies, and the general public. Each and every one of us can play a part in cutting down our greenhouse gas emissions with a view to contributing towards achieving the proposed target in carbon intensity reduction. It will require immense effort and whole-hearted support from all walks of life in Hong Kong, as well as inevitable changes in our own lifestyles and behavior. Bring Your Own Green Building!

KS Wong, an architect with over twenty years of architectural practice and recognized by both local and international awards, is director of Ronald Lu & Partners, and leads the in-house Sustainability Steering Committee. His current projects range from building design, master planning, urban regeneration to research studies, and include the first zero carbon building in Hong Kong. He also served as the PGBC Chairman and the HKIA vice president in 2009-2010. He currently chairs the Green Labelling Committee of the Hong Kong Green Building Council.

Urban Spectacles

Laurent Gutierrez | Valérie Portefaix

// essay

As far as I am concerned, I try to direct my telescope through the bloody haze upon a mirage of the nineteenth century, which I seek to depict according to those features that it will show in a future state of the world liberated from magic.

– Walter Benjamin

In a letter to Werner Kraft, dated 28 October 1935, Walter Benjamin described his struggle to see beyond the general theory of materialist civilizations. At this particular moment, Benjamin was about to solve the puzzle that was to become the 1935 introductory essay for the unfinished Arcades Project – "Paris, Capital of the Nineteenth Century." The visionary telescope, or the technical device Benjamin created, is now known as phantasmagoria or the art of making ghosts come alive. The invention of phantasmagoria coincides precisely with the spectacle of nineteenth-century capitalist development. The turning point for Benjamin was to identify "haze" as the nature and foundation of modern development. Therefore, the telescope became the optical-intellectual tool to see through the haze, and to see beyond the present into the past in order to foresee the future.

Learning from Benjamin's struggle to construct an understanding of early capitalist development amidst the newly bourgeois Paris, we ask ourselves if a similar visionary optic might not allow us to see through the haze of present-day Hong Kong and China's so-called contemporary evolution toward global economic colossus. Once we looked at it from a temporal dimension, however, versus a purely abstract condition, the binocular vision became the visual, structural, systematic, and technological apparatus by which we could construct a new, penetrating perspective – a properly neo-Benjaminian "gaze." In other words, the haze is the necessary condition for the Hong Kong-China relationship and their common ambitions at the moment. The use of binoculars, as magnifying apparatus, allows for the creation of a new panoramic vision transforming the prosaic real into a surreal spectacle, playing with notions of visibility, hyper-visibility, and invisibility – or the co-existence of multiple states typically hidden by the authorized view.

For the Biennale, the skyline of Hong Kong is the proper subject (analysand) for an optical and sensorial transference, making this panoramic spectacle the vehicle for expressing the capitalist self-image and its representational bias. From the perspective of West Kowloon, the frontline of skyscrapers takes the shape of a fragmented heroism. Each of its components disappears, combining to form a singular mass, a single mediated image that allows it to acquire its status *as skyline*. The Hong Kong skyline is the best physical graph of Hong Kong's successful *material* development and is directly related to China's economic achievements. From an evolutionary perspective, it had to battle with natural elements, the sea and mountains, simply to exist. This first evolutionary stage lasted for more than one hundred years – a small eternity. But then, coinciding with the handover a decade ago, The Center was created – that is, a giant lighthouse that lit up Victoria Harbor, serving to show the direction of capitalist investment for China's merchants. This initial illumination eventually engaged the entire skyline in a nightly light-sabre fight for the crowds of mainland Chinese tourists, proudly coming to harvest what they identify as their own – prosperity and the future phantasm of Hong Kong fully integrated with China, with the resulting giant strolling the world.

So, if there is an impossibility of seeing through the haze today, one may at least foresee the future of the Hong Kong skyline as a phantasmagoria under Chinese command, becoming the simple representation of its frenetic development. Therefore, the doubling of binocular vision – inverted and maxi, reducing and magnifying – is the visionary optic par excellence that will provide the extreme variations or elliptical intellectual torsions needed to perforate this atmospheric condition, toward a strategy of *invisibility* nonetheless, or hiding in plain sight, a bifurcation of purpose within difference; an "ecological" and harmonious development for China: always so far away … yet so close!

Laurent Gutierrez and Valérie Portefaix are the principals of MAP Office. Both teach at the School of Design, the Hong Kong Polytechnic University.

Bloody Haze
Inverted Binocular and Maxi Binocular

MAP Office // exhibit

Examining the interplay of visibility and invisibility, the distorted image of a city's skyline, as illustration of capitalistic development, is perhaps its best representation.

The two binoculars are mounted on fixed poles aimed toward Hong Kong's skyline. The skyline is a physical graph of the "successful" economic development of Hong Kong. Importantly, the pair of binoculars are pointed in the exact same direction; one is positioned in a close-up (magnifying) mode while the other offers the "long distant" (inverted) view. Each comments on the traditional "optic" of perspective, suggesting as well that Hong Kong "looks back."

Ice Formations

Jason Kelly Johnson | **Nataly Gattegno**   // essay

Live models are dynamic formations that register and continuously adapt to shifting atmospheric and microclimatic conditions. These models can be used as analytical engines to understand the patterns around us, and in some cases, as conceptual frameworks for architecture that also reveal emerging organizations of energy, form, and flow in visually discernible patterns.

Glaciarium is a portable interactive instrument, a live model, which engages visitor's senses through the sight and sound of a melting ice core. Somewhere between a microscope, acoustic device and an atmospheric peep show, the installation allows one to observe, quantify and participate in the changing phases and formations of melting ice. *Glaciarium* employs interactivity and the senses to turn an abstract global issue into an intimate, almost visceral experience.

Throughout the day, the infrared sensors tracked the ice core formation. Increased observation amplifies the internal lighting effects and, depending on the duration of interaction, dramatically accelerates the melting of the ice core. The quickening rhythm of dropping water registers the observers' prolonged presence. The more one looks through the viewing aperture, the more one participates in the degradation of the ice core. *Glaciarium* is simultaneously a projection of an imminent environmental condition and the subtle materialization of how contemporary political, social, and ecological trends might be channeled towards a more productive future by engaging the senses, in this case through the sight and sound of a melting ice core. In a sense, the environmental imperative is no longer debated but instead rendered personal; the influence of the individual is linked directly to the materiality and sensation of the installation.

Jason Kelly Johnson and **Nataly Gattegno** are design principals of Future Cities Lab, which is an experimental design practice based in San Francisco, California. FCL earned second prize in the Seoul Performing Arts International Competition, and was a finalist in the History Channel's City of the Future competition. Most recently, they received the Architectural League of New York Prize and were New York Prize Fellows at the Van Alen Institute in New York City.

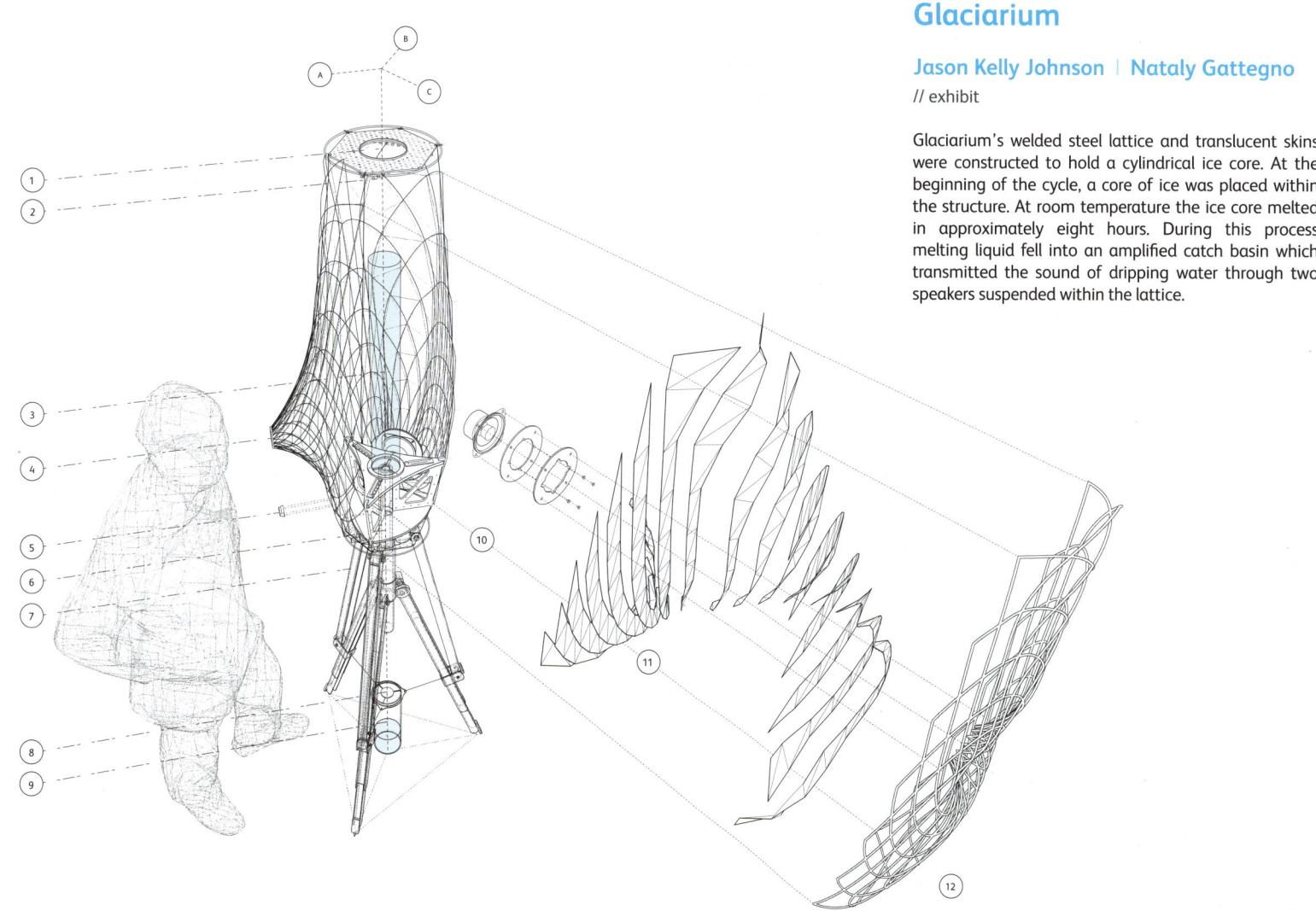

Glaciarium

Jason Kelly Johnson | Nataly Gattegno
// exhibit

Glaciarium's welded steel lattice and translucent skins were constructed to hold a cylindrical ice core. At the beginning of the cycle, a core of ice was placed within the structure. At room temperature the ice core melted in approximately eight hours. During this process melting liquid fell into an amplified catch basin which transmitted the sound of dripping water through two speakers suspended within the lattice.

Greenville Design Competition

Aedas | South China Morning Post   // exhibit

The 2008 earthquake in China devastated huge areas of Sichuan. Chengdu, the capital city of Sichuan, is taking a leading role in the post-earthquake rebuild as a China Urban and Rural Integrated Experimental Zone. The *South China Morning Post*'s Homes for Hope and the Aedas Architects Foundation have organized a design competition open to students in China, seeking creative, sustainable, and quake-resistant affordable housing designs for Sichuan.

Finalists

Shaking Houses
Xiong Xin, Harvard University

Overlap
Yi Nian Zu, Tsinghua University

Hang House
Kong Di, Beijing University

ISO*Union
Kwan Chun Sing, University of California, Berkeley

Rebuild for Those Who Lost Homes
Jia Wei, University of Hong Kong

Exefuy Honk
Ginger Zhong, Tongji University

Tree House
Liu Yi Lin, South China Normal University

Coexistence
Wu Hui Biao, ETH Zurich

Encounter with Qiang Flute
Tem Wu, Sichuan University

The Pinwheel House
Chui Ying Chee, MIT

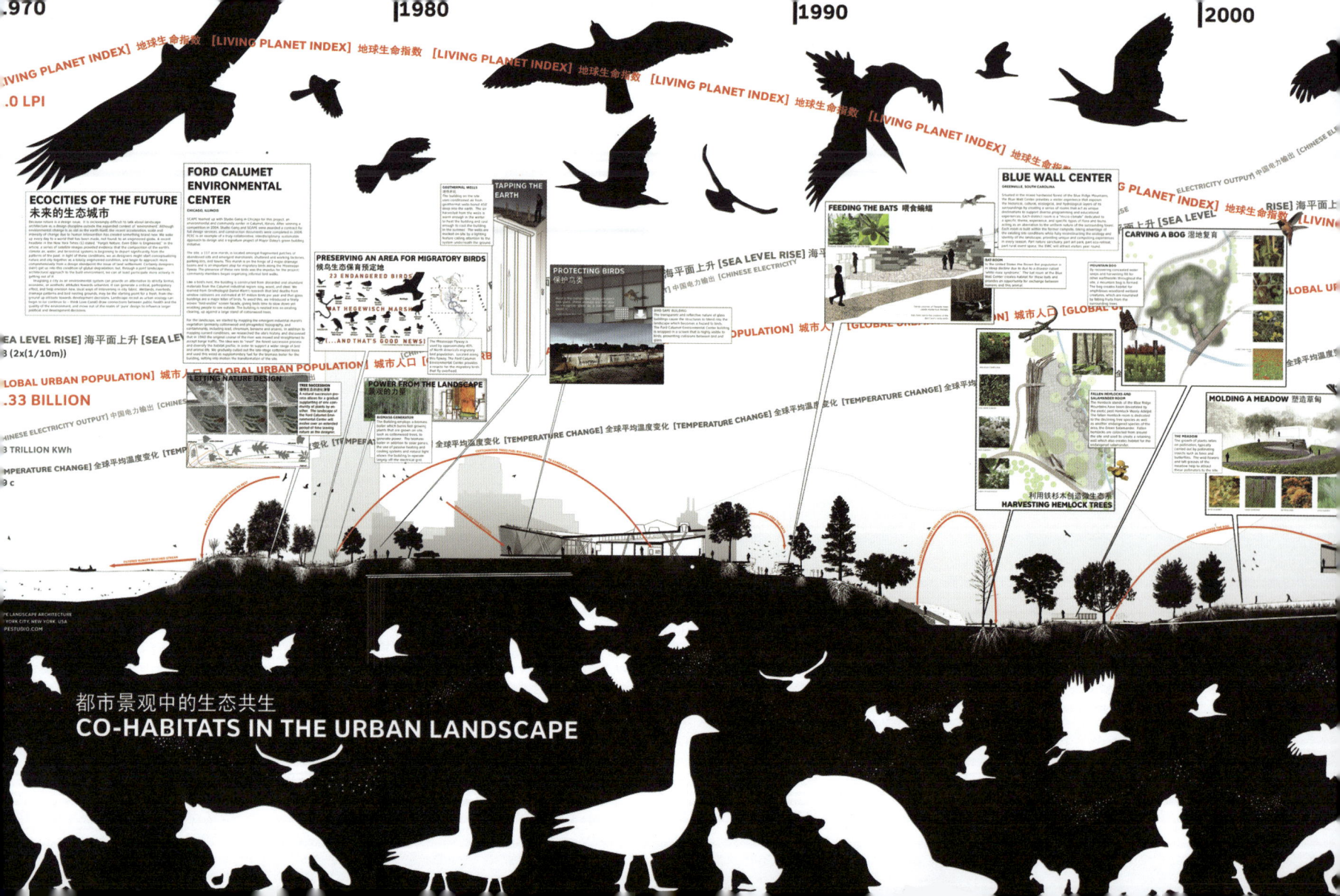

都市景观中的生态共生
CO-HABITATS IN THE URBAN LANDSCAPE

Design for the Anthropocene Era

SCAPE Landscape Architecture // exhibit

Design for the Anthropocene Era threads together three SCAPE projects illustrating the joint natural and human habitats generated by new construction and earth work. It is vital to expand architecture beyond "design for us," or beyond a built environment conceived exclusively for human consumption and comfort, to address the wider global ecosystem as a shared space for all species. Urban design can be recast as a form of new, activist, joint urban and environmental stewardship in order to manage biodiversity and begin to reverse the trajectories of mass extinction on a hot, crowded planet.

165

IN HONG KONG THERE ARE
56 SPECIES OF MAMMALS,
100+ SPECIES OF
AMPHIBIANS AND REPTILES,
115 SPECIES OF DRAGONFLIES,
238 SPECIES OF BUTTERFLIES,
490 SPECIES OF BIRDS

100 TO 140 HECTARES OF LAND
WERE CREATED BY RECLAMATION
EVERY YEAR FROM 1985 TO 2004,
DROPPING TO 17 HECTARES
FROM 2005 TO 2009

The Crab-Eating Mongoose's Right to the City

Mari Fujita // essay

From the recent immigrant, to the crab-eating mongoose, to the lesser bamboo bat, to the red lacewing butterfly, the battle for space in Hong Kong transcends species. The land-use zoning system under the Town Planning Ordinance, as well as the Conveyancing and Property Ordinance, the Wild Animals Protection Ordinance, and the Environmental Impact Assessment Ordinance are among the many regulatory mechanisms that determine how much of what can be built where, when, and for whom. As the two sides — that is, the developers and the conservationists — engage in a battle to increase the occupiable space for their respective constituencies, (multi-national banker or stateless mongoose), the distinction between human space and animal space in Hong Kong becomes further contested, marked, and codified.

A less antagonistic form of urbanism would require the eradication of the artificial division of nature and culture as well as the long-standing asymmetry of human life privileged over all other life forms. Conceived for a more inclusive definition of the "collective," this urbanism has the potential to radicalize mainstream notions of sustainability by having a more profound impact on the way the city's space is imagined. Vertical towers with nooks for crawling, winged, and bipedal species; hard, smooth, and soft horizontal surfaces layered in section for the enjoyment of creatures of all scales; lush, warm interiors that encourage the colonization of plants and insects; continuous water and greenways that weave habitats above, below, and through the hard infrastructure of the city all come to mind as possible-impossible scenarios worth exploring.

The first task toward such a smoothing of the urban condition is to reframe the city from a series of codified territories to that of a continuous, uninterrupted milieu. For sociologists, milieu "refers to our ability, but also the necessity, of creating our own environment according to our intentions and always in co-operation and conflict with our fellow-beings."[1] Operationally, the subjectivity implicit to the use of milieu in sociology demands the capacity to understand places as inherently multiple. The subjective aspect of milieu was explored much earlier through the theories of Jakob von Uexküll, a German zoologist who was interested in how living organisms perceive their surroundings. His quirky interest in the tick, amoebae, sea urchin, and other less-obvious subjects of study led to the development of his theory of the *Umwelt*. Uexküll believed that each living organism occupies his or her own *Umwelt*, a subjective and spatiotemporal world, mutually conditioned and mutually altered. The *Umgebung*, or the objective world (if such even exists), is composed of multitudes of *Umwelten*.[2] The application of Uexküll's theory to humans has been contested because in classical, Western philosophy (and in modern science), there is the assertion that humans possess rationality, which places us firmly in the realm of the *Umgebung* (the objective, empirical world of laws and reason). However, the imagining of simultaneously existing worlds that have their own subjective and spatiotemporal logic shares sympathies with postmodern notions of subjectivity, and, while in part a reaction against modernist rationality, suggest archaic views that predate science per se and Western rationality in the specific.

Concurrent with this self-assumed rationality of humans is the objectification of other species manifest in the form of zoos, menageries, cabinet of curiosities, and nature preserves. Underlying such an impulse for objectification is an historical attitude toward animals that shares sympathies with "parallel histories of colonization, ethnocentrism and the discovery of the other."[3] As postcolonial theory gains ground in a broader set of disciplines, could a phase of post-objectification follow, according all species the right to the city?

Currently, 57% of Hong Kong's land area is developable for humans while 43% of the land area is reserved for other life forms.[4] To imagine Hong Kong as a continuous milieu composed of overlapping, embedded, multi-scalar *Umwelten* would be to stimulate wonderful, surreal, invigorating consequences for a city that already distinguishes itself with its density and programmatic diversity.

Mari Fujita is Assistant Professor at the University of British Columbia School of Architecture and Landscape Architecture, as well as the principal of Fujitawork, a Vancouver based design studio. Mari's research is focused on the spatial and cultural affects of globalism. Her design studios and seminars explore emergent forms of urbanism with a focus on Vancouver and other cities experiencing rapid growth.

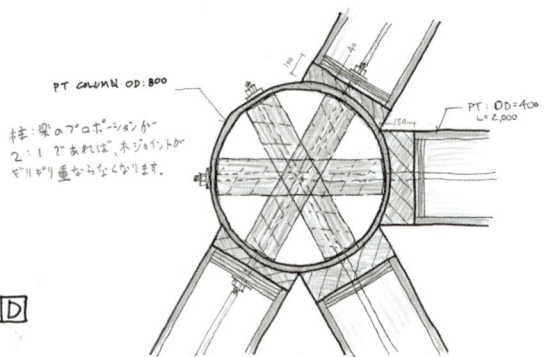

PT COLUMN OD: 800

PT : OD = 400
L = 2,000

柱の梁のプロポーションが
2:1 であれば、木ジョイントが
ギリギリ重ならなくなります。

D

2009.06.25
HONG KONG-SHENZHEN BIENNALE PAVILION   COLUMN-TRUSS JOINT DETAIL Sc:1/10

SHIGERU BAN ARCHITECTS
PAVILION DESIGN 1
25 JUN 2009

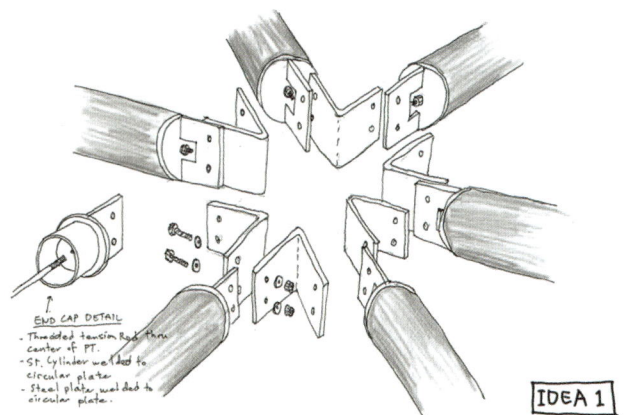

END CAP DETAIL
- Threaded tension Rod thru center of PT.
- St. Cylinder welded to circular plate.
- Steel plate welded to circular plate.

IDEA 1

2009.07.20
SHIGERU BAN ARCHITECTS
HONG KONG-SHENZHEN BIENNALE PAVILION   DOME INTERIOR HEXAGON JOINT

SHIGERU BAN ARCHITECTS
PAVILION DESIGN 2
20 JUL 2009

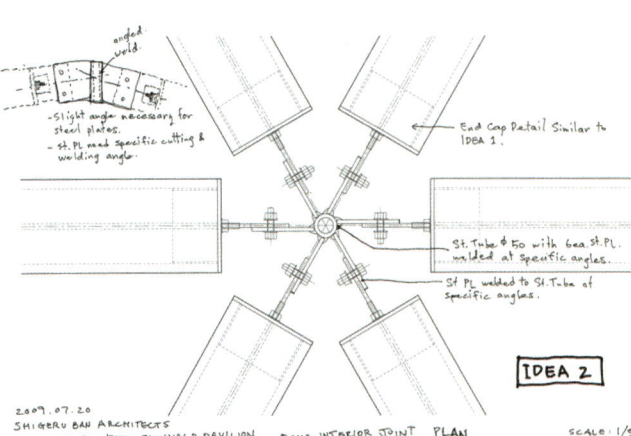

angled weld.

- Slight angle necessary for steel plates.
- St. PL need specific cutting & welding angle.

End Cap Detail Similar to IDEA 1.

St. Tube Ø 50 with 6ea. St.PL. welded at specific angles.

St. PL welded to St.Tube of specific angles.

IDEA 2

2009.07.20
SHIGERU BAN ARCHITECTS
HONG KONG SHENZHEN BIENNALE PAVILION   DOME INTERIOR JOINT   PLAN

SCALE: 1/5

Pavilion Process

Shigeru Ban // essay

The temporary nature of the Main Pavilion led to the decision to create a paper tube structure that also strived to minimize foundation requirements. The initial design went through many challenges and alterations to arrive at the final creation.

The original site allocated for the pavilion was triangular. The first plan was, therefore, a thirty meter equilateral triangle broken up into a finer grid of three meter triangles. The perimeter of the pavilion was composed of large columns at a three meter pitch to create a colonnade that defined the interior space of the open-air structure. These columns supported the entire roof structure, which was to be composed of a series of trusses comprised of smaller diameter paper tubes. Atop the truss was to be a light, translucent, corrugated polycarbonate roof. The structural innovation for this design was at the column-to-roof-truss connection, where wooden joints, inserted into the paper tubes, would create a new resisting joint; a first-time challenge for a paper tube structure.

The second design kept the same plan form of a thirty meter triangle but the paper tube structure was a three-dimensional dome structure that would come down to meet the ground at the three points. Because there were a minimum number of supports to carry the whole load of the roof, it was necessary for the foundations to become very large and heavy to support the massive beams that would span between the foundations. The hexagonal steel plate joints of the roof grid had to be made of inconsistent angles and connect to paper tube segments of differing lengths. The predetermined geometry of the geodesic roof made this proposed structure a sleek, low-lying form.

When it was determined that the location of the pavilion would be elsewhere within the larger biennale site, there was no longer a restriction to make a triangular structure. The third design proposed a square plan using shipping containers as foundational piers. Shipping containers are very much a common sight in Hong Kong, and are appropriate for creating temporary foundations, first, because they can be leased and returned after use, and second, because they themselves are rigid structures with a broad surface coverage for load-bearing purposes, and third, they can be filled with sand bags to achieve the necessary resistance against uplift forces. In this semi-final version, three containers per side were spaced at approximately six meter intervals for an even arrangement of walls and openings. A continuous steel beam was secured to the top of the containers using standard container connection joints to make up the perimeter support for the paper tube roof. The paper tube roof was composed of four equilateral triangular faces that leaned against each other to make a pyramidal form. Each equilateral triangle, similar to the first design, was composed of a smaller grid of triangles using all similar steel plate connections.

The form of this design would create a prominent presence within the Biennale landscape, and would also be visible from across the bay. The plan would have enclosed a large, regular-shaped interior accessible from all sides with a high ceiling. The openings could be closed off in numerous arrangements to flexibly accommodate various events. Additionally, there was a second option to this design that reduced the number of containers to two per side, resulting in a smaller interior space and a lower overall height.

The final design was a take-off from the previous design but incorporated a trussed paper tube roof in the form of a vault. The vaulted roof of this version has a broad span of thirty meters, a depth of thirty meters, and is supported by two rows of evenly spaced shipping containers. The roof covers the same regular thirty-meter by thirty-meter plan as in the previous design, but is open on either end of the vault. Within the Biennale site, the structure is oriented to allow the open end or aperture of the vaulted form to frame the view of Hong Kong Island.

Throughout the design process, discussions and input from the building authorities made the design process quite difficult. Because this was the first paper tube structure to be built in Hong Kong, there was a reluctance to approve the building as other typical temporary structures in other cities. Therefore, the built structure was somewhat compromised to meet these demands, resulting in an over-engineered structure. Subsequently, the depth of the structure had to be shortened to compensate for the extra costs incurred. The realization of this project was made possible by the tireless efforts of a collaborative team of architects, engineers, curators, consultants, and builders.

Shigeru Ban, born in Tokyo in 1957, graduated from Cooper Union School of Architecture in New York. In 1985, he established his private practice, Shigeru Ban Architects, in Tokyo. From 1995 through 1999, he was a consultant of the United Nations High Commissioner for Refugees, and at the same time he established an NGO, Voluntary Architects' Network. Ban's world-renowned projects include the Curtain Wall House; the Japan Pavilion, the Hannover EXPO 2000; the Nicolas G. Hayek Center; and the Centre Pompidou in Metz, France. He has received numerous distinctions, including the Grande Medaille France Academie d'Architecture, the Arnold W. Brunner Memorial Prize in Architecture, and the National Order of the Legion of Honor; he was a Professor at Keio University, Japan from 2001 to 2008, and has served as a jury member for the Pritzker Architecture Prize.

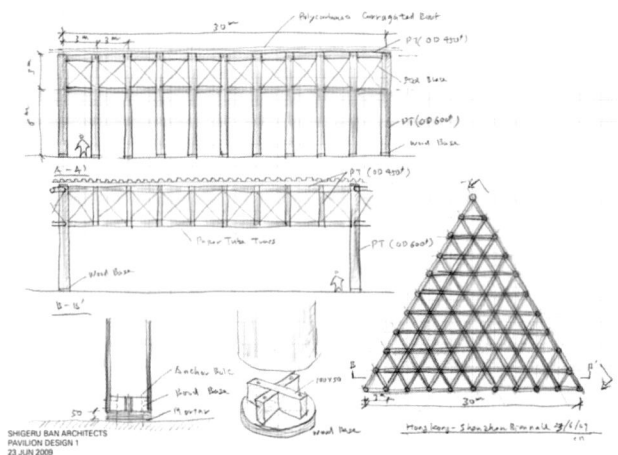

SHIGERU BAN ARCHITECTS
PAVILION DESIGN 1
23 JUN 2009

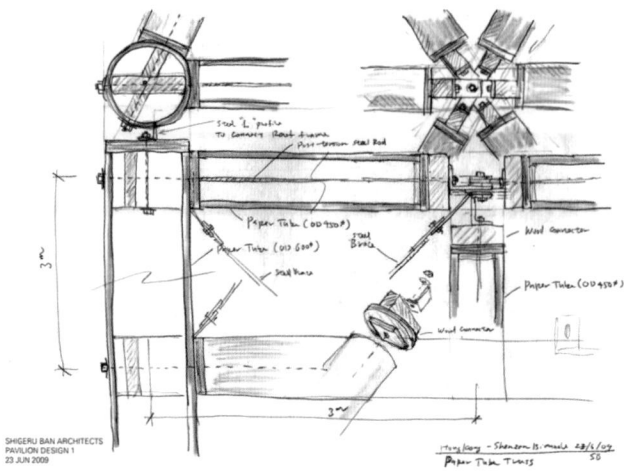

SHIGERU BAN ARCHITECTS
PAVILION DESIGN 1
23 JUN 2009

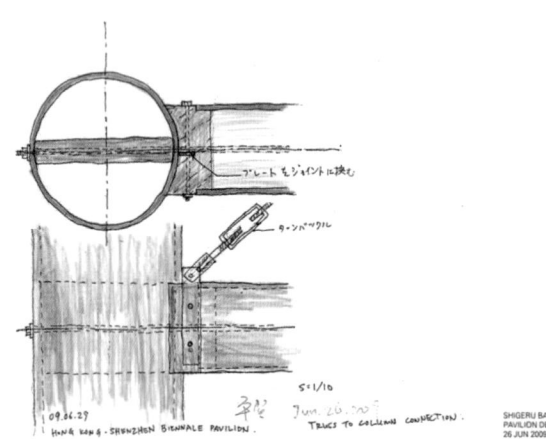

SHIGERU BAN ARCHITECTS
PAVILION DESIGN 1
26 JUN 2009

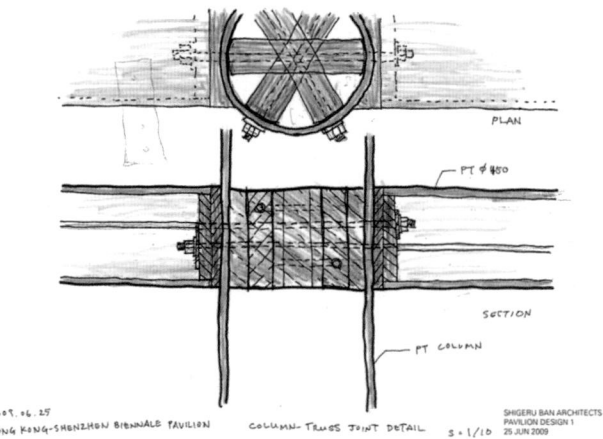

SHIGERU BAN ARCHITECTS
PAVILION DESIGN 1
25 JUN 2009

174

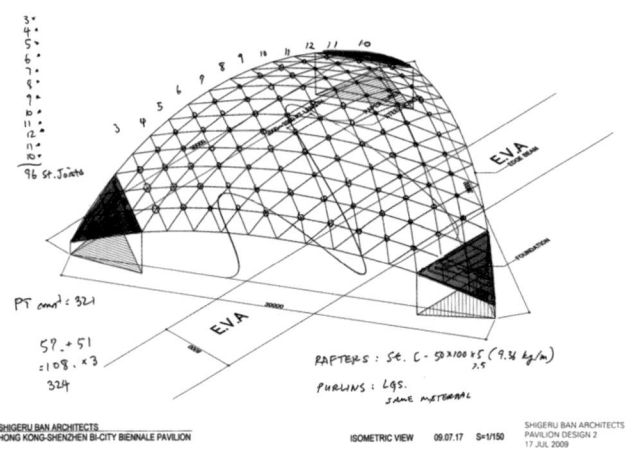

3.
4.
5.
6.
7.
8.
9.
10.
11.
12.
13.
10

96 St. Joints

PT cont = 321

5? + 51
= 108. x3
324

RAFTERS : St. C - 50 x 100 x 5 (9.36 kg/m)
7.5

PURLINS : LGS.
SAME METEREAL

E.V.A.

E.V.A.

SHIGERU BAN ARCHITECTS
HONG KONG-SHENZHEN BI-CITY BIENNALE PAVILION

ISOMETRIC VIEW   09.07.17   S=1/150

SHIGERU BAN ARCHITECTS
PAVILION DESIGN 2
17 JUL 2009

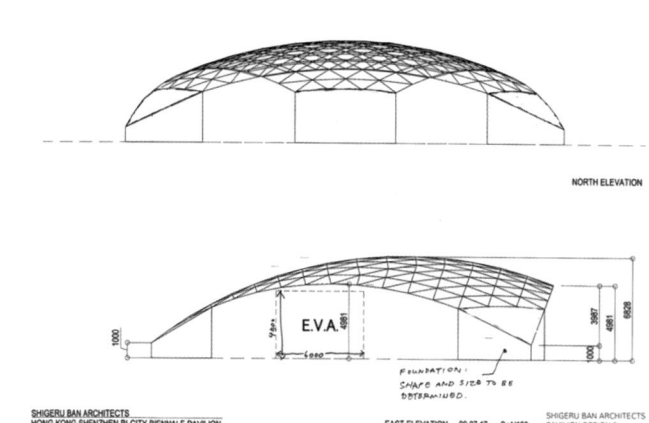

NORTH ELEVATION

E.V.A.

FOUNDATION:
SHAPE AND SIZE TO BE
DETERMINED

SHIGERU BAN ARCHITECTS
HONG KONG-SHENZHEN BI-CITY BIENNALE PAVILION

EAST ELEVATION   09.07.17   S=1/150

SHIGERU BAN ARCHITECTS
PAVILION DESIGN 2
17 JUL 2009

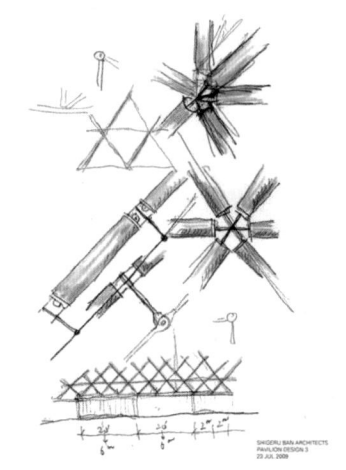

SHIGERU BAN ARCHITECTS
PAVILION DESIGN 3
23 JUL 2009

Hong Kong Biennale   23/7/09

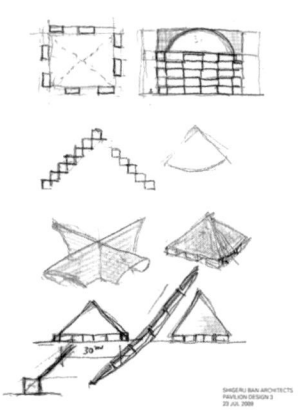

SHIGERU BAN ARCHITECTS
PAVILION DESIGN 3
23 JUL 2009

175

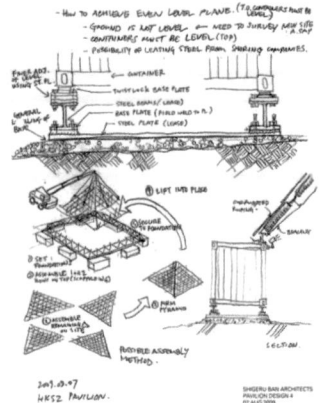

2009.08.07

- HOW TO ACHIEVE EVEN LEVEL PLANE (TO CONTAINERS MUST BE LEVEL)
- GROUND IS NOT LEVEL → NEED TO SURVEY NEW SITE A GAP
- CONTAINERS MUST BE LEVEL (TOP)
- POSSIBILITY OF LEADING STEEL FROM SHARING COMPANIES.

2009.08.07
HKSZ PAVILION.

SHIGERU BAN ARCHITECTS
PAVILION DESIGN 4
07 AUG 2009

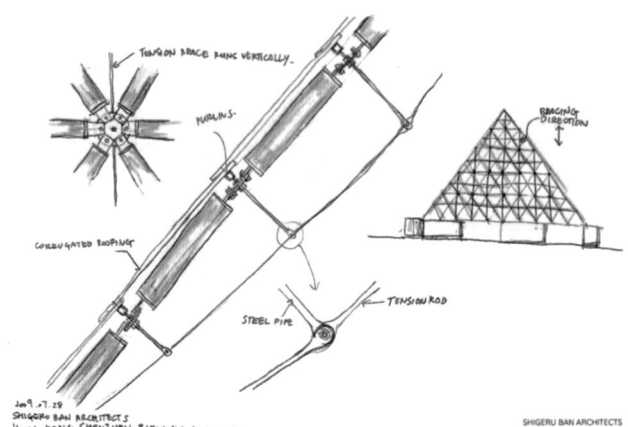

2009.07.28
SHIGERU BAN ARCHITECTS
HONG KONG SHENZHEN BIENNALE PAVILION

SHIGERU BAN ARCHITECTS
PAVILION DESIGN 3
28 JUL 2009

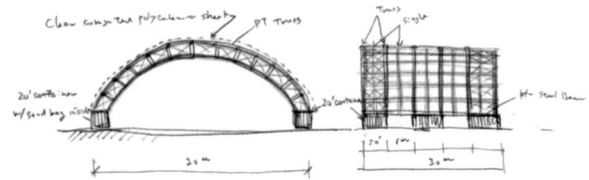

Hong kong SZ Biennale 19/8/09

SHIGERU BAN ARCHITECTS
PAVILION DESIGN 4
19 AUG 2009

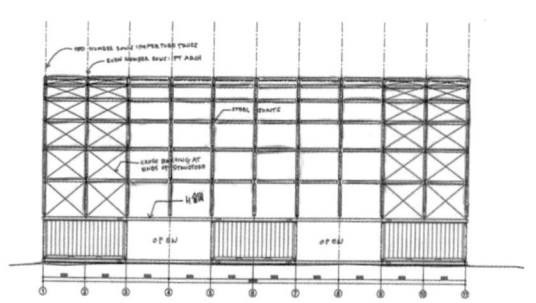

SHIGERU BAN ARCHITECTS
PAVILION DESIGN 4
20 AUG 2009

S = 1/300   SIDE ELEVATION

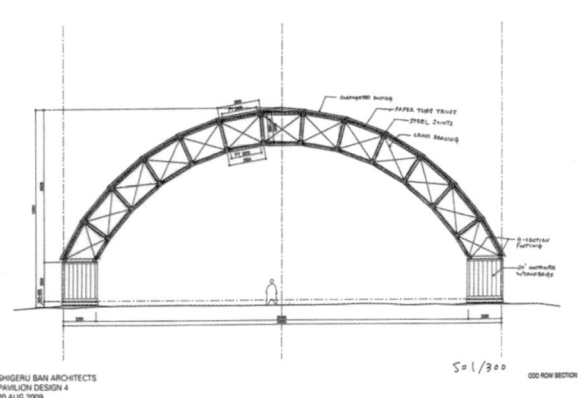

SHIGERU BAN ARCHITECTS
PAVILION DESIGN 4
20 AUG 2009

S=1/300   ODD ROW SECTION

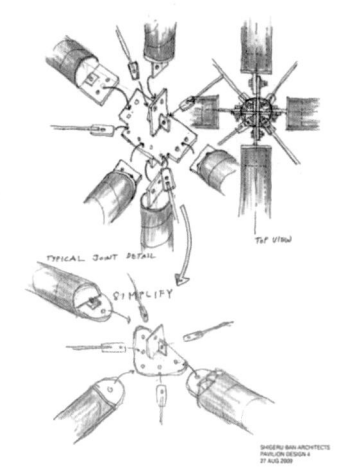

SHIGERU BAN ARCHITECTS
PAVILION DESIGN 4
27 AUG 2009

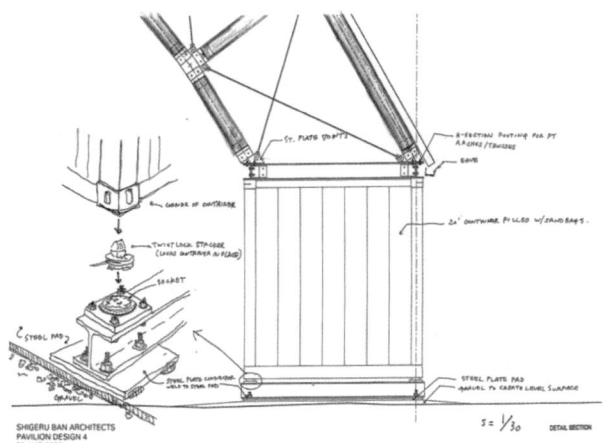

SHIGERU BAN ARCHITECTS
PAVILION DESIGN 4
20 AUG 2009

S=1/30   DETAIL SECTION

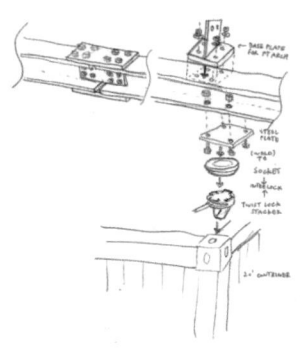

SHIGERU BAN ARCHITECTS
PAVILION DESIGN 4
27 AUG 2009

177

After I started designing temporary structures I discovered my own definition of what is temporary and what is permanent. People think the buildings I build in paper are temporary, but many of them have stayed much longer and become permanent. I also discovered that when I work in the larger cities, many constructions which are built in concrete only stay for a few years. And after I experienced many earthquakes, I realized that concrete buildings are easily destroyed in earthquakes. So then I thought, what is permanent? Because concrete buildings are very easily destroyed by an earthquake or by a developer who makes a concrete building and then destroys it to make room for a new structure. So it is very temporary.

— Shigeru Ban

Hong Kong Experience

Shigeru Ban // essay

Historically architects have worked primarily for the privileged to visualize or embody power and money, which are effectively invisible. Yet many natural disasters are happening all over the world, and these events are no longer so much natural as man-made; for it is not an earthquake itself that kills people, but the collapse of buildings, which, of course, is the architect's responsibility.

Thus, it comes full circle; people need temporary housing after such events, but, there are no architects working in disaster areas because they are too busy working for the privileged few. I, too, would like to design monumental buildings, as well as temporary houses for the world's poor or disadvantaged. In this way I might merge my experiences designing beautiful and functional temporary houses with my desire to design monumental buildings.

When I build temporary houses in disaster areas, I always work with students. It is part of my educational activity, for it is important to teach students about the responsibility of architects and to provide opportunities for them to work with real building materials.

Although Hong Kong is physically very small, there is a strong desire on the part of the people to grow and expand culturally. Hong Kong's unique geographical and political positioning, in close proximity to many Asian countries but still a little bit away from mainland China, is very advantageous and critical; it is only natural to be, in this way, Asia's de facto cultural hub. Therefore, the development direction for West Kowloon should be very different from the strategies used in other cities. It has to be a concentration of Asian ideas and talents versus an importation of exterior influences.

iPhone Orchestra

Samson Young // event

The Hong Kong iPhone Orchestra is, first and foremost, a community project with the aim of empowering non-specialists with the tools to make music in an ensemble situation, something that was previously only available to those with years of training in music.

The core belief is that musical instruments are nothing but physical gesture-to-sound interfaces. iPhones are similar to an instrument in that they have built-in gesture detection in the form of the touch screen, as well as a voice-level input detection system. Specially developed software could transform these input data into output sounds. A "musician" could then use these gestural input features to create sounds in an intuitive manner.

This is something that was not possible until the last few years, and I think it is very liberating. It means in the future musical performance in a group setting will not necessarily be the elitist affair that it is now. I see technology enabling non-specialists to finally take a significant role in serious music-making. This liberation of the non-specialists has already happened in dance, theatre, and the visual arts. Nobody is going to criticize a conceptual artist who cannot paint a realistic self-portrait, but music is accepting this idea very late in the day.

The mass media has certainly helped in spreading the word, and a community music project such as the iPhone Orchestra depends upon the participation of the community. We particularly need input from those in the community that do not have musical training, and the media has been instrumental in our ability to reach out to those people.

Another project, the West Kowloon *Sound Walk*, also involves the participation of the local community. It consists of a walk split into two parts; the first part was conducted near the waterfront, the second part was conducted inside of the construction site where some of the biennale installations were placed.

For the first part, I went ahead of time to the site and recorded the sounds of people's activities. I did this at different times of the day for several days. I pieced these soundscapes together into a thirty-minute track. At the soundwalk, which took place at 6 a.m. in the morning, we sat on that same bench where the sounds were recorded and listened attentively to the track.

For the second part, I gave everybody a pair of silicon earplugs to wear. These earplugs would block out up to thirty decibels of sound, which in the early hours of the morning means that you can pretty much only hear your own breathing when wearing them. With the earplugs in our ears, we took the longest path around the construction site.

Samson Young is Assistant Professor at the School of Creative Media at the City University of Hong Kong, and a PhD fellow at Princeton University. His work combines a formal training in classical music, electro-acoustic music, and musique concrète with interests in new technology, site specificity, and moving images.

Hong Kong WaterWorks
Memory, Water, and Architecture

Kanta Kochhar-Lindgren // event

Waterfront Bi-City Conversation

date: 21 December 2009
participants: Colin Ward, David Gianotten,
Michael W T Ng, Rem Koolhaas,
Rocco Yim
moderators: Eric Schuldenfrei, Marisa Yiu
respondents: Donald Wun Hing Choi,
Laurence Liauw, Tao Zhu

How does the profession of architecture contribute towards the production of a culture of experimentation? If the Biennale becomes a platform for change by serving as an instrument for the participation of the public, then how could this mechanism have impact in the practice of architecture? What is the role of a biennale in society, how is it significantly different than the role of a singular installation?

Rem Koolhaas: Maybe I will take a more bitter approach and talk about the idea of a biennale. I want to share some experiences of different biennales in which we have participated in and also say something about how and what a biennale can do, including this one.

I think there are two types of biennales. Biennales that bring together what is of the moment; that is, things that are based on affinity, and not so much with a very strong message but with something the Germans describe as the zeitgeist, a word for the spirit of the times. And then there are other kinds of biennales that are very rigorous and really have a message that can act directly on architecture as architectural propaganda. In 1980, there was a famous one in Venice that was called "The Presence of the Past." It was a single exhibition that destroyed modernism and put post-modernism on the map in one go. It was really spectacular because the power of that exhibition, the power of that kind of editing, and the power of that kind of selection, was extremely impressive to see. So, biennales can be very, very strong. In that sense, they have a very important role to play in how architecture develops and communicates both to the public and within itself. I think that it is the intriguing thing about biennales. Most biennales are the dialogues of the artists and architects who participated, and of the art which is presented to the public, but not necessarily at the same time.

So, I think here in Shenzhen and Hong Kong, we have a different kind of biennale. This is a biennale without a strong message. Maybe we have become nervous about strong messages.

There is no longer much enthusiasm
for the kind of explosive development that
China has pursued in the last ten years;
instead people seem to be looking for
a more intimate, maybe smaller scale and
more participatory kind of work.

— Rem Koolhaas

Therefore, it seems more like a case of mutual affinities, and much of this is between the lines, saying something about architecture rather than explicitly making a message or pronouncement. I think what is addressed here between the lines, perhaps more evident on the Shenzhen side than in Hong Kong, is the problem of the way new cities might create vital urban communities. What is very, very clear is that the Hong Kong-Shenzhen Biennale is taking stock of the state of urbanism in China and trying to look for more sensitive alternatives. That is very, very clear. There is no longer much enthusiasm for the kind of explosive development that China has pursued in the last ten years; instead people seem to be looking for a more intimate, maybe smaller scale and more participatory kind of work. So, I think this is the partly hidden agenda. Maybe it is inevitable.

My only worry is that in that kind of soft message there is not enough energy to really deal with what I think is the most important task for Shenzhen and for Hong Kong, which is to engage each other and to really define what their future or imminent connection will be, and what role they are going to play in each other's life. I think that there is an enormous latency. Everyone knows that it will be very important, but nobody is willing to assert it or define it, so I feel that a kind of vagueness is very much a part of the West Kowloon Cultural District. I am interviewing a number of Biennale participants in Shenzhen tomorrow and I hope I will be able to press them to really say, overtly, what is going to happen. So I think that this is what a biennale can be used for too.

> I think one of the
> issues is we always tend
> to think very big;
> participation and
> process become things
> that are so huge
> and so difficult to handle
> that there is never really
> time to think, research,
> and pursue questions
> at a small scale
> with somebody who
> really lives or works or
> experiences the
> outcome of the process
> we are engaged in.
>
> — David Gianotten

David Gianotten: I want to focus on what architects could do to stimulate experiments, or try to look for new ways to engage cultural production – to break the mold perhaps. I think one of the issues is we always tend to think very big; participation and process become things that are so huge and so difficult to handle that there is never really time to think, research, and pursue questions at a small scale with somebody who really lives or works or experiences the outcome of the process we are engaged in. We go through all sort of political processes and compromises, and never reach a point where the outcome could provoke a new kind of result and a new approach to things. We do have to deal with complexity, but the outcome can be without complexity, without all the complications and compromises. Therefore, we need to try to engage people more often and more thoroughly, and also to give them an opportunity to respond and really participate, to not simply be confronted by the end result, which they do not have any role in and may not support anyway.

Rocco Yim: I think participation and process are really the essence of this Biennale. Participation is only fruitful, in my point of view, if it is interactive and it is a true dialogue and communication between participants. And process is only meaningful if it contributes positively to the end product with the product being the definitive, or in this case, the purposely non-definitive. Now, when I say the Biennale is a success, it is because I have witnessed, not immediately, but throughout these weeks, this phenomenon of interaction between the participants and the site. For instance, we have the *Eco Farm* interacting with the ground. We have *Projecting Window* interacting with the harbor by using a very mundane building component of which we are all familiar with. At the same time, we have *Bloody Haze* also interacting with the skyline in a different way. They all try to, in some key way, confuse us by giving the skyline a different meaning than the one we had.

And then there is interaction between exhibits themselves, either accidental or intentional, like *Live Nature* just behind the matrix of *Boundaries*. So, all of this is evidence that the exhibits do talk to each other despite the fact that they are displayed in a very casual way. They talk to the site, they talk to the surroundings. Now the process itself seems to contribute to a lightness and impermanence to the exhibits; they all seem to rest, just barely touching the ground, including this pavilion, which could disappear at any moment. This impermanence, perhaps a product of the site itself, seems to give credit to the idea that it is an evolutionary process, an ever-changing process that will bring you surprise, spontaneity, and, therefore, heightened expectation. Now having given a rather crude critique of this Biennale let me say that I have some worries about the West Kowloon Cultural District project.

It is the very element that contributed to the success of this Biennale – that is, participation and process – that are needed when we embark on the design and implementation of the West Kowloon Cultural District. We do need interaction, we do need dialogue, and we do need a process that ensures a degree of expectation and freshness, not just during the design phase, not just during the construction phase, but throughout the lifetime of this project. Apparently, what we need is maybe a curatorial team that orchestrates and directs such a participatory process and such an evolutionary scheme. However, we also understand that the nature of the West Kowloon Cultural District should be very different, unique. It should not be just about monumental projects, about high-

sounding purposes and structures – it needs and requires very different scales, something people could touch and lie on. So it requires an interpretation of how this process should be executed.

> This impermanence, perhaps a product of the site itself, seems to give credit to the idea that it is an evolutionary process, an ever-changing process that will bring you surprise, spontaneity, and, therefore, heightened expectation.
>
> — Rocco Yim

Colin Ward: When we were wandering around the Biennale site recently we were struck by Urban Rethink Tank's *Graham' Super,* which has to do with the Graham Street Market in Central. As many of you know, Graham Street Market is this intense piece of urban landscape that sits in the middle of the city. It is a fish and meat market, one of those fantastic places that is a real link in the community of Hong Kong, for it is a real touchstone for many people, and it is a place people grew up with and associate with.

There is real participation in the community and it has a strong cultural legacy for people; it is one of those things that we need to keep hold of.

The whole open market hawker tradition goes back to the very beginning of Hong Kong; we were looking into it and initially 50% of the people in Hong Kong traded in this sort of open-market way and that has been slowly, tragically, diminishing over the years. As of 1970, the government has no longer issued these licenses. So these areas are diminishing and dying, although the Urban Renewal Authority has sort of relented to try to enhance and support these open markets, but they are dying because people are not given any chance to forward these licenses and they are not passed on from generation to generation. These markets are echoes of Hong Kong's fantastic trading position. I guess we need to ask, and repeatedly, how can we maintain the fine-grained local perspective in light of the universalizing global?

So if we have these markets which are the epitome of the local, how do we maintain that in the face of the global? Jeff Wong is one of the designers that put the booth together, and he used to work with us, and we met him to talk about it. He was saying that Hong Kong is slowly becoming only the international, and the local is dying, and, therefore, we are left with a Hong Kong that is predominately what we see here across the water. Although it is truly an astounding backdrop for this incredible event, is that skyline the future of Hong Kong? Is this what we want for Hong Kong, only the international, high-powered life of a hyper-metropolis? Where is the local?

Hong Kong is slowly becoming only the international, and the local is dying, and, therefore, we are left with a Hong Kong that is predominately what we see here across the water.

— Colin Ward

You land in any high street in the United Kingdom, and you actually do not know whether you are in Nottingham, Manchester, or Liverpool – it is all the same. That is not a good sign. There is a crying need to make sure that we maintain difference as a key part of what we do as designers and urbanists. Imitation is a large part of the global metropolitan culture; people imitate what they are flattered by, what they are envious of, and so what are we all imitating here? What are we flattered by and envious of? And what do these edifices that signify monolithic success in commerce and finance mean in relation to Hong Kong? Is it the only vision? Where is cultural difference or social difference? What makes Hong Kong different to New York or London?

Speaking of the Kowloon Walled City, which I believe was pulled down in 1993, was that the indigenous architecture of Hong Kong? Is it more relevant than this skyline or this *Paddling Home* installation? Is this where we should be heading, toward only the super dense? And then if we have the super dense, do we have any green space? Does super dense possibly mean a more sustainable environment through hyperexploitation – an obvious paradox?

Michael WT Ng: The first thing that really dawned on me in coming to West Kowloon for the Biennale is that there are a lot of fences around the site. There is this kind of alienation about this place; here we are facing the magnificent Victoria Harbor and somehow it is this strange lack of accessibility that is the most prominent characteristic.

To go back to one of the major themes of this Biennale, we talked about the Bi-City, which is Shenzhen and Hong Kong, and how we are now blurring into China, the way we work and how we influence architecture across the region and vice versa. Part of the discussion here regarding Hong Kong's top-down approach to design is critical. I have been observing this while also considering axonometric drawings, and the types of alienating views they create. You see very iconic components without really knowing what is down on the ground and in between buildings. This is a very Western way of looking at space – an idealized and rational, or Cartesian way.

The Chinese way of looking at space is totally different. For example, when you look at a Chinese painting, there is a very intricate organic way of looking at things – of seeing. There is also an alienated way of looking at things, and in the design of cities, one can see this in the different forms of representation. I would really like to have more discussion about how the way we visualize things. For example, in the exhibits I think there is a very strong recurrent theme about the problem of the environment. But I like several pieces better than others. This is because there is a kind of message or rationale that some of the exhibits carry that is less effective, for me, than those that engage the landscape and the public in a direct, perhaps non-rational way.

Donald Choi: Hong Kong is a city of commoners. Why are we not using architecture to better serve the majority? We definitely need a democratic participation mechanism in our city and the process needs to be inclusive. The problem with architecture is it is not inclusive enough. With so much energy and eyes on West Kowloon, we can really develop a new process, new participation of the city and create our own local unique architecture. We must remember that as architects we have a social contract with the community to create a better living environment and to improve the living standard. Architecture is not for individual architects or creating monuments, or giving signature to the city. That is only the by-product; the real product is how architecture proves that it is good for the society.

BYOBands

Kung Chi Shing |
Giorgio Biancorosso |
William Lane // event

Participating bands were A Roller Control, Poubelle
International, The Yours, Unixx, SaxMax, Jing Wong, Mike
Yuen, Shadow Kim, Yank Wong, Wilson Tsang, Les Fong,
Suitman, Him Lo, and the Hong Kong New Music Ensemble.

Nam June Paik: One for Violin
Solo (1962)
–
'Destruction of a Biennale'

The outdoor concerts were a wonderful experience for both the audience and musicians, with one of the most spectacular views in the world as the backdrop. They also served to underscore how much this city needs high quality public performances, and by extension, the way our government's policy regarding the usage of public space has acted as a hindrance to promoting Hong Kong as a world class cultural city.

— Kung Chi Shing

Live Music

Giorgio Biancorosso // essay

The live presentation of music does not only stimulate the creation of new and wholly indigenous forms of performance, it also helps create temporary sites for public enjoyment, reflection, and contemplation. The live musical performances held during the Biennale, for instance, completely altered the conventional postcard-view perception of the city skyline. By bringing people to the edge of the promenade, the organizers effectively invited them to view the Hong Kong skyline as an element interlinked to the Kowloon waterfront across an imaginary, three-dimensional stage – the harbor itself.

The city's canyons of high-rise buildings and all manner of enclosed spaces call for just such a recreation. Sound works around corners, so to speak, and its reach defines the limits of a shared place, turning it into a destination and ultimately a "site." Indeed, by travelling to and fro in all directions, and returning precious information about it to our ears, strategically organized sound specifies and describes a space in ways that no photograph or other form of visual prosthesis can interpret.

Naturally, there are obstacles to the creation of a vibrant public music scene. The temptation to retreat into arenas is difficult to resist. But those obstacles must be addressed and, when found unreasonable, impugned. For public music performances are not just needed for the enjoyment of the people, as a patronizing policymaker might put it; rather we need them to understand, interpret, and – in the admittedly extreme case of Hong Kong – remake the very urban space we inhabit.

Giorgio Biancorosso is Assistant Professor at the University of Hong Kong who studied music and film at the University of Rome and King's College, London, before obtaining a PhD in musicology at Princeton University. He has taught at Northwestern University and was a Mellon Fellow and Visiting Assistant Professor in the Music Department at Columbia University. He is the Review Editor of *Musica Humana* and a member of the Programme Committee of the Hong Kong Arts Festival.

Urban Adapter

Rocker Lange Architects // exhibit

While variation is apparent in the style of Hong Kong's civic furniture, there is a lack of uniformity in the formal expression that could potentially foster a unique Hong Kong character or signature style. The contemporary civic bench seeks to provide multiple design solutions instead of just one single arrangement. The Urban Adapter is based on a parametric model that uses data to interact with the surrounding environment to produce its own type. Rather than have a fixed form, the furniture can mutate into various shapes with the same DNA dependent on different site conditions.

ffformica

Xu Tiantian // exhibit

ffformica experiments with color, translucency, and spray technology to highlight the capability and versatility of Formica, highlighting the potential of furniture as an object that is not only defined by a certain function, but, rather, improvised by different users to activate its possibility.

cultural education

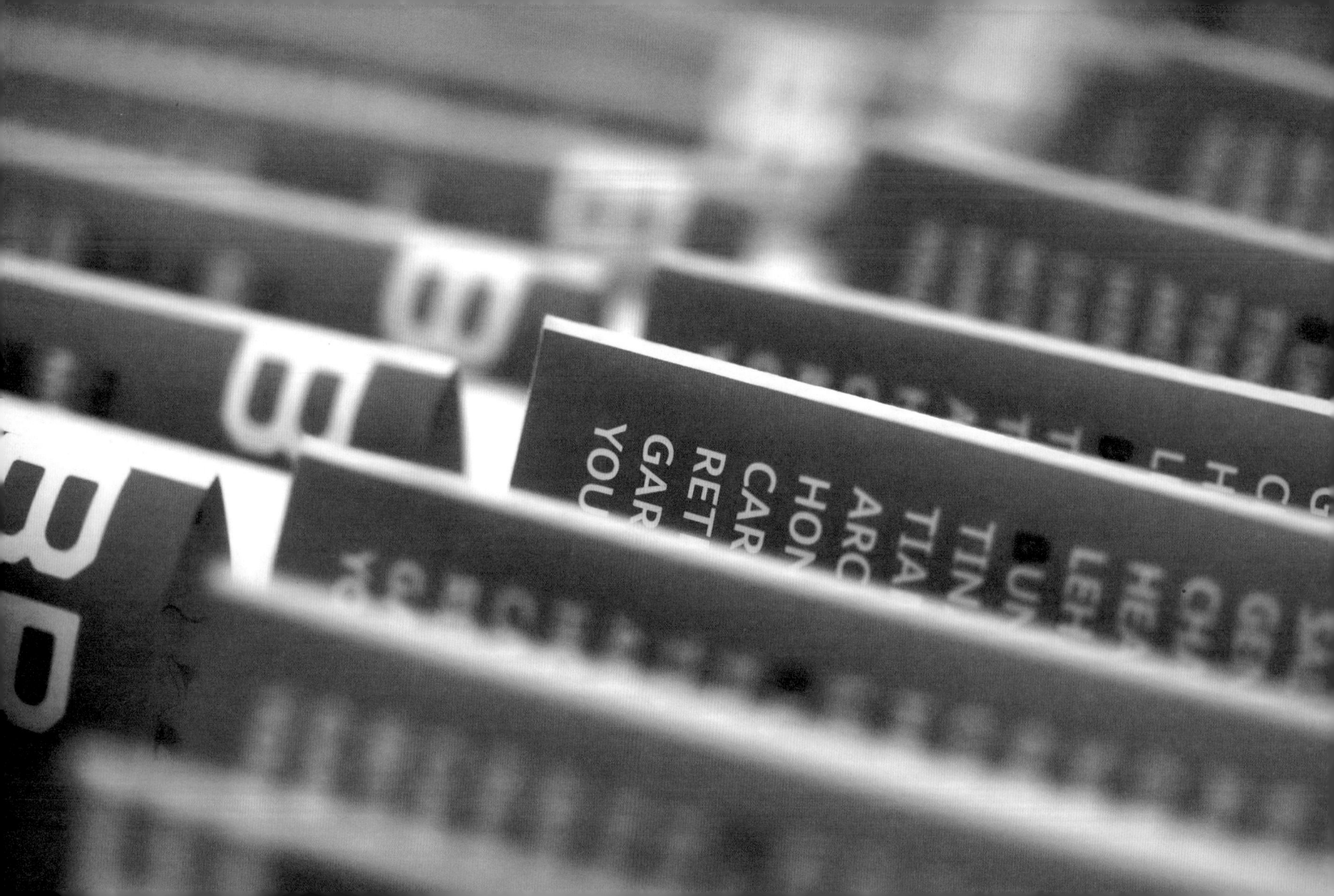

ATTENTION ALL SNAP-HAPPY PHOTOGRAPHERS!
各位攝影發燒友！

BRING YOUR OWN BIENNALE
West Kowloon Waterfront Promenade
西九龍海濱長廊　　　**Dec 2009 - Feb 2010**
"09香港·深圳城市\建築雙城雙年展"

"2009 Hong Kong & Shenzhen Bi-City Biennale of Urbanism\Architecture"

城市动员 CITY MOBILI-ZATION

BYOB

transformative
landscapes

Itinerary

a) Rosary Church
b) St. Mary's Canossian College
c) Kowloon Cricket Club
d) Kowloon Bowling Green Club
e) Lands Tribunal
f) Tin Hau Temple
g) Yau Ma Tei Car Park
h) Yau Ma Tei Police Station

Yau Tsim Mong Tour

Sharing Architecture

Platteen Tsang | **Iman Fok** // essay

Choosing Tsim Sha Tsui and Yau Ma Tei as the canvas for these guided tours, we traced the developmental history of Kowloon, from Great Britain's takeover to the present times. The significant changes to the coastlines on both the eastern and western side of the Kowloon peninsula was also one of the major concerns explored in the tours.

Urban fabric does not appear out of the blue. Similar to architecture, urban fabric is a reflection of the living style, and includes, but is not limited to, demands of living spaces, transportation, and community facilities. These elements are important variables affecting how humans interact. Moreover, the continuous demand for better living conditions changes through the history of mankind, subject to the variations of culture and technology. Therefore, history, urban fabric, and people's lives are all closely interlinked.

In Yau Tsim Mong, for example, the original location of the Tin Hau Temple was by the seaside, purposely built to protect the fisherman from storms and other natural hazards. Due to dramatic development and reclamation, today the Tin Hau Temple is located inland – stranded. Although the purpose of the temple as a place for worshipping the Chinese gods remains, the building is now being regarded as a tourist spot and the space in front of it is used as public open space. These changes reflect the changes of culture and are derived from the unique history of Hong Kong.

Platteen Tsang is actively involved in organizing cultural tours and social events for members of the general public. Platteen studied architecture, town planning, and construction project management. He is also a part time graphic novelist.

Iman Fok worked as a social worker for thirteen years, and serves as the executive director of HULU Culture, a non-profit organization which was established in 2004 dedicated to protecting Hong Kong traditional culture and heritage.

Community to us is the subject matter. Without a prescribed institutional burden, the Community Museum Project is able to concentrate on testing new methods, where values and legitimizing processes include the underrepresented. We curate "things" creatively and are not bounded by the physical and conceptual constraints of a traditional walled museum. By opening the museum projects onto the street level we create new visual, museological, and civic forms through collecting and interpreting the city's artefacts, documenting individual stories, and exhibiting the wealth of visual manifestations from our public culture.

— Siu King Chung

Here to Tai Kok Tsui

John Batten // essay

Tai Kok Tsui is a pocket of old industrial and residential buildings near Mong Kok that was, until recently, fronting Victoria Harbor. In the dramatic and often confusing years prior to Hong Kong's return to China in 1997 and before Kai Tak Airport closed, and well before the public realized what was happening, a frenzy of reclamation was undertaken along this shoreline to accommodate the train lines to the new airport on Lantau Island, and to provide land for new high-rises and a park that, infamously, morphed into a future site for the arts: this temporary Biennale site.

All of Kowloon's older urban low-rise areas are under threat of redevelopment due to the old airport's flight-path building height restrictions being removed: a chip, scratch, scrape, demolish at Hong Kong's unique urban character. So, for a moment, can I lead you away from this biennale of BYOB ideas and events for a walk around the landlocked Tai Kok Tsui.

Catch bus 905 or 971 from Hong Kong Island to quickly arrive in Tai Kok Tsui via the Western Harbor Tunnel. Disembark at the Chung Wui Street bus stop, skirt down to the Lok Kwan Street Park, marvel at the concrete Chinese pavilions, and consider the lurking dangers that prompted a sign warning that the artificial lake is 0.41 metres in depth. Walk down Tai Kok Tsui Road, and at the corner of Tung Chau Street, you will see a kitsch reminder of the area's marine past: a concrete reconstruction of fish, coral reefs, and a green-tiled seabed.

Turn right into Tung Chau Street and enter an industrial corner of lathes, metalwork shops, and guillotines with metal carefully stacked into different gauges, this location justified by the previous proximity of sea and ships. There is an old world aura of real physical objects being manipulated into real physical uses, emphasized by the 1950s-era factories carrying old signage: "Golden Girl Brassiere" (with the by-line "SUPER Non Iron Quality") and "The Great Wall Thread Company, Ltd."

Wander around the treeless streets named after trees; note the funeral parlour on Maple Street surrounded by flower shops supplying black and white trimmed wreaths; cross Tai Kok Tsui Road again and buy great Chinese cakes at Zho Fu Bakery (149-157 Tai Kok Tsui Road); turn left into Tai Tsun Street with its many restaurants: Malaysian laksa at number 26 and dessert at 20B.

Cut back across Tai Kok Tsui Road to the historic Tin Hau Temple; next-door is a classic cha chan teng, Shun King Café (corner of Fuk Tsun Street and Lime Street) with its wonderful 1960s interior and recalcitrant outdoor seating for smokers. A brisk ten-minute walk will take you to Nathan Road or, by negotiating a labyrinthine route, to the Biennale.

Look behind the Biennale site towards the International Commerce Centre: the new high-rises are fenced, road-locked and lacking community-energizing street-side shops, street markets, and pockets of quiet. I am sure the view is fantastic, but where is the friendly local character that makes a great city?

John Batten lives in Hong Kong and regularly writes on art, culture, and urban planning issues. A former gallery owner, he is the organiser of the annual charity art event ArtWalk and co-convenor of the urban planning and heritage pressure group, Central & Western Concern Group.

Tai Kok Tsui Tour

Itinerary
a) Chung Wui Street Bus Stop
b) Lok Kwan Street Park
c) Corner of Tung Chau Street
d) Willow Street lathes, metalwork shops, and guillotines
e) Zho Fu Bakery
f) Tai Tsun Street restaurants
g) Shun King Café

Is Architecture's Discipline in Crisis?

// forum

date: 27 February 2010
participants: Ada Wong, Duncan Jepson,
Duncan Pescod, Eugene Tan,
Jason Forster, Kacey Wong
Mathias Woo, Syren Johnstone,
William Lim
moderators: Eric Schuldenfrei, Marisa Yiu

How do Hong Kong architectural installations in a biennale setting reflect questions regarding the greater discipline of architecture? Are they statements of progress or reflective models for the way cities can do better, to create a greater level of exchange between disciplines? If architectural forms reflect core aspirations and values in society, then what type of strategies can produce such exchanges?

Duncan Pescod: Frank Lloyd Wright said, "A doctor can bury his mistakes but an architect can only advise his clients to plant vines." One architectural issue is that it is very evident when something goes wrong, but it is not so evident when something goes right, at least not until years later. Iconic buildings are controversial and that is one of the issues architects have always had to address. My own personal belief is that architecture is not in crisis any more now than it has been in the past, or will be in the future.

I believe architecture, like all disciplines, has to work with other things and other disciplines. It is about working with designers, artists, and all of the creative industries; trying to reflect what society is all about. When it comes to getting things done, we need fewer architects and more bricklayers. And that appeals to me because this

is actually one of the other issues that we need to think about, which is the practical application of what architects can create. We were just talking a couple of minutes ago about this fantastic pavilion designed by Shigeru Ban. But one question was asked: is it suitable for the purpose for which it was designed? The consensus seems to be it is a beautiful piece of architecture. But how practical is it in the middle of Hong Kong's coldest winter? Aesthetics and function somehow must be one thing.

Ada Wong: I do not know. But as I sit under this pavilion, I think we do have to solve one issue. Where should we put this pavilion next week? This has to be dismantled by next Tuesday. Could we not leave this here longer? This district will not be in development for awhile. Because it is a temporary structure and there are many regulations and

laws that we have to work around, if we want to keep it we will have to move it.

In 1997, when I was an urban councillor, we were asked to build the central library; that was the first incident, the first time when public architecture was on the front page of the newspapers and people started talking. The public was discussing whether this building was pretty or not. Well, I think it is nice. But did we organize an architectural competition for it? It was then that I believe architecture was in a complete crisis. The government architects are doing most of the important work. There is simply no platform for the local architects to perform.

These forums should be more like a movement than an event with a beginning and an end.

— Ada Wong

There needs to be more initiatives, like this one, for organizing competitions to provide opportunities to more designers and encourage more participation. That is the missing piece in the big puzzle. I see the Biennale as a great platform for promoting architecture in the public realm. I was amazed that so many people came to the Biennale with their families. How do we continue this momentum? These forums should be more like a movement than an event with a beginning and an end. The Biennale is coming to

an end and that is very sad. I want to see this as a long-term commitment towards sustaining a movement to make our public spaces better.

Frank Lloyd Wright said, "A doctor can bury his mistakes but an architect can only advise his clients to plant vines." One architectural issue is that it is very evident when something goes wrong, but it is not so evident when something goes right, at least not until years later.

— Duncan Pescod

Mathias Woo: Maybe because there is always a suspicion about practicality in Hong Kong, we need to somehow be more cautious about our environment. The government is building a lot of impractical buildings, such as the Wan Chai office tower. There is always this issue in Hong Kong: the culture of architecture is static when compared to London or New York. Hong Kong has not been innovative for a long time. The last time we were on the world map was with the Bank of

China building, after that there is nothing. West Kowloon is a scandal. There has been no impact in terms of architecture yet. In this city we have been building a lot of utilitarian buildings. I do not know why we call this practical. It is not practical. I would say if we can generate more intellectual debate about architecture, it will be good for the promotion of architecture. Let us not just talk about architecture in terms of financial return. We need different types of architecture as well. The government plays a very important role in the promotion of architecture; events like this one are important in facilitating discussion. Architecture is about the making of buildings and space, but we need many types of buildings and many types of spaces.

I think the crisis is that we do not share a common agenda. Architecture is something essential to improving the quality of life. This is a perception that is shared in Korea, Japan, Taiwan, and China, but not in Hong Kong yet.

— Mathias Woo

We should create some pilot programs; it is completely possible for the government to do pilot projects by only extracting 1% of the budget allocated for the public projects. The works coming from this small percentage would have to be selected through a type of design competition with different types of construction management positions available. It is difficult to start alternative types of programs because of all the bureaucracy that we have created for ourselves.

I think the crisis is that we do not share a common agenda. Architecture is something essential to improving the quality of life. This is a perception that is shared in Korea, Japan, Taiwan, and China, but not in Hong Kong yet. Hong Kong still thinks of personal tastes, and then about its practicalities and impracticalities.

William Lim: I guess now the discussion is about Hong Kong architecture in crisis. It is sad to be an architect in Hong Kong. Many architects in the industry are shunning work in Hong Kong, because of what we have to face, such as the problems you have to face with the building authority. I designed something a few months ago, a bamboo bridge. That experience is amazing because of what we had to go through. Because of the many rules and regulations imposed, in the end we either had to close the event or make the bridge inaccessible to the public.

To really understand the problem, we have to compare our situation with our surrounding neighbors. What are they doing to promote architecture? Many other cities realize art and architecture projects as an incentive for

people to visit. Ever since Bilbao, it has been an important incentive for the city to improve its image through architecture. As far as Beijing, Shanghai, Shenzhen, Guangzhou, and Macau are concerned, they are creating interesting work. In a way, Hong Kong is lagging behind in what the city is constructing in terms of architecture. I do not see architecture here. I just see buildings. Architecture is space and it provides inspiration. For example, Singapore has a good art incentive program. There should be a group of experts to curate art and architecture. That is what Hong Kong needs to learn.

The old fabric of Hong Kong is being lost to podium style architecture; not public space so much as the street fabric. If architecture is in crisis, then the people are in crisis.

— Jason Forster

Jason Forster: The old street fabric of Hong Kong is being lost to podium style architecture. If architecture is in crisis, then the people are in crisis; as people experience these changes directly. I organized the Clockenflap music festival in Cyberport. Cyberport is not built to be an artistic hub in Hong Kong, but is actually modified by the usage of it. The limitation was posed by the buildings itself. The lifts were not big enough for the equipment to fit in. It could not fit in anything larger than a table. The sound production team had to rent a crane to get the equipment over. In terms of public space, I think they need to have more open dialogue to find out what is required. This whole cultural project needs to be more open. It should not be about designing pretty buildings, but ones with functionality as well.

Duncan Jepson: The conversation has drifted to the Hong Kong Government in crisis, and I offer you my sympathies. I am both an investment lawyer working quite happily in the private sector, as well as making films. Filmmakers have asked whether the government is doing enough for the film industry as well. The government is in crisis, and, strangely, the worlds of art, architecture, and film probably could do more to help them out. All the documentaries made in the world could do more, but you do not get back a lot from filmmaking or architecture when it is experimental.

So is architecture in crisis? Looking around in the schools, it certainly looks like a crisis. And, I cannot be quite so positive as others here, for it is in crisis, and it is not a good crisis. We have so many edifices such as Central. Many people work in Central, but they do not like going into Central because they do not feel comfortable. Architecture needs to serve the community, and architecture needs to reconnect to whom they are serving. As a final note, I was born in the north of England, which was very industrial at that time. There were more artisans on the street and a lot of effort was put into building proper buildings. The estates or terrace houses they built are still in good shape after a hundred years. I am not sure if that is occurring right now.

> Architecture needs to serve the community, and architecture needs to reconnect to whom they are serving.
>
> — Duncan Jepson

Syren Johnstone: The topic of today's forum is the engagement of the community in the development of an architectural project. What is it exactly with which the community can engage within the architecture process? West Kowloon is symbolic in relation to the crisis in Hong Kong. What should be put here? There are three factors that we can discuss, the first being ownership. If the project is thrust onto the architects without the community's involvement, they will most likely not accept it, as it will be a foreign object to them. Second, what is necessary to get the community properly involved? Generally, we hear a lot of language from architects about engaging the community, followed by a token engagement, for example, a round of presentations. How can we get the community truly involved; to hear their views? This is a classic problem. Third, we

are living in an era when the expert knows best and the layman just needs to shut up and listen. When we talk about West Kowloon and the WKCD plans, it is obvious that the plans need to be connected in a real way to the neighborhoods, rather than disconnected, as if they constitute a parallel reality.

Kacey Wong: Let me tell you a secret. The secret is that I am honest in what I believe. Architecture is the foundation because we – as humans – do not last that long. Architecture lasts much longer than us. When we are gone, architecture will still be here and other generations will witness it. It is the testimony of our civilization. I am honest but inside myself, I feel that sometimes the government is not honest, or perhaps extremely dishonest. All you need to do is look at the housing projects and see how laughable they are. We can look at other cities, and we can always be envious. At this stage of globalization, compared to all the cities that look alike, we are only a tiny dot anyway. The mainland now looks at Hong Kong as if we are some kind of left-behind species, an anachronism. We still think that we are living in the golden 1980s. Mainland China looks at us as if we are a museum piece, for we smell like the Qing dynasty.

Eugene Tan: A crisis for architecture or art is not such a bad thing. What interested me about this Biennale was not the visual aspect, but the way architects and artists might collaborate on creative projects, some of which are just architecture, and some of which are responding to the environment. I think this notion of getting the artists and architects to rethink their discipline with the help of other professionals is important. And as a platform of production, this Biennale is also important. Hong Kong is known in Asia as a marketplace for art, but not a place for production. It is important to make Hong Kong into a vibrant place for production.

Ever since Bilbao, it has been an important incentive for the city to improve its image through architecture. I do not see architecture here. I just see buildings. Architecture is space and it provides inspirations.

— William Lim

Cabinet of Curiosities

Esther Lorenz | Li Shiqiao | Puay Peng Ho
// exhibit

A Cabinet of Curiosities is a space to keep objects whose categorization is yet to be defined. A museum, despite its connection to thinking (a space in which to muse), is often shaped by the underlying forces of curatorial screening; a Cabinet of Curiosities, in contrast, offers genuine freedom of thought. How does this reflective space of a Cabinet of Curiosities reposition the effort to provide cultural facilities in Kowloon? Can we imagine Kowloon culture through a different trajectory from that of an economy of goods and services, including "cultural capital"?

The Unclassified

Esther Lorenz // essay

Curiosity is a fundamental driving force for culture. It is humankind's urge to explore and to explain, to know and to learn, to classify and to cultivate. A cabinet of curiosities is a space to keep things which have not yet been categorized and evaluated. The items stored in such a place are in a state of transition between intuitive marvel and institutionalized knowledge. The German word *wunderkammer*, which literally means "a chamber of wonder," implies both the notion of amazement and of questioning. This distinguishes it from *Schatzkammer*, a treasure chamber, which is a place to store objects of monetary value. A cabinet of curiosities is a place to state cultural value.

Cabinets of curiosities emerged in Europe in the late sixteenth century. At the beginning, these rooms were spaces for self-expression of the collectors themselves and for the amusement of their guests. In their further development into rooms for collection and classification of natural and cultural peculiarities, they started to play a crucial role in the formation of science and knowledge, as early predecessors of institutions to keep and to display objects of recognized cultural value.

The architecture of a cabinet of curiosities, in line with the ambiguity of the term, oscillated between a room and a walk-in armoire: apart from being furnished with chests of drawers and showcases, the walls and the ceiling were formed to take in objects found to be "curious" as well.

The installation *Cabinet of Curiosities* displays an open collection of marvels found in everyday life of Kowloon. It is designed as a room turned inside-out, and at the same time it functions like a piece of furniture by containing a series of smaller cabinets, each of which is specifically created for keeping one particular curiosity found in Kowloon. The curiosities are chosen by individuals, following a sensation of wonder, they are not institutionally curated. Just like its historical counterpart, this cabinet does not make any distinction between nature, art, science, and the humanities.

Cabinet of Curiosities is a space for reflection. It functions following the principles of curiosity and intuition. The juxtaposition of objects of different kinds and categories allows free association and the generation of new meaning.

With the enormous scale of a cultural district such as West Kowloon, it is important for a city to be aware of its cultural characteristics and inherent dynamics, especially as a precondition for building institutions to facilitate culture to take place and to develop further. *Cabinet of Curiosities* formulates a challenge for Hong Kong and at the same time offers a device to step back from established categories, in order to focus on the nature of its own culture.

Esther Lorenz is Assistant Professor at the School of Architecture, The Chinese University of Hong Kong. She is a registered architect and has practiced in the Netherlands, Australia, and Austria. In her research work and teaching she investigates cultural issues in regard to contemporary cities and architecture with a focus on socio-cultural sustainability, space perception, and the intersection between media and architecture.

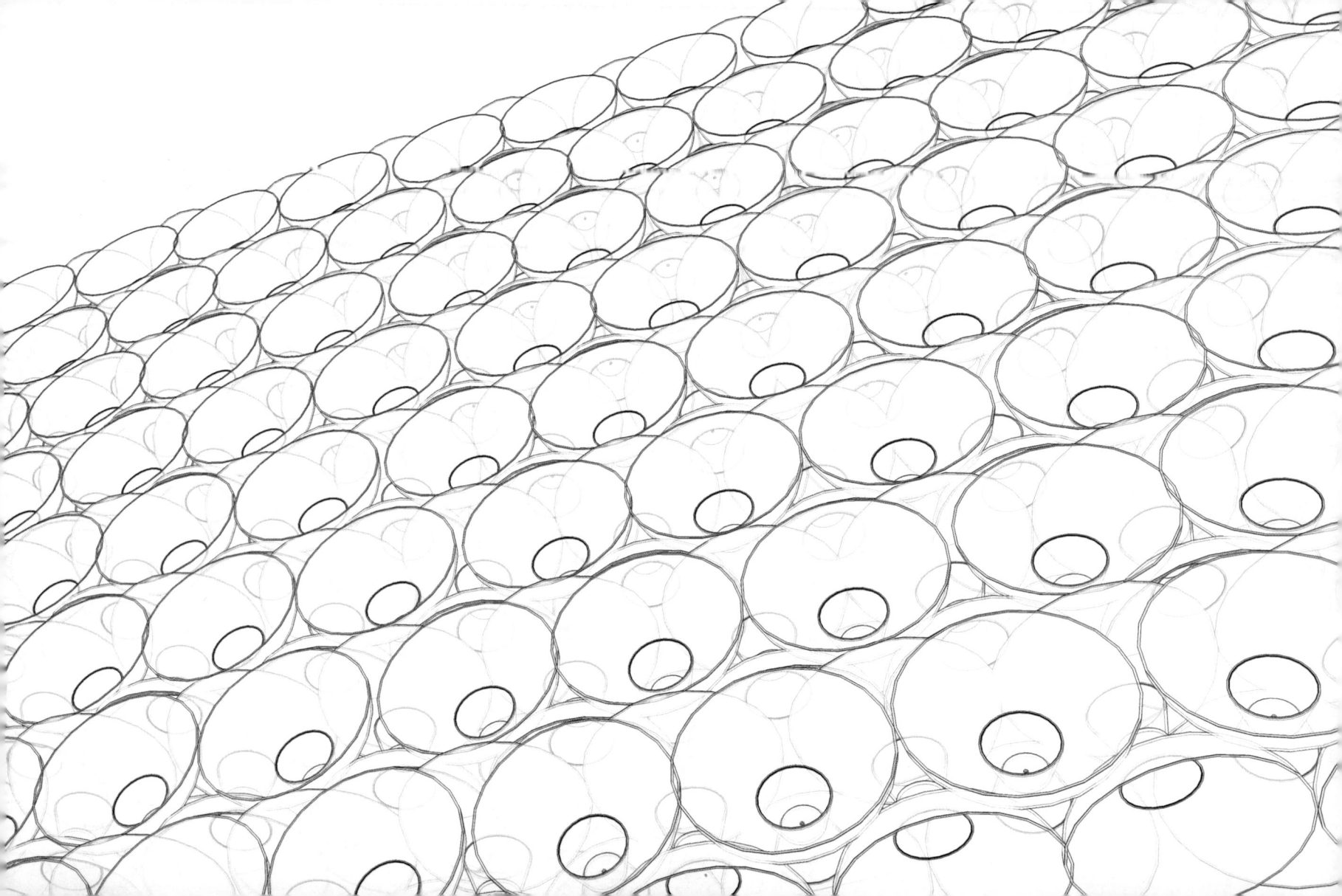

There are "LINKS" and "links"

Manuel C S | Clara Brito // essay

For us, when faced with the task of expressing the historical *links* between Macau and Hong Kong, those LINKS are yet to be made. Of course, we are not forgetting the common past, wherein both territories were ruled by foreign countries. But apart from this, the depth of the formal interrelations is, and was, very superficial, for we also have to take into consideration that the economic realities of these cities are dramatically different.

Therefore, we should rather try to learn and dream about the informal LINKS that are and were created or broken between the people who currently live, work, eat, sleep, drink, gamble, shop, make love, invest in or stroll between the two cities.

M.I.R.AGE is the result of a *redesign* process that intends to extend and revitalize the life of all-ready-made products that we accidentally encounter. In 2003 we created the M.I.R. (Made In Red), a lounge lamp made by the simple reassembling, in a back-to-back position of two traditional lamps found in municipal markets across the Guangdong Province.

M.I.R.AGE is a *fata morgana*, consisting of vertically stacking 1,000 M.I.R. lamps to form one rapidly changing M.I.R.AGE.

When we started working on the challenge posed by the Biennale, and after we visited the site of the main venue, we were happily surprised by its location at the West Kowloon promenade facing Victoria Harbor. For it was during a boat trip from Macau to Hong Kong that we started working on the M.I.R.AGE concept. The word comes to English via the French *mirage*, from the Latin *mirar*, meaning "to look at or to wonder at." As such, the installation presents an analogy of the image created by the interpretive faculties of the human mind when traveling from city to city.

The Hong Kong-Zhuhai-Macau Bridge could be a good symbol for the future interrelations between the people and the cities' economies in the Pearl River Delta, as the bridge will add an important infrastructural element for the economic development of the regional creative industries. As infrastructure is fundamental for economic growth, there is the continuous need to build a strong and collective network between the different industries and creative agents of the greater Pearl River Delta.

As for the added value of Macau, it rests perhaps ironically in the privileged connections with several emerging economies of the Portuguese-speaking countries, such as Brazil and Angola. Thus, links the region to a significant portion of the world's population through a shared past connection.

Lineslab is a venture with a contemporary orientation based in Macau, committed to the equation of objects, people and events. Headed by Manuel C S, an industrial and urban designer, and Clara Brito, a contemporary fashion and product designer, the spaces they inhabit are laboratories for the synthesis of creation and risk.

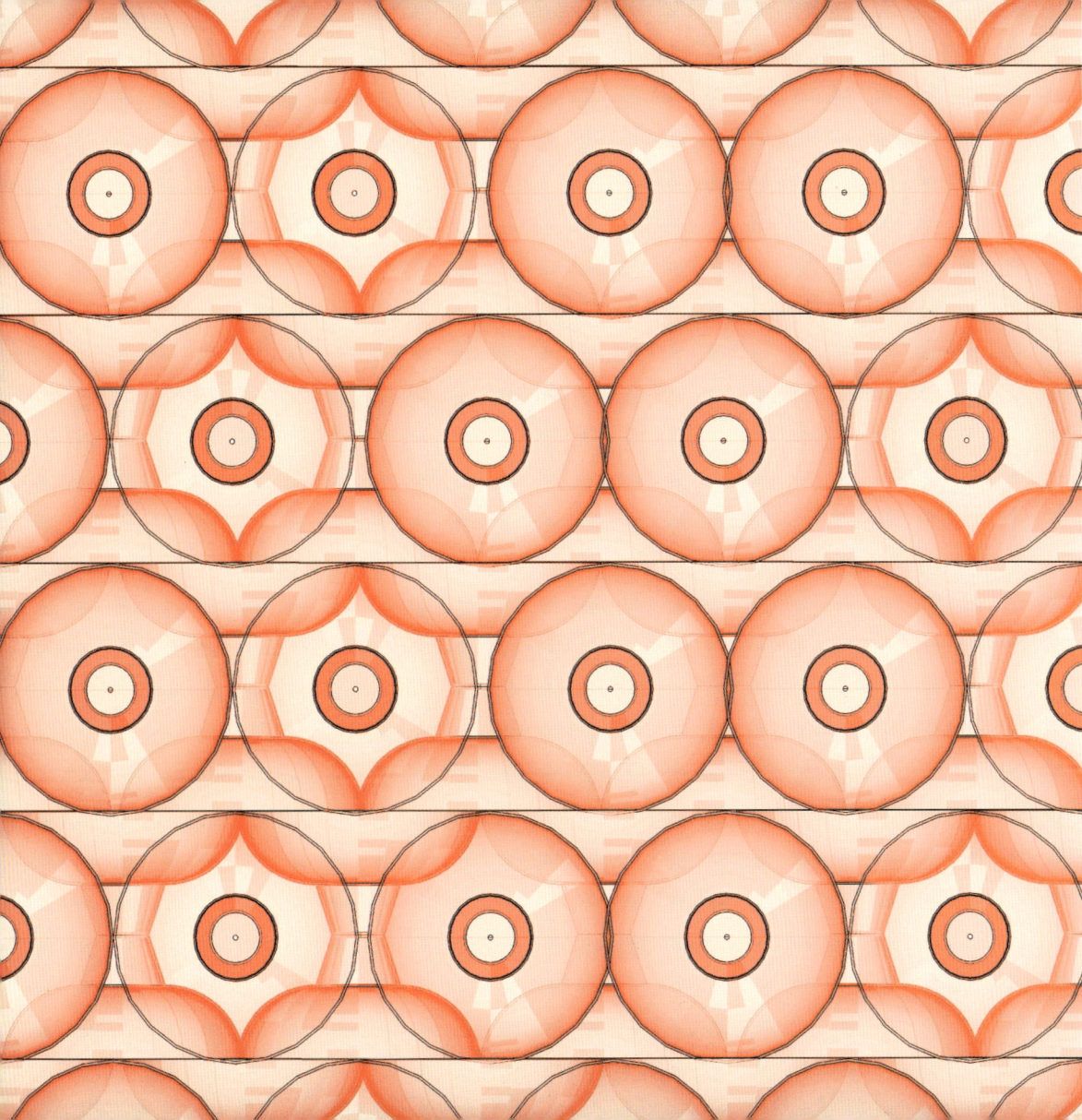

m.i.r.

Lineslab // exhibit

The m.i.r. project poses the question: why design, when you can redesign? It utilizes the traditional red light domes that can still be found throughout markets in China and reinvents them by joining two together in a new lighting object.

Fa Pai Rides WKCD

HKICC Lee Shau Kee School of Creativity

// exhibit

Fa Pai Rides WKCD is a joint effort of Mr. Wong Lai Chung and the Hong Kong Institute of Contemporary Culture (HKICC) Lee Shau Kee School of Creativity students, integrating traditional craftsmanship with innovation. The artwork explores the relationship between the proposed West Kowloon Cultural District, urban development, and cultural conservation. In this regard, Mr. Wong, a local Fa Pai master, took up a three-month residency at the School of Creativity as a craft artist. During the residency, Mr. Wong shared his story and Fa Pai craftsmanship with students.

Jungle Fever

Budi Pradono Architects
with Angki Purbandono // exhibit

Jungle Fever is a disease scanner – a mobile medical apparatus. It is designed to detect a single disease and ameliorate its repercussions. When deployed in a series, the booths create a corridor of cleansing filters, with the final provision of a recovery booth to replenish the user's systems before continuing on their journey.

The booth can vary in shape and size and can be used in any location. It is easily constructed and dismantled on site. Light, elements of construction, recycled material, and plants create an interesting volumetric-therapeutic space, and the pipe work that links the booths adds structural-tectonic value.

face[GUARD]

Erik M Hemingway | Allison Warren
// exhibit

The premise of face[GUARD] is that it hybridizes the cough guard of a typical retail establishment with the traditional hawker booth. The cut and perforated plywood can be easily transported and assembled. This exterior skin allows the level of transparency to be controlled by the person inside the booth. Moveable even by bicycle, the booth takes its mobility origins by cultural transportation systems, and upon completion of the exhibition, the structure's modular system can be added upon over time, to extend the booth into an upgraded residential unit.

"3:15's Rain Catcher"
Let´s Celebrate Rain,
Hong Kong, and Hawkers

YS GROUNDWORK // exhibit

Let us celebrate rain within Hong Kong and Shenzhen's monsoon climate. We love rain, we hate rain, we Cantons LIVE rain. Have you ever seen the color of rain? A shelter shields us from the weather. A shelter can be simple, a house, a cave, a space suit, an umbrella. The hawker center embodies the simplest manifestation of a shelter— a shelter to cook, eat, and interact. Have you thought of an inverted umbrella? The nature of the umbrella changes radically when it is simply inverted. It becomes a rain collector. We are creating a collective rain collector, to experience the true color, the sound, and the poetics of rain.

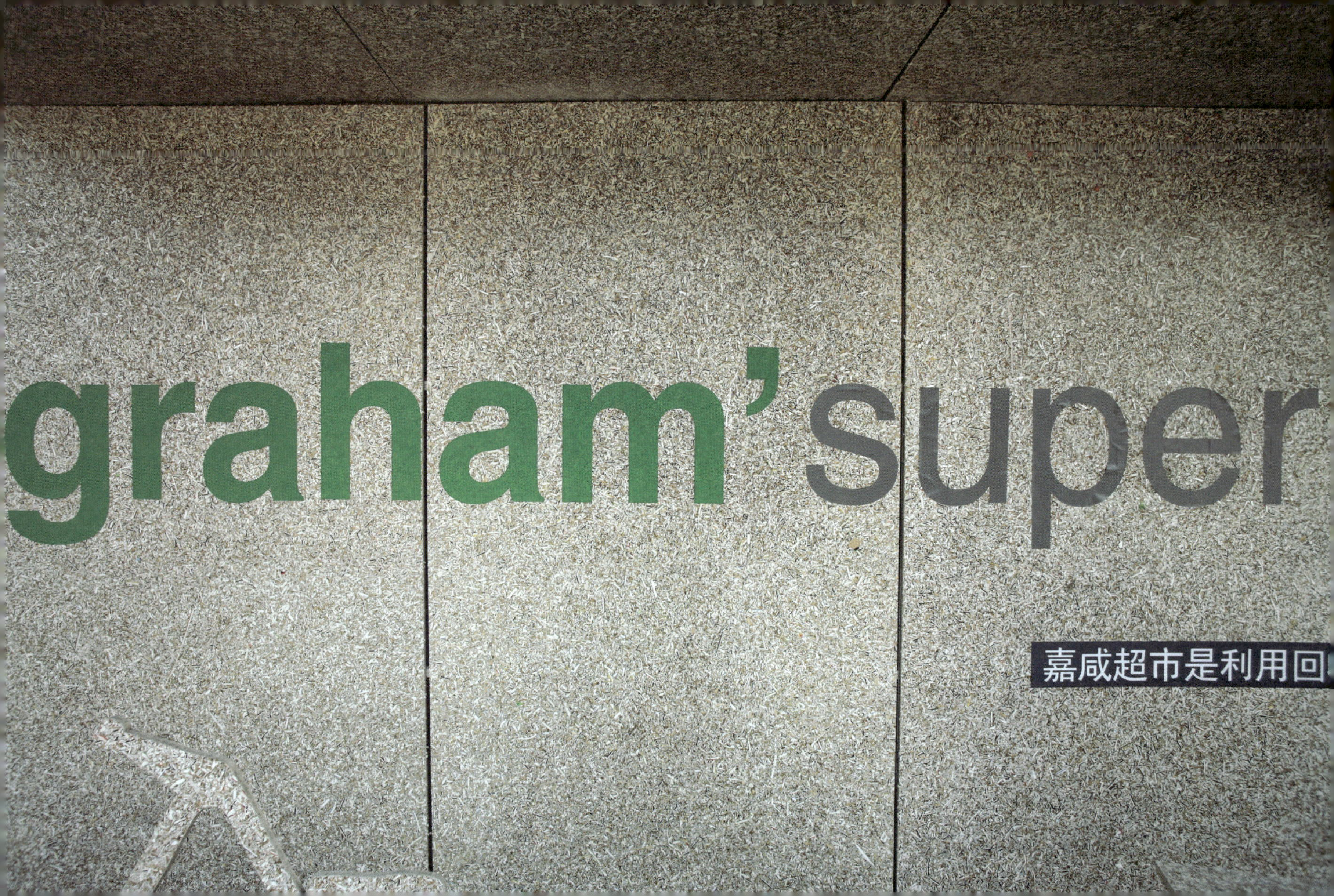
graham's super
嘉咸超市是利用回

is made by recycling **200,000** nos of
used beverage paper cartons

收 200,000 個紙包飲品包裝盒再造而成

Graham' Super

Urban Rethink Tank with Re-Records |
No One Pulse Alok | Edwin Lo // exhibit

A hyper-realistic metropolitan texture is mapped onto an extremely localized labyrinth. As we look upon the urban fabric of Graham Street Market in Central, and its evolution throughout the decades, we want to consider the theme of cultural fabrication from the meanings and practices of Hong Kong's self-made urban vernacular.

Our interests are, therefore, twofold. First, we are inspired by the existing textures and community character of this vernacular texture as manifestations of incremental cultural processes, while we are also intrigued by their disjuncture with the legacy of Hong Kong's modernity. Second, we want to make sense of the ongoing situation through creative "architecture," using re-, inter-, and trans-actions to explore this disjuncture.

"excavation"

Kingsley Ng | **Syren Johnstone** | **Daniel Patzold** // exhibit

"excavation" uses Hong Kong's urban furniture to demonstrate the impact of absence – when things we know in our public space disappear – by fabricating a future archaeological site on the West Kowloon peninsula. At the "excavation" site, remnants of a former market place are discovered along faded lanes where a few remaining artefacts sit in the larger shadow of what was once there. This site of future archaeology presents a kind of interactive parallax across time that facilitates the contemplation of present day urban development issues. Uncle Hung, the only intact green booth on the site, is the personality which bridges the present and the future. You can find him at Facebook/hungbak.

MS1 - GZ/FPT - AERIAL VIEW

"regeneration"

// off-site installation

> Looking up at the fair moon,
> I lower my head and think of home.
>
> – Li Bai

We engaged the community in an off-site part of the Biennale by constructing a new booth for street hawkers in the Central Market, built to their specifications. Our regeneration of the booth contains within it a memory of the older booth, which once stood in the same spot: only at night can one see the old signboard that once hung there, and only at night with the help of lights or a camera flash can one still see the old graffiti. The "regeneration" booth is, therefore, the only Biennale work outside of West Kowloon with a continuing life.

"community"

// event

Looked at but cannot be seen;
listened to but cannot be heard;
held but cannot be touched.

The public was invited to come and create an
archaeological dig in West Kowloon. Children and
curious adults built their own miniature paper cutout
booth, which was an exact replica of the one we
relocated from the street market.

Street Life

The Living // exhibit

Imagine you are eating a bowl of soup noodles at a dai pai dong. Halfway into the bowl, you sense that your food is glowing and that there is a scrolling LED message at the bottom of your bowl, and the message is a provocative observation written by an architect from the Biennale. Encouraging micro-exchanges mixed with the element of surprise, Street Life mobilizes existing street life and creates unexpected interactions between international participants and local citizens.

City Image and Identity

// forum

date: 22 January 2010
participants: Carol Willis, Christine Brucker,
             Greg Yager, Hendrik Tieben,
             Ian Hau, Katty Law, Laurence Liauw,
             Phil Kim, Puay Peng Ho, Stefan Al,
             Sylvester Wong
moderator: Sujata Govada

The city's image and identity is not only determined by the buildings and the natural setting, but by the quality of the public spaces. Cities often undermine their own competitiveness by not capitalizing on their natural and built heritage, and the advantages of building on and emphasizing the city's unique features and local character. How can Hong Kong improve its image and identity to compete with other cities?

Sujata Govada: This is a great venue for this event, a great waterfront site with a spectacular view of the famous Hong Kong skyline. The city's image and identity automatically jumps to prominence when we talk about vertical density and the public realm. The city image and identity goes beyond the famous skyline, it includes the public realm and heritage.

Most people who come to Hong Kong are quite impressed by the city, with the spectacular skyline, which you can actually see at night time even better. Views from the Peak also allow people to get a great overview of the city from above. But I think the image and identity of a city goes beyond the snapshot view from afar. I think that we have been struggling in Hong Kong for some time to ensure that we use our urban environment wisely and create

long-term value for the city. Especially with the waterfront, you can see how accessibility becomes an extremely important issue, as does continuity. Accessibility and integration are critical issues, water access in the form of water taxis with floating pontoons should be a priority in the future. Better land-marine interface and integration of new development with existing adjacent developments will also help the future West Kowloon Cultural Development District.

Sylvester Wong: Steve and I used to live in San Francisco, but we came here ten years ago. It has been fantastic, and not just working in Hong Kong. We have had a lot of opportunities to deal with waterfront reuse issues, such as Kai Tak, Central Waterfront and even this place where we are standing now. We have also had a chance to work in waterfronts all over the world.

Many cities, for example, New York, San Francisco, Shanghai, Hong Kong, and Singapore, have all undergone profound changes, from a mostly working waterfront to a mostly living waterfront. These changes impact the identity of the city, what constitutes a front door, for example. And the change presents rare new sites in the midst of density, chances to create new front doors. With this comes a new responsibility: if you place projects not just where land is available but where a larger picture is framed, then you create a series of fantastic spots with which to engage and further construct and evolve the image of the city.

Navigability is one of the great things about urban waterways. Whether it is a river, or a bay, or a harbor, in most cases they will never change, and the mental map or spatial image that forms in your head as you move around the waterway becomes embedded in the very identity of the city.

And hopefully, in Hong Kong, we have finally come to an end of changing the waterways and the waterfront, of altering that image. Whether you are looking east, north, or west, the climate, the sense of sun and orientation gives you a sense of where you are in the city.

And right now we are planning Bandar Seri Begawan in Brunei. It is a low density place; it is not a vertical city. Just the same we are creating a whole series of places along its waterfront that are different, that engage in different ways, whether it is a hard waterfront, soft waterfront; whether it is hotels and visitor-oriented, or it is about students and the growth of the city. All of those uses turn out to be impossible to attach directly onto the river that runs through the city; and, therefore, to try to force the waterfront to be an integral part of every type of activity in Bandar Seri Begawan is a mistake. But it is an integral part of the city's identity nevertheless.

> We are creating or recreating a system of interlocking ecologies. Beneath every city is an eco-structure, an earth, water, and wind system that's supposed to actively work for or support the city.
>
> — Sylvester Wong

This illustrates an important point: waterfront identity is not just about daily life or activities that we plan at the water's edge as much as it is about the eco-structure of the river itself; that is, one of the things we are creating or recreating, a system of interlocking ecologies. I think beneath every city is an eco-structure, an earth, water, and wind system that is supposed to actively work for or support the city.

Carol Willis: Hong Kong has repeated and realized some of the dreams of the visionary architects working in New York during the early twentieth century such as Harvey Wiley Corbett's dream of multi-level transit and Hugh Ferriss' idea of tower clusters linked by high-speed transportation. It was part of the visionary city that New York was reacting to, from tremendous technological change to issues of immigration and huge growth that New York experienced at the turn of the twentieth century. These same rapid clusters of development are now apparent in Chinese cities today. Yet Hong Kong stands somewhere in the middle of an urban evolution that keeps repeating itself. With regulations in response to growth, zoning that is imposed on the city; then planning, then master planning, and then over planning, there is then a reaction against planning. You see that evolutionary sequence repeats itself in almost every city of the world.

In this reaction to planning I have observed that there is a surprising lack of interface between the university and the professional community of architecture. The university does not seem to be represented in that public dialogue to the same extent as it is in New York. It is much more common to have professors come to a professional presentation where government officials are also present. It is not so much a dialogue, but maybe a contestation on certain points. I think it is necessary for the academy to insert itself into the public debate in Hong Kong.

Hendrik Tieben: I want to talk about public space. I think the first issue is the transformation of society: public space in Hong Kong has a completely new dimension or significance since the city has undergone rapid and radical change in the past decades. We have more elderly or retired people now who need parks and open space, and we have more people who have free time on weekends, who can also enjoy public open space, which was not the case twenty years ago. So there is much more need for unqualified, easily accessible, open space in Hong Kong just as it is disappearing.

Yesterday, in the Shanghai presentation we heard some discussion about public space in China, especially in regard to the percentage of open space in cities. But measuring the percentage of open space, or of green space, does not necessarily translate into quality and actually it can sometimes destroy a city. In fact, in certain Chinese cities there is a lot of open space, but it is fenced by the government because there is not any money to maintain it.

Laurence Liauw: So the subject of today's panel is the image of the city and identity, right? I am actually going to avoid talking about the waterfront view and talk about our back door, the Hong Kong-Shenzhen border which is actually a political issue; that is, the relationship between Hong Kong and Shenzhen. This is an issue I addressed two to three years ago. I tackled this issue out of frustration, because if you look at the two skyline views, 1997 and 2007, the so-called image of Hong Kong has hardly changed. What these pictures really show you is how much or how little our government has done.

There are a lot of different ongoing discourses about public space, policy, and planning. It is in most of the libraries. But if we really look at the image out there, of our neighbor Shenzhen,

which, by the way, in the ten-year period between 1997 and 2007 actually doubled in population, you see the lack of progress in Hong Kong. The population of Shenzhen in 1997 was six million, Hong Kong was six plus million as well, Shenzhen population is now officially at twelve, and probably, unofficially, at fifteen million. So their population has increased to twice Hong Kong's in ten years, and I think people who have been to Shenzhen can see and feel it in the urban growth, in terms of city image.

Obviously, Hong Kong is very different from Shenzhen; we have one country and two systems, but in terms of imagery, I think the Hong Kong effect has definitely influenced Shenzhen. The Shenzhen CBD has a similar kind of tower structure and a lot of generic housing. So, if this is the so-called prototype image of Hong Kong, Shenzhen has matched us already, but instead of a beautiful harbor they have big parks. The border area, of which I feel very strongly, is maybe more of a political issue than an architectural one; and I think it is something completely ignored by the Hong Kong Government. In 2047 there will be no border, so actually by 2030 if we do not have a plan, if we do not start building by 2030 we will not be ready. And I think most of you know that the restricted border area, two years ago, suddenly shrunk to become a kind of Berlin Wall; the so-called Frontier Closed Area. So, this is a very big opportunity, for it is a really, really big area. And it is actually the busiest border region in the world; for example, on one Ching Ming Festival day, when the Chinese people go to visit their ancestors, 6.7 million people crossed the border in one day.

But what about all the people who come from Shenzhen to Hong Kong to buy watches and milk powder, or visit Disneyland? What do they see at the border? And how is it different? What kind of image of the city are we presenting to them? Nothing. I think that is a big problem, we are talking about the busiest border in the world and Hong Kong has done nothing to present a good first impression image to all these people who flock here and help our economy.

The Shenzhen side of the border has been more or less completely urbanized. They have a commercial district, a business district, a new government district, parks, residential areas, and, still, they have villages. It i really the whole spectrum of what a city includes. On the Hong Kong side of the immediate border, apart from maybe two or three vernacular villages which I believe should be preserved, there is really not a lot there; it is basically containers, trucks, highways, barren landscape, a few graves, and three planned isolated new towns. The government is planning new towns, but I am not sure what the three new towns are going to look like, so let us wait and see.

The Planning Department in Hong Kong actually uses the word buffer for the border. Buffer — meaning we do not want Shenzhen or that Hong Kong needs to be protected from the mainland psychologically, politically, and environmentally. HK-SZ border conservation is a good thing and ecological planning is a good thing; but actually what the Hong Kong Government is trying to do is use this kind of green barrier as a kind of permanent wall from Shenzhen. This so-called green void is erected against what Shenzhen is

trying to do. Shenzhen is trying to integrate with Hong Kong, and there are plans from the central government and the provincial government for our two cities to be a lot more integrated. Yet, by the time we get to 2030, it is going to be too late — there is too much resistance still on our side. They may move on without us, leaving us marginalized.

> HK-SZ border conservation is a good thing and ecological planning is a good thing; but actually what the Hong Kong Government is trying to do is use this kind of green barrier as a kind of permanent wall from Shenzhen.
>
> — Laurence Liauw

Greg Yager: City identity is about creating a brand; yet it is about transport, integration, and the future. There is a lot of speculation about what Hong Kong is going to need for the future when it becomes an integrated megalopolis with Guangzhou. When the border disappears we are going to have a metropolitan region that is similar to Los Angeles. Currently in China all these transportation networks look the same, where it is well engineered transportation, but it is not humanized. It is difficult for us to change transportation patterns, but there is still a need to make educated decisions about transportation-oriented development. In Chinese cities, we can make a difference on where the stations are placed, where transportation lines might go, how we can avoid building on top of villages, and how we can keep the city fabric intact. One of things that I find here in Hong Kong when we look at urban development around transport stations is really the real estate is on top of train stations, and the real estate drives a lot of the transportation decisions. In China it is the opposite, the rail industry does not want anything around the stations. They treat them like airports with lots of cars, lots of rails, lots of connections, a hundred metres of clear zone around their stations so they can handle taxis and buses. At one end, we look at that and believe that is an opportunity to make use of this type of development. But in reality the volume of the people, the volume of trucks, the volume of buses coming to these stations is phenomenal, so in some ways that hinterland around these stations becomes important, but how can we humanize it?

Ian Hau: Global density is a global issue, it is everywhere in the world. How do we make places liveable not just socially, politically, and environmentally? There are potentially twenty-one mega cities that will evolve around the world, out of which there are four here in China. The Beijing-Tianjin corridor, the Chongqing region, the Yangtze River Delta and Pearl River Delta. The Yangtze River Delta region will grow to 87 million people in the next twenty years.

In order to plan better we need place making strategies for people and to form land and resource management policies to address the potential fusion between agricultural landscape and urban environments.

> There are potentially twenty-one mega cities that will evolve around the world, out of which there are four here in China. The Beijing-Tianjin corridor, the Chongqing region, the Yangtze River Delta and the Pearl River Delta. We need land and resource management policies to address the fusion between agricultural landscape and urban environments.
>
> — Ian Hau

Katty Law: Over many months a force is already building up in Hong Kong. Numerous protests in Central tell us exactly how many people in Hong Kong nowadays are against development, the over-development that is happening everywhere has destroyed communities, harmed the environment, and damaged our overall livelihood. I think the movement against over-development is becoming a very important social movement to which the government and the professionals will have to pay heed. I saw many young people, students, housewives, and grannies from all walks of life protesting. I was really touched just sitting next to two old ladies, for example, who were actually discussing the problems of the express rail line. I cannot imagine that something like this could have happened ten years ago. Now it happens. It is indeed a wake-up call. Hong Kong has façades with skyscrapers, but what is behind them? And what do you think people really cherish? It is not this slick high-rise image, not at all. What we cherish is our life style, the freedom to choose, whether it is farming in Choi Yuen village or whether it is just to live in a tenement in an old district.

> What we cherish is our lifestyle, the freedom to choose, whether it is farming in Choi Yuen village or whether it is just to live in a tenement in an old district.
>
> — Katty Law

The Floating
Grassroot Market

Wallace Chang | Yin Mo Tse |
Marta Bohlmark // exhibit

The long history of street trading is one of Hong Kong's most significant and unique attributes. How the street market can continue to thrive in a city that is becoming increasingly compact and where space holds exceptional value is, therefore, a highly relevant question? There is an urgent need to save the remaining markets, while street markets need to be reassessed and reconsidered as a valuable resource for maintaining local skills and knowledge, and as a dynamic means of building community, with the added potential to become models of successful micro-enterprises. Are there spaces in the city that can become markets of specific and interesting character, without taking away the current attributes of the space? Can we test this concept and develop it to see if it can prove itself to the larger business community?

Along the Kai Tak River Project

Wallace Chang // essay

The interdependent relationship between the human world and the natural world illustrates the seamless co-existence of cultural ecology and local living. Incidentally, the Kai Tak River has escaped from being covered, thus inviting the recovery of an ecological sensibility in the city and the rediscovery of the human relation to the cyclical rhythms of nature. *The Floating Grassroot Market* evokes a cultural recovery from collective and individual eco-amnesia when fish might once again follow their ancestral navigation routes through watercourses that were once polluted, or when birds might retrace their flight paths that were once disturbed or obliterated by aviation traffic. For this recovery to take place, there must be a datum in place to anchor the flows of lives, be it visible or invisible. So, how should human beings respond to this recovery of the flows other than to allow it to happen, to observe, and honor it?

As a natural corridor penetrating the districts of East Kowloon, the Kai Tak River hinges on the rediscovery of a naturalistic landscape. Thus, in *The Floating Grassroot Market* the observant exhibitor holds momentarily a positive and open attitude in a multi-level collaboration with different organizations and stakeholders from the community toward a humanistic ideal of "planning together, building together, and sharing together," while, through suggesting an open, spatial system for everyone and everything, bringing back from the past what was almost lost to the future.

If the West Kowloon peninsula is to host an artificially created cultural district, created *ex nihilo* (out of nowhere), by nobody, East Kowloon's Kai Tak River project is to be a self-generating process by which a multitude of lives are rejoined in patterns that once coincided – a true cultural district rooted in the natural world.

Wallace Ping Hung Chang is Associate Professor at the Department of Architecture, Chinese University of Hong Kong and was a visiting scholar at Harvard University.

dreamgrove

DRIFTING CITY // exhibit

dreamgrove is a virtual, ongoing, participatory project. It connects a database of dreams to an interactive garden, recording narratives in a public field, organized by mood, writer, number, or color. Currently accessible from a Web page and an iPhone App, it contains clusters of over 350 texts. A temporary garden, narrating dreams through an interactive soundscape, *dreamgrove* interfaces the collective unconscious by combining the digital and the botanical, transforming text into virtual public space.

Site as Garden Interface

Petros Babasikas // essay

The *dreamgrove* project has been a work in progress that consists of the tending and design of a multilayered interface: a compound of different kinds and orders of space (botanical and digital, physical and virtual, linear and topographic, planted and drawn, settled and incomplete), all fed by global participation and networked upon a common core: a database of dreams. Different versions of the garden interface were assembled and disassembled, proposed and archived, drawn and restructured, in museums, biennales, online, on the iPhone, or on paper. Each version investigated common organizational structures of information, narrative, growth and landscape, and variations on a previous design. For each realized version, there were at least two unrealized ones – project proposals that, in their majority, remained on paper.

The *dreamgrove* project will soon fill up its dream-narration quota. At that point it can expand, or it can close down. It has already succeeded in its first premise: to create, out of texts, a new kind of public space. It has yet to realize its second premise: the recombination of the digital and the botanical. This would input transformational plant growth and fructification data into the database and output transformative information onto growing and fructifying plants. The ensuing digital-botanical space would produce a new type of local weather: data returned as gravity and inertia onto a hybrid sound.

Petros Babasikas is founding partner of Drifting City, a collaborative based in Athens and Los Angeles working in architecture, media and public space. He teaches architecture studio and theory at Patras University. An associate member of International Academy of Digital Arts and Sciences, Petros studied Comparative Literature at Columbia University and received a Master of Architecture from Princeton University.

Abandoned Furniture

Rosly Mok | Vanessa Chan
// exhibit

The stories behind abandoned furniture are precisely what make it come alive. The mystery and layers of history create sentimentality, and perhaps extra eagerness and meaning. In terms of public usage, are the stories of abandoned furniture not more meaningful in comparison with the rows of monotonous and dead "public" benches lining the typical urban park? Join us with the chairs or sofas you do not need anymore. Share your memories and history with the public and contact us to add your piece to our project.

participatory
protocols

BYOBlanket: Yoga

Tiana Harilela // event

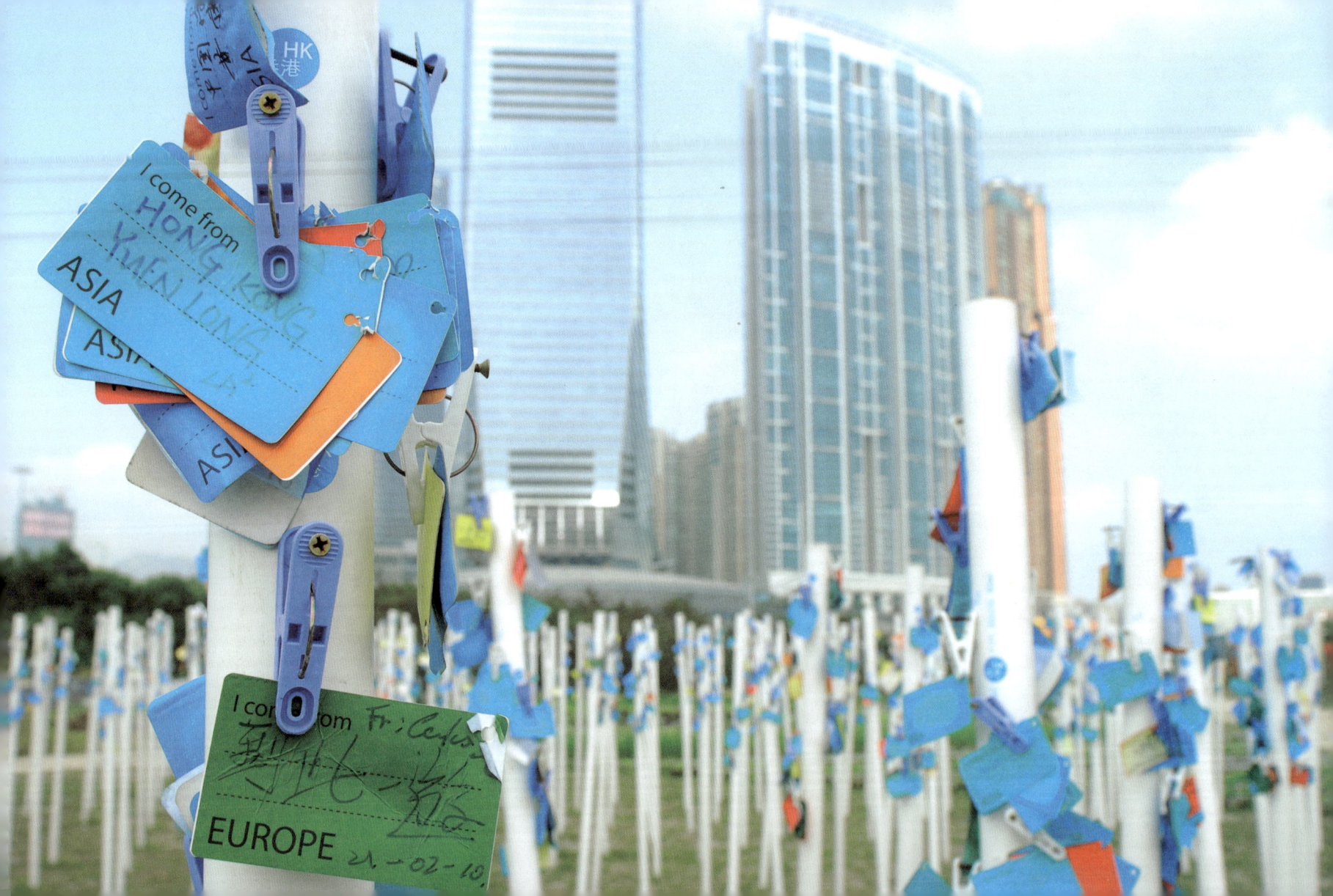

community interaction
cultural reflection

YOUtopia

Eunice Seng // essay

Of late, the battle cries of the social activists to take to the streets and the spaces of liberation envisioned by the neo-avantgarde groups of the 1960s have been the go-to sources for curators and artists of many Asian art and design events. The more informal and unexpected the spaces, the more desirable they present themselves as alternatives to the official state museums and the white box spaces of art galleries.

Around the same moment when Pop art appeared to challenge the norms of high art, architects rode the same euphoric wave of the 1960s, producing megalomaniacal visions of walking cities, space pods, monumental grids, and networked environments. Intended to liberate city dwellers from the sterile and monotonous, post-war environments of bleak urban blocks and large housing projects, they proposed, instead, to place the liberated subject in capsules within mutable megastructures, within psychedelic and multi-media-filled environments. As much technological as they were socially-driven, these new social visions were predicated on new architectural forms. Paradoxically, play was contained within oppressive totalitarian environments. The notion of the freedom to choose was wired to a heavily technological aesthetic, labelled by the architectural critic Reyner Banham as "dinosaurs of the modern movement." When sociologist Henri Lefebvre called for a revolution of the environment, such alternatives offered by groups such as the Situationists, Superstudio, and Archigram remained primarily academic, and were even decried by critics as dystopian.

Utopia was temporarily denounced, albeit by a select group of European and American architects and intellectuals, when Manfredo Tafuri's 1976 *Architecture and Utopia* presented the architectural project as an accomplice to capitalist development. Colin Rowe's provisional attempt to resuscitate utopian interest in his 1984 *Collage City* by demonstrating that all cities are composed of overlapping utopias – a visual representation of Foucault's heterotopias to some extent – could at best be seen as an historical apology to a generation that witnessed modernist utopia's failure to live up to its self-avowed, emancipatory promise. By the time Michel de Certeau offered ways to thwart "the system," in his *Practice of Everyday Life*, published in English 1984, but part one of *L'invention du quotidien*, 1980, the impossibility of any real revolution against capital was no longer questioned.

Toward the end of the second millennia, the site of utopia shifted, at least in the global imagination. The Chinese city became the popular site for the modern utopia. While the authors of *The Architecture of Everyday* invoked Lefebvre to make a case for the ordinary, banal, anti-monumental and non-heroic architecture, it was figures such as Le Corbusier and his city blueprints that were summoned to design the Chinese city. The rational and monumental plan could be readily implemented on a large tract of cleared land. Post-1990s Shenzhen exemplifies the modern plan. In contrast, Hong Kong with its differentiated geography and a history entangled with two empires – the most violent occurrence being the leftist riots of 1967 – is the prodigal city that has thwarted any overall urban plan. The deeply corrugated, extruded towers of Hong Kong embody a highly differentiated mass, unique and ubiquitous at once. Dense and conducive for acupunctural-type schemes and interventions, the present city offers the preconditions for the kinds of utopia heralded by the west in the 1960s, with a focus on "you" – differentiated from earlier universal notions of the "individual" – both as a singular and collective representation.

YOUtopia thrives on the situationistic, participatory, and generative utopian thrust of design projects, but rejects totalitarian tendencies. It recalls the modest playgrounds of Aldo van Eyck, the "supports" of Nicholas Habraken, the projects of Lucien Kroll, and the cities of Paolo

Soleri. The new millennium sees a blurring of the contrast between Hong Kong and Shenzhen as increased population flows, business transactions, and intensified collaboration calls for diverse and multi-scalar approaches. Rather than setting itself directly against capitalist development, YOUtopia operates within it, borrowing the soft and hard-sell techniques of Hong Kong's shopping culture that permeate every level within and beyond its shores, from informal stalls to high-end malls to exclusive clubs. It focuses on a designed and calculated impermanence to produce new materials and dialogues between the two cities. A site of contesting identities and imbued with an underlying pragmatism, Hong Kong is a viable breeding ground for YOUtopia – BYOB is its facilitator.

Eunice Seng is Assistant Professor in the Department of Architecture at the University of Hong Kong and founding principal of SKEW collaborative, Shanghai-Singapore-New York. Her research interests include: modern architecture and urbanism; modernity and housing; histories and theories of the metropolis; politics of power and post-colonialism; inter-disciplinary and comparative approaches to architecture; utopias; artifacts and their cultural translations.

Boundaries

Gene Miao | **Frederick Wong** // exhibit

The exhibit explores two aspects of social formation. One is how communities that are adjacent, yet distinct and separate, come together at their borders to create a shared space and common identity. The other is how individuals make diverse and creative imprints on societies and thereby create communities that are diverse, vibrant, and perpetually changing. Over time the exhibit takes on the imprints of the visitors who have stopped to participate in its creation, making the two "worlds" of the exhibit colorful and lively.

Signage
Performance

Big Mad // event

Chinese
New Year
Pun Choi Feast

O.S.J. Fund for the Elderly |
Kowloon Federation of Associations |
Hong Kong Institute of Architects

// event

On Active Ageing

Philine Bracht // essay

By 2050, Hong Kong is forecast to rank fifth in the world for cities with the largest percentage of older adults, according to the World Health Organization. Today advertising strategies show an intrusive approach to the marketing of commodities and technologies in our "barrier-full" public and private environments. Our global social fabric seems woven with a focus on the youth. However, there is a change of demographics and statistics that shows a new proportion of ageing in societies. According to the recent census in China, "there are 177.6 million people above the age of 60 in China, or 13.6% of the total population ... China has more senior citizens than in all European countries put together. China's aged population and its proportion to the total population both are higher than expected. ... China will reach a critical point in 2015, when elderly people are expected to outnumber children (0 to 14-year olds). And by 2050, the aged population will reach 437 million, or about 30% of the population" (China Daily, May 19, 2011).

At the same time advances in health care and lifestyle find people living longer and healthier lives. Sixty is the new forty. People in their sixties and seventies have more income and education than any previous generation. They remain energetic and productive members of society making meaningful contributions to their communities. There is a great need for universal design, one that is human-centered and will accommodate the needs of larger user groups. And one that will not exclude those who need glasses to read, or who may not be able to climb high steps, or that may want to rest in-between different activities.

Philine Bracht is a consultant of universal and sustainable product design and Visiting Associate Professor at the Hong Kong Polytechnic School of Design. She is the project leader of the International Design Opportunity (IDO), a workshop at the School of Design which combines ethnographic research with cross-cultural and multidisciplinary learning.

A POPULATION IS GENERALLY CONSIDERED TO BE AGED IF PERSONS OVER SIXTY ACCOUNT FOR MORE THAN 10% OF THE WORKING AGE POPULATION

AGEING IS AN INEVITABLE MATHEMATICAL CONSEQUENCE OF TWO DEMOGRAPHIC TRENDS: DECREASING TOTAL FERTILITY RATE AND INCREASING LIFE EXPECTANCY AT BIRTH

Curating A Feast

Marisa Yiu // essay

With the goal of producing a biennale that is truly inclusive, one that has the potential to attract an audience largely unfamiliar with the concept of what encapsulates a biennale, the steering committee and the curatorial team collaborated with the Kowloon Federation of Associations, the St. John's Fund for the Elderly, local architects, and community groups to create a large-scale gathering of elderly Chinese to welcome in the New Year. Officiating guests from the Social Welfare department and the Elderly Commission of Hong Kong joined the opening ceremony with guided tours led by a team of dedicated student volunteers on the Biennale's grounds.

The event is a Pun Choi feast and it draws upon a custom of communal eating honored throughout China's history. Pun Choi is special in that it is composed of many layers of different ingredients and is eaten layer by layer instead of stirring up the slices. Pun Choi translates to "basin food," where a large basin traditionally made of wood holds the culinary relic originating from Hong Kong New Territories walled-villages. Pun Choi consists traditionally of over ten ingredients. These ingredients are layered in tiers usually starting with braised turnips, bamboo shoots, pan-seared prawns, fishballs to roasted duck.

In addition to the hot pot feast, the elderly enjoyed entertainment provided by local celebrities, speeches given by various government leaders on the importance of continuing to promote large public gatherings and home affairs, health, and social good for the elderly. Dancers performed traditional Chinese dance and meandered through a dense field of more than 200 circular tables crowded with diners at the West Kowloon waterfront. The event vividly demonstrates the joy of communal eating and the new meaning it achieves in a reinvented context in which tradition is celebrated alongside the present. The event was conceived to be an anti-spectacle, but it became spectacular nonetheless because of the enchanting mass activity of 2,000 pairs of chopsticks intersecting and peeling the layers of the hot shared meal.

Grassroots / Diversity / Community

// forum

date: 4 December 2010
participants: Agnes Ng, Daniel Patzold,
John Batten, Kacey Wong,
Kingsley Ng, Paul Zimmerman,
Platteen Tsang, Syren Johnstone,
Tao Zhu, Valerie Doran
moderators: Alan Lo, Marisa Yiu

Grassroot movements are driven by the politics and diversity of a community, yet, how do these movements affect change? Speakers responded to concepts of community from perspectives of value, scale, and ideology. Can bottom up strategies react against or work with the larger metropolises found in Asian cities? What values of history can construct new identities and new communities that mobilize diversity and change?

Alan Lo: Our curatorial vision is to form a biennale that transcends exhibits; one that also interacts with the participants and at the same time extends beyond the physical boundaries of the biennale site, reaching out to neighborhoods and reaching out to the different communities.

Agnes Ng: When I received the invitation to the Grassroots, Diversity, and Community Forum, I thought how these three words are very, very important. People sometimes think they do not have any influence on the city, but in another way of thinking, they are the most important force for the development of a city like Hong Kong.

Wikipedia, a community created Encyclopedia, states, "A grassroots movement is one driven by the politics of a community. The creation of the movement and the group supporting it are natural and spontaneous, highlighting the differences between the orchestrated and traditional power structures." Pursuing this metaphor further, grassroots extend under the soil, and, because they are mostly unseen, some think that they are not important. But all these roots are natural and spontaneous; most importantly they go where they are needed, they search for what is needed in terms of water and nourishment. The above-ground portion or power structure will wither or topple over without this supporting network. Therefore, if we are doing anything that does not feed back to the grassroots, it will wither.

Paul Zimmerman: We are at a very interesting point in time because the community is now very receptive to change. There are several underlying causes and I do not know whether anybody has recognized how strong the force is going to be.

First of all in 1997, after Hong Kong returned to China and the world went through numerous crises people stopped leaving Hong Kong and Chinese people from around the world decided to make Hong Kong their permanent home. In 2003, SARS changed the awareness of the value of a quality living environment. In 2006, the government created a five day work week, effectively doubling everyone's leisure time, while allowing far more time to explore the city. From now to 2030, the number of people over 65 will go up from one out of eight to one out of four. People will have more time to demand and create a better living space. Hong Kong has all the assets to become one of the best cities to live in China.

These different kinds of communities have an inherent diversity, forming a very colorful and rich form of life that shapes Hong Kong. It is organic yet organized; and it is not organized in the sense that we need rules and restrictive regulations to keep it all functioning harmoniously.

— Platteen Tsang

Platteen Tsang: I did not live in Hong Kong for over ten years, then I returned two years ago. Because there are so many foreign nationals in Hong Kong and because so many natives have gone abroad for extended periods, different kinds of people with similar lifestyles have combined to form unique communities. These different kinds of communities have an inherent diversity, forming a very colorful and rich form of life that shapes Hong Kong. It is organic yet organized, but it is not organized in the sense that we need rules and restrictive regulations to keep it all functioning harmoniously. It is, however, organized or orchestrated along the lines of social means: a balance between work, relaxation, and living.

Tao Zhu: Whenever we talk about community, the first point is always local. The second point of reference, however, is constructive — for Hong Kong is not the centre of the cosmos and we should not do things in total isolation. In this way, a new mental map is in order to connect Hong Kong, mainland China, and Taiwan. Hong Kong should be much more conscious of its political role as a point of balance between mainland China and Taiwan. The second point, in terms of this larger constructive community, is illustrative of an imbalance: mainland China, while large and powerful, and Hong Kong while tiny and wealthy, are actually in a position to learn from Taiwan. But the problem, in terms of this possible three-way constructive community is that Hong Kong never pays much attention to Taiwan. Hong Kong can be a major intermediary between China and Taiwan, because the two parties are still treated as two separate families, and it is not always possible for them to talk to each other directly. This brings it all back to the local: by protecting

Hong Kong's core values — the freedom of speech, respect for human rights, active engagement in the construction of a community, and also the proactive role played by the professions — we can facilitate an accord between all three players in this regional or "family" construct.

This brings it all back to the local: by protecting Hong Kong's core values — the freedom of speech, respect for human rights, active engagement in the construction of a community, and also the proactive role played by the professions — we can facilitate an accord between all three players in this regional or "family" construct.

—Tao Zhu

Kacey Wong: When I was in architecture school a lot of my colleagues dreamed of building the biggest, tallest building in the world. However, at that time I just wanted to do a little apartment. Unlike in the West, where you can have your own little house and decorate it, in Hong Kong we do not have an independent exterior world as such because it is under the control of other forces – for example, the government or real estate development companies. I realized that the physical aspects of our society here are not really controlled by individuals. And while many aspects of society are often organic and self-grown, from the grassroots so to speak, I think the public misunderstands the role and the power of the architect in providing space for such freedoms; they are actually under the thumb of the developer. They sell their creativity. To do really progressive and interesting projects, you have to be super strong and ruthless. Design is a service after all, architects are paid to design – and then you think about people who cannot afford to pay. Who is helping them? Nobody basically, they are helping themselves.

This year I created a house called *Paddling Home*. I am essentially trying to give a voice to different sectors of the community. The focus is the middle class, which is a large group in Hong Kong. *Paddling Home* is a commentary on the housing market: how we have to live in ugly pink buildings; how everything is very small but very expensive; and how you end up wasting twenty or more years of your life paying off the mortgage. Everything is interconnected in a matrix: if you do not work, you cannot pay your mortgage; if you do not pay your mortgage, you do not have a place to live; if you do not have a place to live, you cannot get married. It is the Hong Kong mentality. It is all expected.

When we find something today that is a relic from the near or distant past, we cherish it, we value it, we say we want to keep it as our own. But today we are in the process of clearing things away, things that we do care about.

— Syren Johnstone

Syren Johnstone: We are interested in the opportunity to speculate about what the impact of grassroots efforts might be on the metropolis. So, we started thinking about a future archaeological site – that is, going forward perhaps a few hundred years into the future and then looking back. But rather than providing an intellectual experience, we wanted a more physical feeling of what it is like to look back onto something lost. When we find something today that is a relic from the near or distant past, we cherish it, we value it, we say we want to keep it as our own. But today we are in the process of clearing things away, things that we do care about. So what we decided to do is actually go out and interact with the community directly. We took a booth from the Central Market and used it as a center piece for an installation giving

visitors a feeling for what is it like to be a thirty year old booth. So the booth has a name, Uncle Hung. Uncle Hung is also on Facebook, and he is currently gathering friends.

Kingsley Ng: When we engage the community there are three stages. In stage one we developed a platform for intervention between ourselves and the Central Market. The process involved understanding the operations and the cultural levels of the market and at the same time breaking down the barrier between the two worlds, such that the people who work in the market do not feel that we are simply interlopers. Stage two involves how to continue the dialogue, this constructed connection between the Biennale and the market. There is a new booth installed at the same location in the market and the old booth is here, so we are intending to do some more intervention over the Biennale period. We can introduce more materials of the Biennale into the market, and vice versa. Stage three involves how we extend this dialogue to a larger audience, how we keep in touch, how we continue the momentum after the Biennale.

Daniel Patzold: We wanted to create a type of showcase displaying how architecture is informed by cultural processes, versus architecture that is self-referential. So the installation is more like a generator, or a model, than an architectural object. It shows how you could create a common or a public view of how architecture should look and feel, for example what the design qualities of a market might be. Because they are vanishing, the installation is also a retrospective look at cultural values that are disappearing or being absorbed into other processes.

We wanted to create a type of showcase displaying how architecture is informed by cultural processes, versus architecture that is self-referential. So the installation is more like a generator, or a model, than an architectural object, and it shows how you could create a common or a public view of how architecture should look and feel.

— Daniel Patzold

Alan Lo: It is amazing how such a small city as Hong Kong can create so much alienation and isolation in terms of community relations. When we look at Hong Kong Island, Kowloon, and the New Territories, all physically right next to each other, in reality the communities are disconnected and alienated from one another, due in part to mega-developments and the rise of large-scale interior environments that are affecting street-level sociability. With the proposed West Kowloon Cultural District, can we manage the development of such an important project without risking further alienation from the local communities?

John Batten: We have this fantastic street culture here in Hong Kong that is very much underappreciated. The dilemma for all of us is how to maintain a balance with something that is worthy of preservation — but that is a dilemma for all the cities in the world, not just Hong Kong. And it is very depressing when there is nowhere to walk in our cities. Our designers and planners are building gated communities. We, as a people, are not the center of their concern. The problem with the West Kowloon Cultural District plan is that same problem. It is something that just evolved with very little thought or preparation. Many of us, from day one, have asked, why here, why now?

Syren Johnstone: I really do not know why we call this the West Kowloon Cultural District. Calling it a cultural district already prejudices how one starts to think about its possible usages in the future. About one year ago I was visiting Beijing. I was walking around the edge of a lake where people were playing some games which I had never seen before. I watched it for quite a while and realized that is cultural activity; you do not need buildings and you do not need museums and so on to define culture.

Valerie Doran: There is a wonderful poem by Hong Kong poet Leung Ping Kwan (也斯). It talks about many things and it is also related in some sense to what is going on here today. I think since we have the voices of architects, designers, and dancers here, maybe we could have a poet's voice as well, so if you could bear with me I am going to read this poem out loud. It is called *Images of Hong Kong*.

Images of Hong Kong

Ya' Si 也斯 (Leung Ping Kwan 梁秉鈞)
Hong Kong, 1990

I am looking for a different angle
to approach the issue of point of view.
This old photograph was
taken at Bright Light Studio on Nathan Road.
Who would bother to colour-touch
    them these days?
Looking up, I see the Midlevels on the screen.
She's from Shanghai, can't forget
    her past glory,
White Russian cafes on Jaffe Road, violin
music. What is going on?
A bottle of Twin Sister Cologne smashed
    to pieces on the floor.
Hawkers throwing 'airplane olives' into
    postmodern highrises.
I agree with her that everyone thinks
    differently.
He studied anarchism in France, came back
and worked first for Playboy, then for Capital.
We gaze at the moon, from different angles
we gaze at the moon. The clock-tower
    in Tsimshatsui Sunset at Aberdeen.
    They plan
to redecorate this roam. Queen's Restaurant.
    China Club.
One press of the button, endless images
too much titillation distracts you,
too many trivial matters, different occasions,
constantly changing identities. When can we –
He is good at writing reportage,
    his specialties are
dogs and pornography in capitalist societies.
When can we sit down and talk?

Reproduced images and sounds of singers
    divert our attention.
Desire is redefined by the expansive screen.
You reach out your hand – what
    do you touch?
History is a series of images
the material for its making can be foil paper,
    plastic, fibre,
the push-button of a laser disc ... We look up
to gaze at the moon. Is tonight's moon
at the beginning or the end of time?
She is a novelist from Taiwan, thinks she is
Eileen Chang, writes romances about
    Hong-Kong, neon light reflection,
Star Ferry spattering waves as it reaches
    the pier, the old train station,
the endlessly reproduced Repulse Bay Hotel.
Exotica for a faraway audience.
We keep changing our position,
we are looking for a different angle
that neither adds nor subtracts,
forever on the margin, forever in transition.
We write with pens of different colours,
but these things, too, easily
    become superficial.
Is this how history is constructed?
He is a good writer of spy stories with an
    Oriental flavour.
Entangled with what others have said
Why is it so hard to tell our own stories?
They plan to redecorate this room,
We look up, searching –

Filming *Tourbillon*
at The Stage

Eason Chan // event

BYOBicycle
Critical Mass

// event

One hundred bicyclists joined together to celebrate people-power and the bicycle's role as a viable form of transportation. With professionals and beginners riding alongside each other in an extraordinary ode to environmental sustainability, Critical Mass brings cyclists of all kinds — commuter, sporting, leisure and beginner — together at the West Kowloon waterfront. Organized by Karta Healy/TWOnFRO, Stijn Deferm/Stijncycles, Hong Kong Cycling Alliance, Hong Kong Critical Mass, HK Strida, and Flwrider.

The Stage

Daniel Wu | Edward Huang | Teddy Lo

// exhibit

In this city where nothing seems to last for long, bamboo scaffolding remains as our only enduring form of traditional architecture. *The Stage* celebrates bamboo construction by re-contextualizing and re-exploring the material with the goal of creating a newfound appreciation, understanding, and respect for a tradition that is unique to Hong Kong. By incorporating LED lighting with bamboo, the design blends the old with the new to show that the two can coexist, creating a unified structure that is at once entirely new, while also referencing local traditions.

frontier closed area

dissolution

49 (+1) Cities

Dan Wood | Amale Andraos // essay

In our increasingly urbanized world, more people will by necessity have to live on less land if the planet is to survive. The truly ecological city is, therefore, the vertical city, which can allow for an efficient and shared public green infrastructure while retaining the possibility of containing development inside cities and retaining natural spaces outside.

In our recent book *49 Cities*, we examine visionary urban plans throughout history to see how these projects would have *performed* had they been built (most were not), by using an "ecological lens" to examine a number of quantifiable factors. One of the most interesting aspects we examined was these cities' relationship with green space. Early examples, from Fourier's Phalanstère (1800) to Howard's Garden City (1902), all took the relationship between cities and the surrounding countryside seriously, making sure to provide a counterpoint – from agricultural lands to wilderness – to the utopian urban propositions.

Within the city, these early visionaries also touted a more radical embrace of nature: lesser known renderings and collages suggested that even Le Corbusier's vision for urban green space – often dismissed as "Towers in the Park" and described as faceless skyscrapers in fields of manicured grass – was, in fact, an argument for a much more untamed or ruralized vision of urban nature, from wild plants in the parks to urban farming.

One of the most exciting potentials of the vertical city is the possibility of eliminating sprawl and concentrating instead on super-dense, super-efficient cities that incorporate prodigious green space and green infrastructure. This would, at the same time, enable a re-thinking of the open space outside cities to provide everything from localized agricultural production to reforestation. A genuinely radical reinvention of the city would concentrate on this larger-scaled vision of Corbusier's original dream, whereby the city itself is conceived of in relation to a surrounding natural zone – call it "Tower-Cities in the Wilderness."

Asian cities provide a tantalizing and exhilarating model for these future cities, embracing verticality and density with a breathtaking exuberance. They lack, however, a counterpoint to density in the form of open green space. Shenzhen's emphasis on development and continuous urban and industrial sprawl, for example, has left too few open spaces *inside* the cities and – more importantly – almost no room for wilderness and its many benefits *outside* the cities.

In comparison, and as anti-intuitive as it seems, one of Hong Kong's most impressive assets is the amount of open space the territory possesses: almost 46% of Hong Kong is protected open space and only about 25% of its land is considered built-up. Given the mountainous geography and the climate, this land is strikingly wild and untamed – in stark contrast to the dense urbanization of its core.

As Shenzhen and Hong Kong continue to grow, it will be important to *reject* urban sprawl and the idealistic-conceptual merging of the mainland with its Special Administrative Region. A far more visionary conception of this emerging megalopolis would be two metropoles separated and connected by an immense terrain of wilderness – creating a shared and jungly green lung for these twinned cities. With the center now a declared void, a new focus on density combined with preservation and cultivation can create a first version of this new symbiosis between city and nature. Instead of an uncontrolled and boundless SZ-HK, a new SZ+Nature+HK can provide a model for the world's cities to follow.

Dan Wood and **Amale Andraos** founded WORK Architecture Company (WORKac) in 2003. Based in New York, WORKac strives to develop architectural and urban projects that engage culture and consciousness, nature and artificiality, surrealism and pragmatism. The practice has international roots; the partners have lived and worked in Europe, the Middle East, and Asia – and WORKac's staff is drawn from different cultures and countries, harnessing difference as inspiration.

PPRD / Parametric Pearl River Delta

OCEAN.CN with Crystal Design and LaN
// exhibit

The rapid urbanization of the Pearl River Delta has been shaped by top-down planning along with profit-driven architectural production, often resulting in cacophonous collages of homogeneous and generic buildings. OCEAN.CN's agenda challenges urbanism formed from featureless, non-specific, bland — and most worryingly — disposable architecture. OCEAN. CN has documented sets of urban and architectural information related to one city from all nine prefectures of Guangdong Province, as well as the two Special Administrative Regions, Hong Kong and Macau. The spatial attributes of these eleven cities were embedded into a series of coded computational models, as well as an interface for visitors to this exhibition to design their own city.

Night and Day HK-SZ
Crisis Fronts Sampler

Michael Chen | **Jason J Lee** // exhibit

The Crisis Fronts Sampler is an interactive exhibition interface and includes components that collect, display, and leverage collective intelligence and social feedback for the purpose of generating proposals for future infrastructural development in the Hong Kong-Shenzhen urbanized region. The primary site of inquiry is the "Closed Area" interstitial border zone immediately opposite the boundary between Hong Kong and Shenzhen and adjacent to Lo Wu and Lok Ma Chau. In the context of the increasing interconnectedness of the two cities and the transition away from Special Administrative status in 2046, this area is a political and territorial gray area.

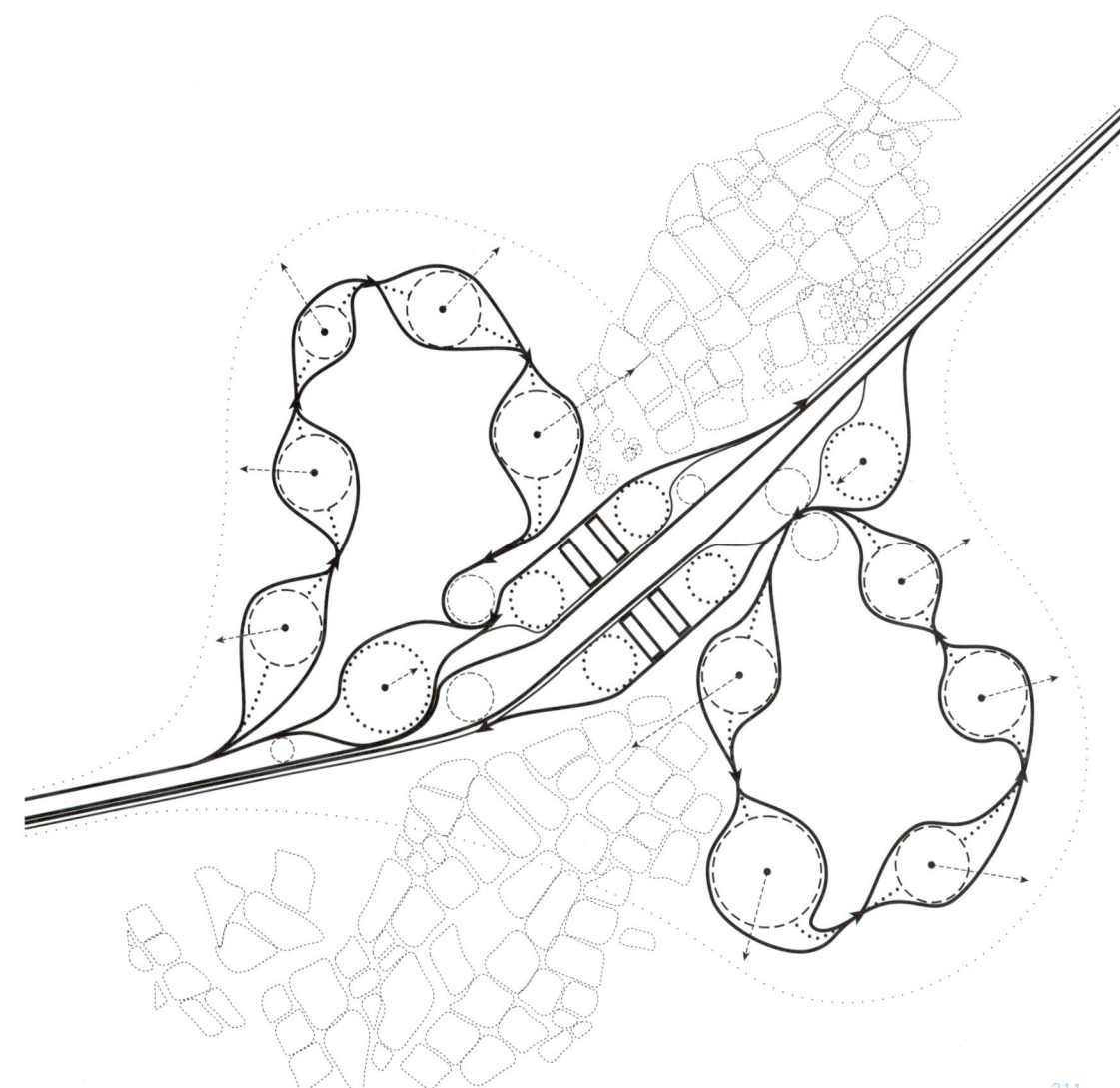

311

Tabula Rasa Reversal

Index Architecture // exhibit left

What do we gain or lose if we have a Victoria Bay instead of a Victoria Harbor? Tabula Rasa Reversal explores this possibility. Urban development on the western part of Hong Kong over the past decade represents a desperate attempt by the Hong Kong Special Administrative Region to incorporate itself, at least in terms of infrastructure, to the Pearl River Delta and China; just consider the Hong Kong-Zhuhai-Macau Bridge and the Western High Speed Train. Tabula Rasa Reversal imagines an urban plan connecting West Kowloon with Hong Kong "island," providing new ground for theoretical urban expansion as well as the physical extension of the Pearl River Delta.

Post Generic City
Learning from Shenzhen

Laurence Liauw with URBANUS
// exhibit right

This project challenges the dominant type of generic cities in China's contemporary urban development produced by centralized government standard control plans. The Dynamic City Model generates multiple scenarios, manipulated by sets of tactical urban interventions that allow the generic and specific to co-evolve. Thirteen types of people and routines are mapped in personal and spatial scenarios, with their routines weaving unique personal experiences and overlapping spatial configurations in this rapidly transforming metropolis.

Landscape Infrastructures

Stan Allen // essay

From the Biological to the Geological

If mere survival, mere continuance, is of interest, then the harder sorts of rocks, such as granite, have to be put at the top of the list as the most successful among macroscopic entities. … But the rock's way of staying in the game is different from the way of living things. The rock, we may say, resists change; it stays put, unchanging. The living thing escapes change either by correcting change or changing itself to meet change or by incorporating change into its own being.

– Gregory Bateson

For the past two decades, the dominant working metaphor in advanced architecture has been biological: a desire to make architecture more "lifelike," that is to say, more fluid, adaptable and responsive to change. Working from D'Arcy Wentworth Thompson's description of natural form as a "diagram of forces," advanced computer technology has been used to simulate the active forces that shape biological form. These contemporary strategies of animate form and parametric design go beyond the bio-morphism of the 1950s and 1960s by suggesting that the architect does not so much imitate the forms of nature as model the natural process of form generation. With contemporary digital technology, it is now possible to grow or evolve new formal configurations in response to specific forces and constraints – structural, climactic or programmatic. While this has produced compelling results, there are conceptual and procedural limits. The design techniques used to generate these new buildings may be dynamic, but the buildings themselves are ultimately static – if they move at all they move very slowly. Despite advances in fabrication technology a large gap still exists between the fluid curvilinear forms generated by the software and the intractability of materials and construction logistics. The metaphor of building as body remains intact and the potential of metabolic exchange or co-evolution with a shifting context is limited.

Arising out of similar ambitions, a counter-trend looks not to the biology of individual species but to the collective behavior of ecological systems as a model for cities, buildings and landscapes.[1] Landscapes change and evolve, and are also shaped by force and resistance working over time. But the time scale of change in a landscape or an ecological system is far slower than that of an individual living body. Architecture is situated between the biological and the geological – far slower than living beings but faster than the underlying geology. It follows from this that working concepts from landscape and ecology – which describe the complex interactions of species and environment over long time periods – offer more fitting models for architecture and urbanism than the current fascination with biological form and captured movement. Resistance and change are both at work in contemporary design production: the hardness of the rock and the fluid adaptability of living things.

This would recognize (following Bateson) that all evolution is co-evolution.[2] Individual species and their environments change and evolve on parallel courses, constantly exchanging information. Ecologies, unlike buildings, do not respect borders. Instead they range across territories, and establish complex relations operating simultaneously at multiple scales, from the microscopic to the regional. The question of process is shifted from design process – the short and limited province of the discipline – to the long life of a building, city or landscape over time, enmeshed in complex social and cultural formations.

Stipulating the usefulness of the ecological model, an additional problem arises. Simply put, what are the real and practical limits to designed intervention within the complex, shifting dynamic of the contemporary city? Cities, unlike buildings, are difficult to delimit and fix in time. Architects are more fascinated than ever with big cities, but at the same time are less and less able to control the form of the city. A further lesson from Bateson: such a complex system, by definition, cannot be designed. Everything we value about cites, it could be argued, arises as something in excess of designed intentionality or engineered performance. The question then is how to design for unpredictability and excess. Contemporary urbanism needs techniques capable of engaging the real complexity of the city as the technologies, politics, social life and economic engines of urbanism continue to change. The city is an intense locus of innovation, its collective creativity always in advance of the disciplines of architecture or urbanism that attempt to control it.

There is a growing awareness that today's complex design challenges can only be effectively addressed by an exchange of information among many disciplines. We need to work within an expanded field that includes architecture, urban design, landscape, infrastructure, ecology and program, and we need to factor in economics and policy. In such a dispersed field, it is easy to see how the specificity of architectural expertise can become diluted. In part, this was the founding premise of landscape urbanism: situated at the point of intersection between regional ecology, infrastructure, open space design, and architecture, landscape urbanism exploited its status as a "minor" field, (lacking a strong disciplinary history) to present itself as a synthetic discipline that could work on the borders of these related areas of expertise.[3] Landscape urbanism works not only in the void spaces between buildings, roadways, infrastructure, but in the space between disciplines as well. But as promising as these ideas are in theory, to date the realized projects of landscape urbanism have stayed within the conventional boundaries of landscape architecture, primarily the design of urban parks and waterfronts, reinforcing the conventional expertise of the landscape architect. An expanded institutional definition is still required, one which would open up to the design of systems and infrastructure: a shift from landscape urbanism to landscape infrastructures.[4]

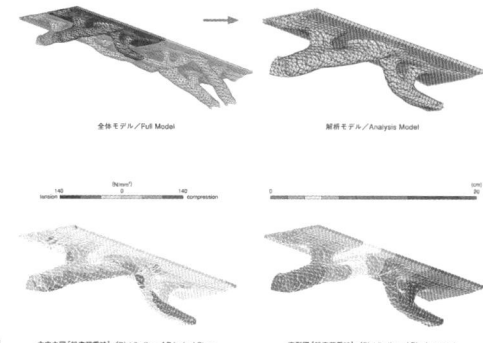

a

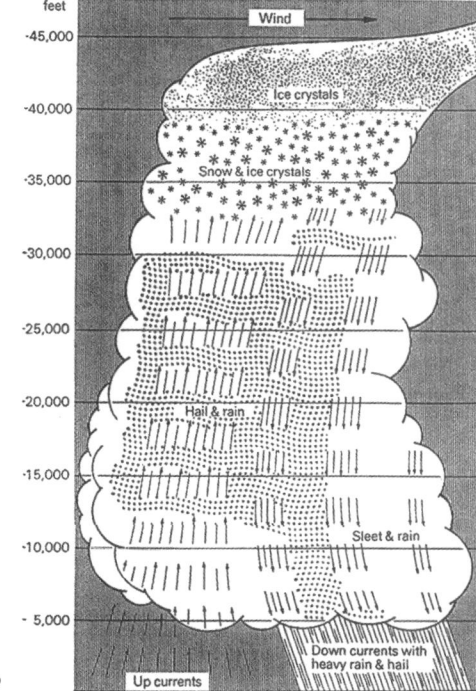

b

315

Infrastructural Urbanism Revisited

> There is a principle specific to environmental ecology: it states that anything is possible – the worst disasters or the most flexible evolutions.
>
> – Félix Guattari

Revisiting the intersection of urbanism, landscape and infrastructure, seen today in the context of the ten year history of landscape urbanism, suggests a productive way forward.[5] Incorporating lessons from the dispersed field of landscape urbanism, this renewed attention to infrastructure represents a reassertion of the specificity of architectural expertise in the design of large scale systems and structures. The design of infrastructure offers a pathway into the complexity of the urban system where design matters: nobody questions the need to design urban infrastructure. What is required is a new mindset that might see the design of infrastructure not as simply performing to minimum engineering standards, but as capable of triggering complex and unpredictable urban effects in excess of its designed capacity. More than forty years ago, Hans Hollein collaged the image of a warship into the natural landscape, suggesting a radical discontinuity between nature and technology. Today his vision can be seen as an anticipation of the present environmental impasse, or alternatively, as a starting point to rethink the relationship between nature and culture under the new domain of contemporary ecological theories.

Although not comprehensive, three primary working strategies may be identified that link back to earlier speculations on infrastructural urbanism while at the same time pointing forward to new techniques and new urban possibilities.

Connectivity

Connection is infrastructure's primary mode of operation. Infrastructures work to move goods, people, energy and information around, establishing pathways and nodes that make connectivity possible. Infrastructures themselves are static, but they serve movement. To shift attention to the design of infrastructure is, therefore, to get out of the double bind of captured movement or animate form.

If conventional, engineering design of infrastructure is based on linear systems, and respects the principles of separation of movement and the minimization of conflict, one valuable lesson from landscape is the potential of connections made not through lines but through expansive surface conditions. These surfaces have the capacity to multiply forms of connectivity. Surface is the territory of landscape, and these warped or folded surfaces contrast to architecture's vertical dimension, which has become associated with partitioned space. Working with surface connectivity, the vertical axis is materialized as building and the horizontal as infrastructure and landscape. This suggests an idea of site as a continuous matrix, differentiated locally as movement, building, infrastructure or open space. The horizontal and the vertical are woven together, and both are understood as architectural material.

Architectural Specificity and Programmatic Indeterminacy

Landscape offers architecture new models for thinking about the relationship between program and site. In the first instance, there is a promise that on an open field, anything can happen: sports, festivals, demonstrations, fairs, festivals, concerts or picnics, as well as any number of informal, unscripted events. In part this is an effect of scale – landscapes are bigger than buildings, but it also has to do with the openness of the landscape field. But that openness is deceiving. The field needs to be "irrigated with potential," to use Rem Koolhaas' suggestive phrase. That is to say, infrastructure creates concentrations of density that in turn trigger concentrations of activity. Program can never be scripted per se; the necessary freedom of the urban realm depends not on top-down determinations but on bottom-up, collective formations. The limits of design need to be strategically reworked to leverage architecture's potential to specify movement, create attractors and loosely steer program. The field is never neutral, and it is infrastructure that creates difference and the possibility for a vital life in time, organized collectively by the multitude of possible inhabitants.

Anticipatory Design

In recent architecture and landscape there is a fascination with self-organization and emergence – the notion that if the correct variables are identified through analysis, the design proposal will "emerge" through self-organization. But the idea that self-organization and emergence lack design intention is a misunderstanding of fundamental principles of ecology, based on a loose appeal to ideas of ecological succession. Emergence does not happen in a vacuum. It is triggered by differences and imbalances in the initial conditions. In the urban or landscape realm – where we are talking about artificial ecologies – you do not get emergence without carefully designed initial conditions. The architect's obligation to design those initial conditions with a high degree of precision and specificity remains. As Jim Corner has observed, "urban infrastructure sows the seeds of future possibility, staging the ground for both uncertainty and promise. The preparation of surfaces for future appropriation differs from merely formal interest in single surface construction. It is more strategic, emphasizing means over ends, and operational logic over compositional design." [6]

The design of infrastructure is therefore open and anticipatory. It has nothing to do with a specific message; rather, it is the design of the system that makes it possible to send any number of messages. It is for this reason that infrastructure is broadly democratic. It represents the investment by the state into systems that allow the movement and exchange of information without specifying the content of that information or the range of movement. This is not to say that infrastructures are utopian; infrastructures are systems of control as well. They can be easily regulated by switches and checkpoints, and shut down when required. And the operation of infrastructural systems depends as much on maintaining separation as it does in establishing connections. Yet we know there is

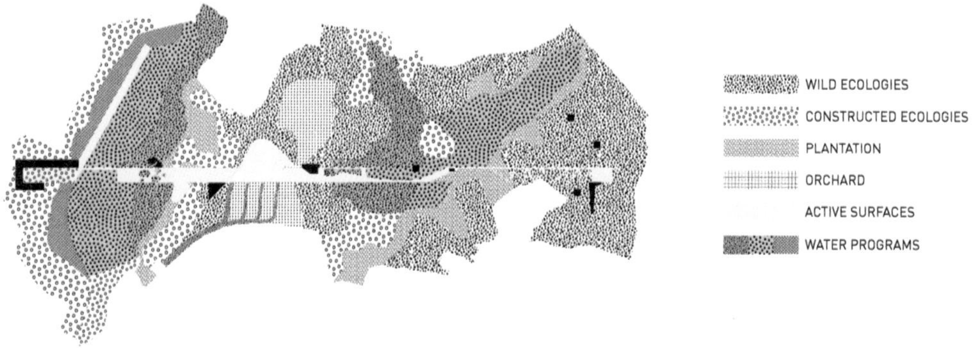

WILD ECOLOGIES
CONSTRUCTED ECOLOGIES
PLANTATION
ORCHARD
ACTIVE SURFACES
WATER PROGRAMS

c

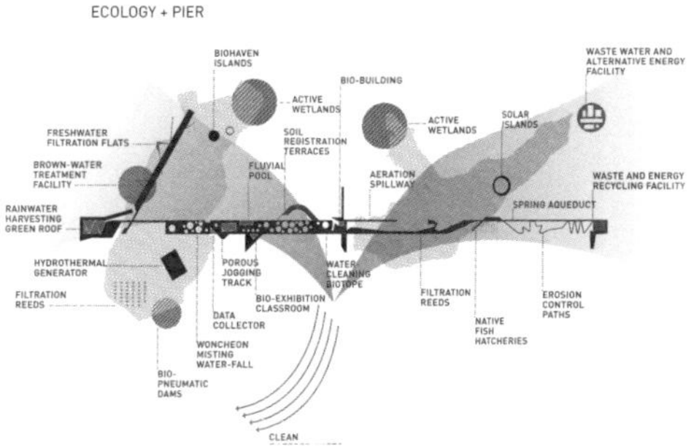

ECOLOGY + PIER

BIOHAVEN ISLANDS
BIO-BUILDING
ACTIVE WETLANDS
WASTE WATER AND ALTERNATIVE ENERGY FACILITY
FRESHWATER FILTRATION FLATS
SOIL REGISTRATION TERRACES
ACTIVE WETLANDS
SOLAR ISLANDS
BROWN-WATER TREATMENT FACILITY
FLUVIAL POOL
AERATION SPILLWAY
WASTE AND ENERGY RECYCLING FACILITY
RAINWATER HARVESTING GREEN ROOF
SPRING AQUEDUCT
HYDROTHERMAL GENERATOR
POROUS JOGGING TRACK
WATER CLEANING BIOTOPE
FILTRATION REEDS
EROSION CONTROL PATHS
FILTRATION REEDS
DATA COLLECTOR
BIO-EXHIBITION CLASSROOM
NATIVE FISH HATCHERIES
WONCHEON MISTING WATER-FALL
BIO-PNEUMATIC DAMS
CLEAN

d

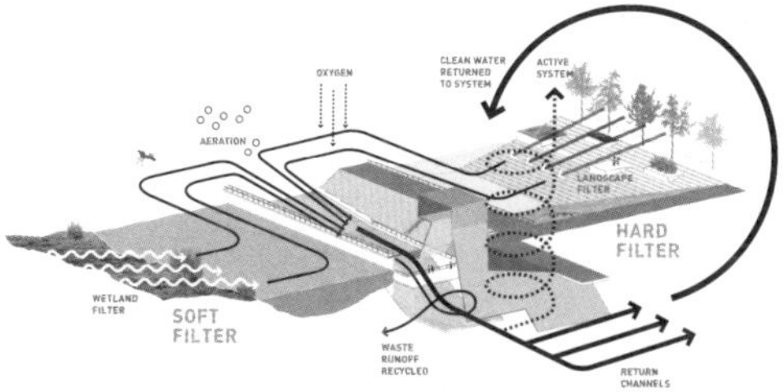

OXYGEN
CLEAN WATER RETURNED TO SYSTEM
ACTIVE SYSTEM
AERATION
LANDSCAPE FILTER
HARD FILTER
WETLAND FILTER
SOFT FILTER
WASTE RUNOFF RECYCLED
RETURN CHANNELS

e

f

g

always something slightly out of control when infrastructures proliferate.

The city today is too complex for unitary strategies or ideological statements. It requires a pragmatic mix of techniques, which parallels the multiplicity of the city itself. Infrastructure plays a key role in each project, but it is one among many available strategies. Each project is a specific response to a particular set of circumstances, but all projects, by virtue of their scale and complexity, can serve as a series of test cases for new urban strategies in the twenty-first century. Each site is large enough to support a diverse programmatic ecology, and we deploy – without apology – an eclectic sampling of techniques, new and old.

We have learned from the experiments of landscape urbanism and landscape ecology. The roadways and civic platforms appeal to ideas of infrastructural urbanism. The architectural strategy in large buildings, while stylistically distinct, is not so far from Aldo Rossi's idea of the architecture of the city, elaborated now nearly 50 years ago. "By architecture of the city" Rossi wrote, "we mean two different things: first, the city seen as a gigantic man-made object, a work of engineering and architecture that is large and complex and growing over time; second, certain more limited but still crucial aspects of the city, namely urban artifacts, which like the city itself are characterized by their own history and thus by their own form." [7] This confirms that current strategies of landscape infrastructure belong deeply to the history of architecture's techniques; yet, at the same time, these old strategies can be reworked in the present with new intellectual templates and ways of asking questions of architectural expertise.

Stan Allen is the Dean of the School of Architecture at Princeton University and principal of SAA/Stan Allen Architect. From 1989-2002, he taught at Columbia University's Graduate School of Architecture, Planning and Preservation, where he was also the director of the Advanced Design Program. Responding to the complexity of the modern city in creative ways, Stan Allen has developed an extensive catalogue of urbanistic strategies, in particular looking at field theory, landscape architecture and ecology as models to revitalize the practices of urban design. His urban projects have been published in *Points and Lines: Diagrams and Projects for the City* and his theoretical essays in *Practice: Architecture, Technique and Representation*.

a) Florence New Station, Florence, Italy
   Arata Isozaki, Architect; Mutsuro Sasaki, Engineer
b) Diagram, cloud formation
c) Gwanggyo Pier, Field Diagram
d) Gwanggyo Pier, Pier Diagram
e) Gwanggyo Pier, Working Infrastructure Diagram
f) Gwanggyo Pier, Spillway and Bridge
g) Gwanggyo Pier, Aerial View
h) Taichung Gateway Park, Urban Strategy Diagram
i) Taichung Gateway Park, Aerial View
j) Taichung Gateway Park, Exploded Axonometric
   of Gateway Complex

PARKWAY

+

CITY FABRIC

h

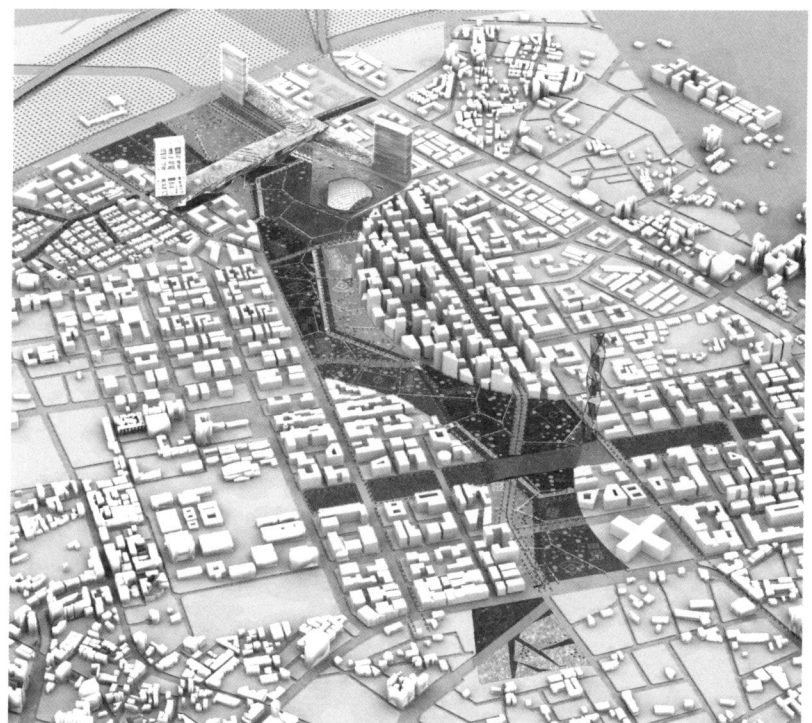

i

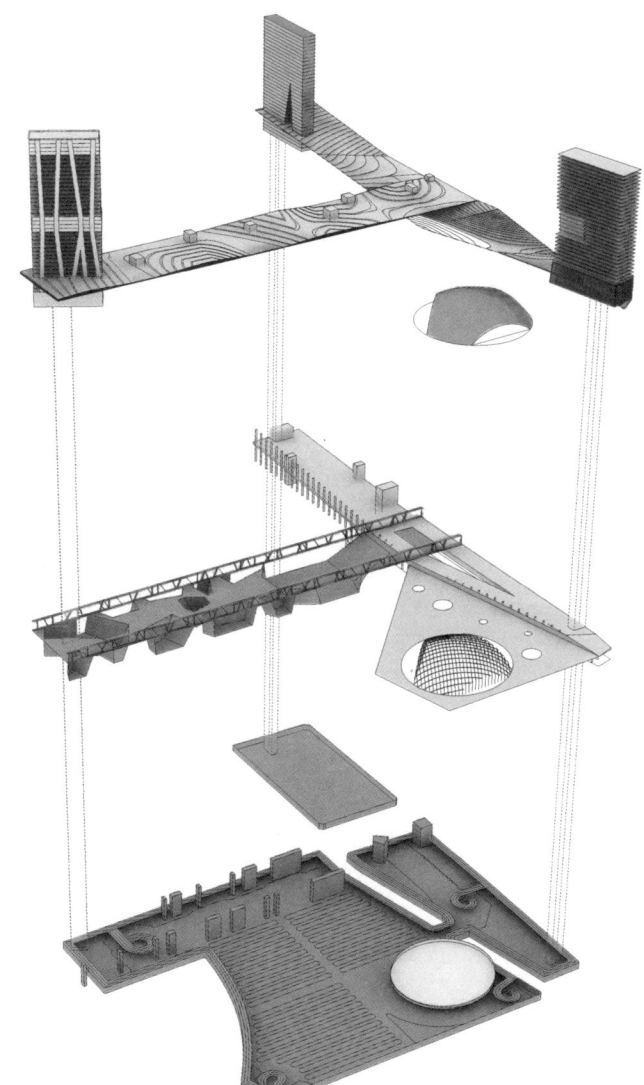

j

319

Pocket Fence

nARCHITECTS // exhibit

A fence may not only divide areas but can also open up to create unique spaces. Pocket Fence is a perimeter barrier for the exhibition and three semi-enclosed areas featuring different plantings and programs. Visitors can weave materials through the chain link, and once inside they can even enclose the space from above. It offers an architectural experience for those entering or leaving the exhibition.

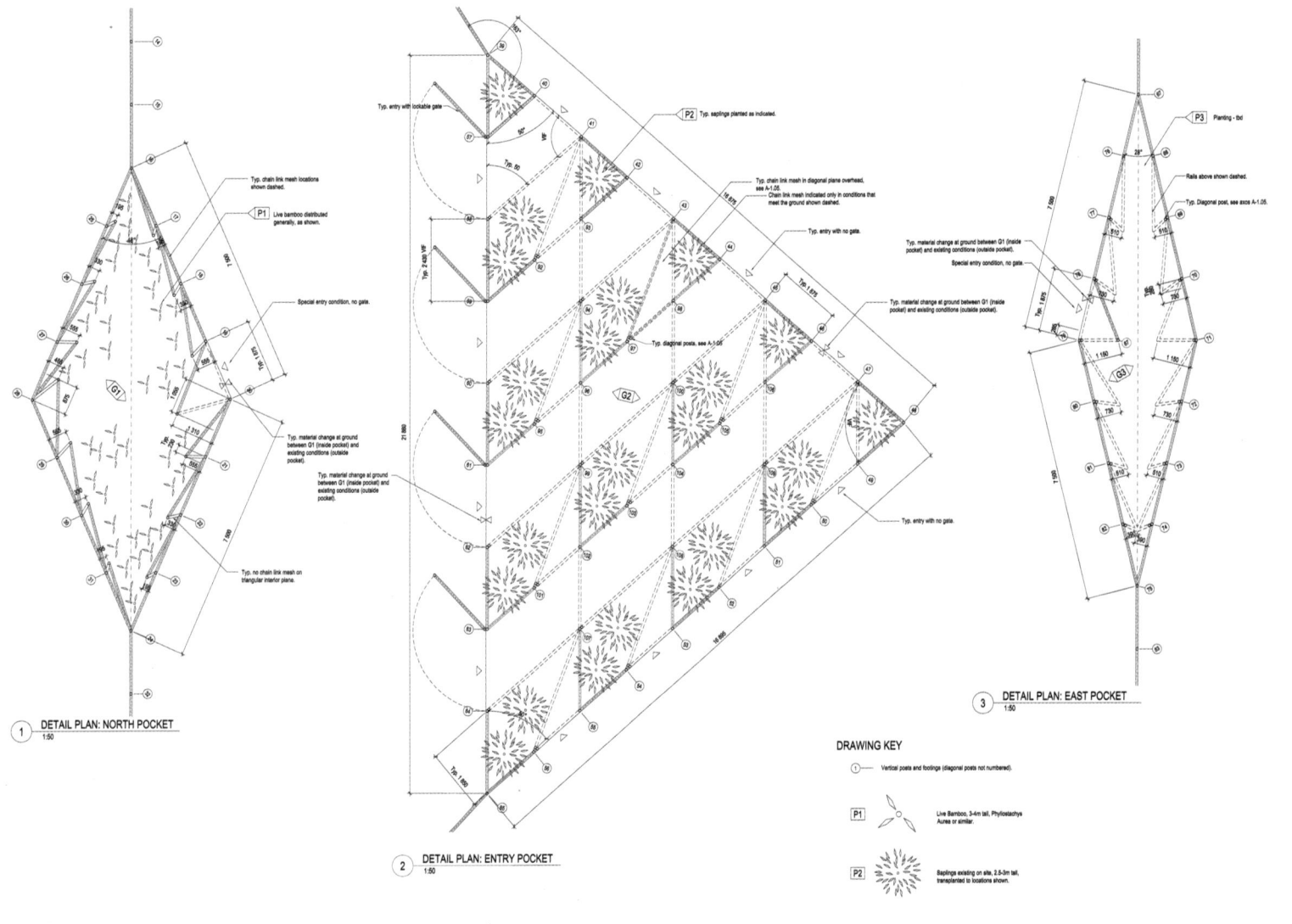

The Learning Cloud

Salottobuono // exhibit

As Hong Kong and Shenzhen citizens are becoming more and more integrated in their daily lives and work, education has increasingly become an important issue. Many people lead a cross-boundary life; with the rate of cross-boundary marriages growing rapidly, the majority of their children have opted to live in Shenzhen and study in Hong Kong resulting in "cross-boundary students." A great opportunity is represented by the Lok Ma Chau Loop and Hong Kong's boundary closed area: a dense development corridor could be realized along the Lok Ma Chau border control point and its connecting roads, while the Loop itself could host hi-tech production activities and tertiary education facilities. But due to the "one country, two systems" policy, these "cross-boundary students" could simultaneously face the conflicting issues of ecology, globalization, transportation, infrastructure, manufacturing, and responsible growth and development as critical components in their everyday lives.

Asia's World City: Hybrid Hong Kong + Shenzhen

Museum of Site | Andrew Lam   // exhibit

MOST's "Winter-worm Summer Herb" structure is curated by Andrew Lam and designed by Berlin based Hybrid Space Lab (Elizabeth Sikiaridi +Frans Vogelaar). It contains nine video works from world-acclaimed artists including Yong Yang, Zhe Jiang, Tan Xu, Eric Van Hove, Meeping Leung, Ng Kwan, Urbanus, and the Hybrid Space Lab. The works focus on the concept of "heterotopia" in the unfolding metropolis of Hong Kong+Shenzhen, albeit, in an era of post-colonial *re-assimilation*.

Interconnectivity

**Brian Wing Hang Chow |
Louis Hing Wai Law | Bill Man Piu Or**
// exhibit

Responding to the theme of BYOB, Interconnectivity emphasizes public participation. Continuous fabric represents the connection between Shenzhen and Hong Kong, and visitor interaction creates movement through the fabric.

As the existing recreational facilities in reality fail to provide interaction between the users, we aim to reuse and improve it, by encouraging public participation in the literal manipulation of the fabric.

On Cultural Education Bi-City Exchange

// forum

date: 4 December 2010
participants: David Benjamin, Jason Lee,
Jeffrey Johnson, Michael Chen,
Soo In Yang, Tom Verebes,
Weijen Wang
moderator: Joshua Bolchover

How do we cross-fertilize to create an active architectural discourse? The Bi-City platform hopes to create a certain kind of educational exchange culture within these cities, yet operate within a global network of educators. How do parametric tools, flexible strategies, and public participatory events formulate architecture and urbanism in an active cultural transformation? Will Hong Kong and Shenzhen consider the Biennale a useful tool for change?

Joshua Bolchover: The difficulty of the West Kowloon Biennale site is a fascinating starting point for discussing cultural education. In part this is because the perception of Hong Kong residents will have to change, as West Kowloon is now going to be a center of cultural production and presentation. Given the New York representatives on this panel, it would be interesting to hear how New York operates today as a cultural center, and how, by comparison, Hong Kong and Shenzhen might develop their own distinct cultural strategy to turn this novel piece of ground into a cultural center for the region. Is Hong Kong a cultural desert, as many people claim? And is Shenzhen, which has just been nominated by UNESCO as a "City of Design" in 2009, really a city of design? Do these two positions accurately describe the present and prescribe the possible future relation between Hong Kong and Shenzhen?

Tom Verebes: I have three general points to make. The first point is in regard to cultural education in a broad sense. Architecture schools do not make architects, they create an architectural culture or discourse. This is what an event such as the Biennale does as well – it creates a certain type of culture within Hong Kong, yet operates within a kind of global network of people. It is interesting that this panel is more or less half Hong Kong residents and half New Yorkers. It is obviously a conscious decision to broaden the local discourse.

The second point I would like to make has to do with urban culture proper and the possibility to fabricate or produce it. I think urban culture or urbanism generally needs to grow, change, and evolve. Hong Kong is a post-industrial city, and Shenzhen is on its way to becoming one. New York and London are also post-industrial

cities; they no longer produce much of anything in terms of material goods, but they produce intellectual property, cultural content, and design; and those are really the centers of design culture for the world. Certainly Hong Kong and Shenzhen, regionally as well as globally, could operate this way.

> ## Architecture schools do not make architects, they create an architectural culture or discourse.
>
> — Tom Verebes

The third point relates more directly to the topic at hand, or how cities grow and evolve. In our research project called *Parametric Pearl River Delta*, we researched eleven cities in the Pearl River Delta. We documented their growth over the last thirty years, from 1979 onwards, demonstrating through a series of descriptive models a range of parameters, or mixes of program, that affects density and typology in the region. What we produced is a kind of planning tool in the form of an interface that one can interact with, a device that is able to engage with the forces that shape the city, harnessing those forces over time toward the development of a type of urbanism that allows the designer to not just catch up with the city, but actually engage it and affect it in real time.

Joshua Bolchover: Regarding the Frontier Closed Area, the border between Hong Kong and Shenzhen and an exemplary site of this undetermined future, what are the critical issues to address in the planning of this region, especially in terms of the cultural plan?

Michael Chen: Jason and I are approaching this topic in terms of infrastructure, not so much in the way of inventive, large-scale public works, but rather in thinking about infrastructure as the intersection between architecture and broader social relations; infrastructure as a means for the city to mediate its own internal forms, its distribution of effects or the arrangement of its cultural parts. So, with regard to the project, we were interested in finding ways to negotiate between the kinds of data that designers conventionally use to orchestrate infrastructure and more indeterminate cultural and social concerns. So we are working initially through the kinds of data that are available, and then looking for new computational or parametric tools to articulate this indeterminate realm that represents the cultural.

Joshua Bolchover: So you are trying to set up a mechanism for participation, public participation, and engagement with the project that can be translated back into architectural means. Yet, I guess people do not associate parametric data with public participation, and this is a shortcoming of parametric methods. I think it is an interesting model to explore and expand. Maybe Weijen could talk about the importance of public engagement and culture, and the differences between Hong Kong and Shenzhen in their relation to Pearl River Delta and China.

Weijen Wang: I think one of the important messages of this Biennale, held in this particular site, is that the Biennale itself is a process for cultural and urban transformation. It is the perfect place to link the past to the future of Hong Kong, to anchor Hong Kong onto Kowloon and China. With the exhibition of multicultural projects associated with the entire Pearl River Delta, it immediately sends a clear message. We sit here under this pavilion, looking back at the urban skyline across the harbor, with history embedded in layers of horizontal and vertical fabrics built through a series of transformations. And at the same time, we are also looking toward the newly developed buildings of West Kowloon and are speculating about the future. It is a view toward a type of structural apparatus – all that is going on over there, including the future culture district and the high-speed rail link connecting to major cities in China, is about to trigger another series of transformations all the way back to where we sit today.

> ## I think one of the important messages of this Biennale, held in this particular site, is that the Biennale itself is a process for cultural and urban transformation.
>
> — Weijen Wang

This Biennale also reminds us of what happened a few years ago regarding how public concern changed the entire first plan for the West Kowloon Cultural District. Today, we have put in place a new concept for this site, including this pavilion and the many exhibitions there – all physical propositions that can invoke a process of public engagement by people and citizens, architects, and planners, by whoever arrives on this site to put their foot on this piece of land. Through the Biennale we begin to realize or envision what West Kowloon might be; the real and physical tangible experience of time and place, versus an abstract conception dictated from above.

Joshua Bolchover: The Biennale can trigger urban change, and suggest new potential uses for sites, as in the past HK-SZ Biennales. I would guess the Shenzhen Government has a very strong interest in adopting this new role for greater Hong Kong, imposed or otherwise, and that Hong Kong proper is somehow now watching in an almost paternalistic way. Do you feel that Hong Kong is actually active in considering the Biennale a useful tool for cultural transformation or is it more passive and simply accepting of the biennial event?

Weijen Wang: I am not sure if the government is consciously aware of that, but I think the organizers, when they selected this site had that in mind.

Joshua Bolchover: Yes, opportunity is a two-way street. The role of the interventions and installations of the Biennale is critical, and one must consider how they mediate between public space and intangible cultural space, beginning by addressing cultural issues and the city, or cultural production with respect to the city.

David Benjamin: It has been interesting to hear the previous speakers reflect on strategies of creating catalysts or triggers, but also tools as a direct response to questions of cultural production, rather than specific proposals. Soo-In and I have been creating a kind of platform, rather than specific messages; creating the medium as much as the message. But in the well-known turn of phrase, "the medium is the message," the medium itself carries the content or becomes a kind of statement of content. So, we are interested in an open-ended, flexible tool for engaging both the individual voice and the collective voice. For example, in *Living City* we created a platform for a dialogue between buildings; we had a building in New York collecting and sending data to a building in San Francisco and vice versa. It was a singular instance of the possibility for buildings to communicate on their own, even without people. We have also recently completed a project in Seoul, South Korea. It is a pavilion displaying air-quality data on a kind of dynamic façade that illuminates and blinks. Yet, probably what is most important to us is the exploration of the way an individual voice can be registered on a building's façade. In this way, the building façade can become a register for exchange – an exchange within a city or between cities, an exchange between individuals, an exchange as an exploration of both civic and collective tendencies, or an exchange between an individual voice and the collective – between the citizen and the larger cultural apparatus. Potentially the model can be expanded to multiple venues and to different cultural registers.

Soo In Yang: Our project for the Biennale consists of a series of soup bowls with an embedded LED.

Scrolling LED text appears in the bottom as a way to distribute messages and questions generated from various sources within the Biennale, both in Hong Kong and Shenzhen. These conversations are disseminated directly to the people by actually serving food inside the bowls in tai pai dong, with four locations in Shenzhen.

> Often there is confusion on the political level where beautification is usually taken as the main purpose of design, without too much thought about the role or site of design.
>
> — Soo In Yang

Oddly, with Shenzhen now being named a UNESCO City of Design, the issue of beautification as design comes up. Often there is confusion on the political level where beautification is usually taken as the main purpose of design, without too much thought about the role or site of design. Therefore, we chose the soup bowl. Using soup bowls to disseminate messages to the people regarding the Biennale is, nonetheless, a powerful design tool because it educates people and truly brings the conversation to the people in an extremely prosaic and provocative manner.

Jeffrey Johnson: What is important here is the notion of cultivation – the cultivation of thought and ideas and bringing people from various backgrounds together to discuss a diverse range of topics, enabling the process of cross pollination. One of the chief challenges is to produce the maximum effect within a certain format. How does one project community? How does one disseminate and broaden the discussion to not only the people within our own circle but decision and policy makers, who in a way control other decisions, whether governmental or developmental.

Michael Chen: I reject the notion that the city of Hong Kong is a cultural desert. There are many ways to read the city and it is in our own interest to find ways to leverage certain social practices and to reconceptualize these according to different sets – for example, scale, intensity, distribution, and frequency – such that it would raise them all to the level of infrastructure. The city is vibrantly cultural. I think that part of the perceived ignorance is because of the unruly and uncoordinated nature of this ad hoc culture.

Weijen Wang: Not through the government but through culture and agencies, the city has found opportunities to build platforms for the public to communicate on design and culture.

Valerie Doran: I think it depends on where you locate this notion of cultural desert. In a sense, it is a metaphysical and a physical issue. The

I reject the notion that the city of Hong Kong is a cultural desert. There are many ways to read the city and it is in our own interest to find ways to leverage certain social practices and to reconceptualize these according to different sets – for example, scale, intensity, distribution, and frequency – such that it would raise them all to the level of infra-structure.

— Michael Chen

metaphysical issue is that, yes, there is a cultural desert, but where is it? I think it is basically a question of cultural policy – an intangible something versus a physical state. And in terms of the physical, the cultural desert is a spatial issue that can be argued via the idea of pubic space. Public space is a huge issue in Hong Kong right now. But people normally control public space and people have begun to feel the squeeze of the developers and the heartless, profit-oriented development of the city. So, when you put these things together, the physical and the metaphysical, what you have is a desert that is rich with potential, but a desert nonetheless – one that is not irrigated. So, it is a real danger. I think the famous rootless cosmopolitanism of Hong Kong is an issue; that is, this rampant culture of excess is no longer grounded in any way.

David Benjamin: The Biennale is a great model for stirring things up, as it is about thousands of tiny initiatives that can equal to some sort of informal, open-ended, flexible movement. The role of such cultural education should always be about enabling students and the public to think and play in a diverse conceptual milieu.

The Biennale is a great model for stirring things up, as it is about thousands of tiny initiatives that can equal some sort of informal, open-ended, flexible movement.

— David Benjamin

Reflections on Hong Kong's Future

Paul Katz // essay

The Hong Kong-Shenzhen Bi-City Biennale offers a much-needed opportunity for reflection on the current state of architecture in Hong Kong, and on the city's future in relation to other world cities. As someone who has travelled continuously to Hong Kong for well over twenty years, I have witnessed the city's rapid transformation into one of the world capitals of business and finance. This is due in no small part to an enormous investment in infrastructure. Hong Kong has quickly become one of the easiest major cities in the world to visit, traverse, and work in, which is why so many businessmen and tourists visit over and over.

The physical facts of this infrastructure-fuelled development are visible throughout Hong Kong. From high-profile projects like the Hong Kong Station and the International Finance Centre (IFC) in Central (as well as the Kowloon Station and the International Commerce Centre (ICC) in Kowloon) to cultural and political flashpoints like the future West Kowloon Cultural District and Central Reclamation projects, infrastructure – and the movement of goods and people – has become the central defining feature of the city.

It has also had a lesser-publicized impact on Hong Kong's culture, and specifically, on the lifestyle priorities of the city's residents. Many Hong Kong residents and visitors now prize convenience and efficiency over other forms of culture. The city's art, music, and architecture scenes have too often taken a back seat to efforts to attract business and finance – arguably the main engines of Hong Kong's past, present, and future. Yet, it is the future that beckons, and commerce has taken its place in lesser cities worldwide with art in ascendance. As a consequence, Hong Kong buildings have oscillated between the extremes of banal hyper-functionality and superficial, prideful, iconicity. Somewhere in-between is a territory that everyone ignores at their own peril.

Unlike in New York, where decades of infrastructural neglect have forced informal initiatives that have transformed the city's public spaces in the form of business improvement districts, pocket parks, and vibrant sidewalk life, development of the space between Hong Kong's buildings, its sidewalks, parks and open spaces has been in short supply. By focusing on infrastructure, planners have too often neglected precisely those spaces that foster the informal exchange of "cultural capital," or, we might say, the production of culture versus mere commerce. Think how hard it is to walk from Central to Admiralty along a sidewalk, for example, or to attend multiple art gallery openings in a single night.

The same impulses have also affected the public's willingness to embrace sustainable design. Hong Kong often lags behind other world cities in major green indices. There are only a handful of LEED-certified buildings. In a city with such progressive ideas about the mass movement of people, the slow adoption of these ideas is disappointing.

Fortunately, many of these tendencies seem poised to change. The continuous reclamation of Victoria Harbor seems halted for good. A new initiative by the government to transform many of Central's historically important buildings is emblematic of a new era of emphasizing public space as a matter of priority. Additionally, planners, developers, and the public seem to be recognizing that vibrant arts and cultural districts are prerequisites to successful business districts, not challenges to them. Privately developed office and residential construction is sponsoring more small stores and restaurants, and top-down investment in infrastructure will soon be accompanied by a matching prioritization of museums, parks, and concert halls.

We have actively participated in the growth of the city as a world capital of business and finance. Our ICC project forms a paired gateway with IFC and our work on Chater House and the Landmark in Central have helped transform that district into Asia's preeminent destination for both retail stores and commercial offices. These types of projects have allowed for Hong Kong's impressive growth vis-à-vis other Asian cities. But the continued blossoming of China's cities will mean that Hong Kong will have to do even more to compete.

We should focus on strengthening the city's unique and varied assets – its harbor, historic legacy, and green spaces. In short, government, developers, and citizens must use the last decade of unprecedented infrastructural investment as a platform for a widespread commitment to architecture, public space, and the environment. Complexity in an infrastructural system is sometimes undesirable. But in a city, it is absolutely essential.

Paul Katz is president of Kohn Pedersen Fox Associates. Since joining Kohn Pedersen Fox Associates in 1984, Paul has led many of the firm's efforts on the planning, design, and development of office, mixed-use and high-rise buildings throughout the world. Some of his projects in Asia include the Shanghai World Financial Center, in Shanghai, the redevelopment of the Landmark commercial complex in Hong Kong, and the Business and Financial Center in Singapore.

The Future of the Bi-City Biennale for Hong Kong and Shenzhen

// forum

---

date: 27 February 2010
participants: Alice Yeung, Anna Kwong,
K K Ling, Liu Xiaodu,
Puay Peng Ho, Raymond Fung,
Tao Zhu, Zhu Rongyuan
moderator: Weijen Wang

Shenzhen and Hong Kong have had their difficulties and challenges in doing the "Bi-City Biennale". In the future, how should it develop further, how should it develop to explore alternative modes of communication between the two cities to constitute new collaborative relationships?

Alice Yeung: Two years ago, when Shenzhen asked us to organize a biennale with them, our objective was not to make a Venice type of biennale in Hong Kong, because we were in a period of discovery. Our objective was to help Hong Kong's citizens to understand architecture and urbanism. And that simple objective remains the same: to engage the public to talk about architecture and urbanism.

Raymond Fung: So far we have accomplished two Biennales. The first was curated by Weijen Wang at the Central Police Station, which was more architecture and urban design oriented; more about technical knowledge and the sharing of the professional aspects of design. The 2009 edition takes a different approach – a very site-specific approach, in part because of the history of this site. Therefore, it became more of an installation in itself – because of the dynamics. So far, these are the two modes. But what is to happen in the third one? Do we find a location that becomes a home? Every year we are in an ad hoc situation, asking for a site, waiting for donations from some departments, and the whole process drags on until the very last moment.

K K Ling: A biennale is both an important platform for communication between the professional classes and members of the public and a platform for professionals in whatever form they may choose to utilize it, as a tool. In Hong Kong, just as it is the role of a civic society to organize activities that the government does not address, the Biennale has been taken on by the professionals. Yet what is needed to make this sustainable is stronger support from the government.

Weijen Wang: I would like to highlight the way the Biennale worked at the Central Police Station in 2007, as well as here in West Kowloon, and how it might work in a future, hypothetical home. Many of us feel that the Biennale, especially in Hong Kong, benefits from having different sites, by moving around the city. Because each time the Biennale becomes a means to activate a specific public place as an urban process. Such was the case with the Central Police Station, where one of our concerns was how to activate heritage buildings; and so is it the case today in West Kowloon as we are all concerned about the role of this site as a public space for future cultural venue.

Liu Xiaodu: Shenzhen and Hong Kong have had their difficulties in doing the Biennale. And this illustrates that to have the government's support and sponsorship, as Shenzhen does, may not necessarily make it any easier. If we are going to formulate an organization to organize the two Biennales, there could be too much linkage. It is fine for now that Shenzhen and Hong Kong each has its own system. It makes the exhibitions and events more complex and distinct.

Weijen Wang: Should professionals constitute the governing body of this Biennale? If not, what other options do we have?

Zhu Rongyuan: The primary intention of the 2005 Shenzhen Biennale, for example, was to provide an alternative mode of communication between other cities and itself. The 2009 Hong Kong-Shenzhen Biennale is a reflection on the increasingly intimate relations between the two cities. These two cities demand a channel to generate mutual understanding and the Biennale is one such tool to accomplish this. Then, there is also the exchange on the cultural and social level. Although the economic differences are shifting and the urban scale of Shenzhen has surpassed Hong Kong's, the difference in the level of civilization as well as governmental systems still exists. It is this difference in civilization, political systems, and social values that makes the Bi-City Biennale different on each side and, therefore, productive of a dialogue. If the difference failed to be retained, then the Bi-City notion would vanish.

Puay Peng Ho: The idea of a biennale being a response to what is going on in a local place is something that we should take seriously. But reaction is not enough; reflection is also what we need. It is an ongoing process. I like this year's theme because mobilization is something very current. In Hong Kong there are many activists and local groups; they are mobilized by government policies or the developers' lack of interest in the public physical environment. If the mobilization theme could be more constructive, producing actual results, then we might make an impact.

Tao Zhu: The issue of the difference is not an issue at all because some of the differences we might never overcome. They are precious. The more important issue is actually the coherence and the continuity. That's why we named it Bi-City.

One of the questions is a horizontal one among the previous, current, and future editions of the Biennale. What is the relationship? Do we need a degree of continuity to make it one single cultural project? One word that could not be better in this regard is ad hoc – that is, the Biennale is logistically, culturally, and conceptually an ad hoc affair. I think now we have sufficient experience to reflect on this quality.

Another question is how can the two cities constitute a more collaborative relationship? After the Biennale, which was kind of like a party, typically everything disappears, with no further elaboration, no further engagement with the media, professionals, and forums. Many great issues in the Biennale quickly dissipate. Due to the current curatorial culture, the Biennale now is more like a presidential campaign and each one has to invent a totally new theme from scratch to try to surpass the previous one. This creates an immense disjunction. We need to impose another layer of coherence.

The Biennale should somehow work together with a common cultural goal rather than individual themes. So, I dare to propose two future visions of the Biennale. And it is not enough to simply say make it an international Biennale. We should actually do more by going back to the local. One vision is to formulate a key element for the Biennale to do systematic research on the development of the Pearl River Delta, as a consistent theme carried forward in each Biennale. The second vision is to promote Chinese contemporary architectural culture in the mainland, Hong Kong, and Taiwan – that is, to construct a common platform, and not as a center but as a key component.

The Imagined Hong Kong Biennale

Jiang Jun // essay

In Hong Kong, large-scale cultural activities have no choice but to engage the urban voids, vacant, somewhat accursed, sites caused by political, economic, or social distress. This is more or less a reflection of culture's marginalized position within the city. In 2009 the Biennale Committee selected the West Kowloon site, the choice symbolizing the essential cultural urban void as a possible generative vessel for new urban visions. Having been idle since the new millennium, the site ascertained a special preeminence or cultural ambition, while at the same time negotiating a fresh beginning through the imminent reformulation of the site as the West Kowloon Cultural District (WKCD). Thus, the Biennale started hurriedly, and with great fanfare, preparing, in a sense, the preliminary cultural software and the formative cultural DNA through architectural and artistic events as a type of prelude to the upcoming, huge, and as-yet-unresolved cultural hardware of the future West Kowloon Cultural District.

What has the Biennale brought to Hong Kong under such conditions? It could be, in fact, the biggest collective imaginative leap from Hong Kong to the Chinese mainland for some time. Hong Kong underwent rapid urbanization well before the recent reformation of its post-British political status. The economic boom of the 1960s and 1970s started the unstoppable golden trajectory of Hong Kong's local culture, and now undoubtedly the rise of mainland Chinese culture in the vicinity is an early sign of the economic center's northward migration, an attempt to draw some of that magic outward and inward. In fact, the program of the West Kowloon Cultural District, as a cultural renewal project, is clearly synchronized with Hong Kong's current economic-political transformation, that is, as a type of relay station for speculative capital combined with art as intellectual capital. However, in mainland China cultural hardware consists typically of a huge museum or large theater oriented by the official ideology, as a standard accessory to the "generic city," such facilities being the long-standing model for cultural patrimony in both the East and West. Meanwhile, the Biennale in Hong Kong relates to a global system of exchange and experimentation and perhaps the drifting status of the cultural projects included in the provocations of the 2009 Hong Kong Biennale and – possibly – as the first signature events of the WKCD, all related to the excesses of success mentioned above. This might show that content is not found in idle or pro forma hardware, but in active and vital artistic activities.

For most Westerners, Hong Kong is most likely just another exotic location, a large-scale Chinatown with higher density. Yet for people from mainland China, Hong Kong serves as a cultural enclave because it is the earliest and most successful Special Administrative Region (SAR) under the "one country, two systems" policy; it is rightly this distinction that gives Hong Kong a temperament different from Beijing, Shanghai, and Shenzhen. The potential of being a cultural SAR could make the north-south communication between Hong Kong and the mainland more productive versus simply competitive. Comparatively speaking, the interaction between Hong Kong and the Western world is more about mobilization or circulation. Another feature of Hong Kong is its generic architecture and the city's rapid changeability, which determines the absence of a respectable museum or artistic epicenter per se. Yet, this absence makes the entire city a potential, surreal, museum-city. These two features of Hong Kong respectively influence the elite culture (based on the conscious north-south cultural communication) and the popular culture (based on informal, innovative strategies). If these two conditions, as a two-way street, can be strengthened through the Biennale, Hong Kong's cultural hardware might allow a gradual reformation of its own dispersed cultural resources as an archive, the latter which will restructure Hong Kong's relationship to both cultural patrimony and the world well beyond its borders.

Perhaps, from 1997 to 2017, and then toward 2047, the development of the Biennale will create alternative spaces, both physical and ethereal, for the people's imagination to inhabit, not unlike the yet-unresolved pieces of Hong Kong, the seminal urban voids of which the WKCD is but the most prescient and pressing example at the moment.

Jiang Jun is a designer, editor, and critic. Born in Hubei in 1974, he received a Bachelor's degree at Tongji University and a Master's degree at Tsinghua University, Beijing. He founded Underline Office in 2003, has been the editor-in-chief of Urban China magazine since 2004, and is Associate Professor at the Guangzhou Academy of Fine Arts, a project director at the Strelka School of Architecture, Design and Media in Moscow, and a visiting scholar at Oxford University.

learning and leisure
as advocacy

Forest Project

Xu Bing // exhibit

Forest Project seeks to establish a self-sustaining system that links art lovers in developed countries with local communities in developing Kenya. The two worlds are linked symbiotically through online auctions of artwork created by students from primary schools in the Mount Kenya National Park area. The income and price disparities between more developed nations and Kenya form the basis for the success of this project. Two dollars is a pittance for many in the West, just enough for a one-way subway ride, but when used to purchase a piece of art created by a student in Kenya, it can be converted into ten newly planted seedlings.

Mission for the Forest Project

Xu Bing // essay

The Forest Project is a mechanism to help restore Kenya's forests by allowing for a continuous flow of funds from wealthy countries to Kenya for the planting of new trees. According to the instructions outlined in the teaching material I compiled, students aged six to twelve compose pictures of trees using writings and symbols invented by our ancestors. Once the works are labeled they are then displayed in the gallery on the dedicated website and within art museums. Through the online shop, auction, and a transfer system, art-lovers from around the world who are deeply concerned about the environment are able to bid on these drawings, allowing the children's creations to reach art galleries and collectors worldwide. All the proceeds go to the Bill Woodley Mount Kenya Trust. Therefore, the trees on paper are transformed into real trees growing in Kenya.

Many years ago, on my second visit to Kenya, local teachers brought their students to the conservation centre where we set up a temporary classroom. Over a four-day period I gave lessons to students of different ages, introducing them to various forms of writing, symbols, and artwork related to trees. The children were then given a piece of paper to let their imagination run wild. After gathering some of the drawings, I began to feel that this project could make a long-lasting, if not life-changing, impact on the children in Kenya.

I went through their work one by one. All their trees were exquisitely drawn while also revealing each individual's personality and thoughts. These trees thrived and flourished amid the assorted flowers and fruit that were made up of various alphabets and symbols. What amazing trees – how did they end up in all those brilliant colors? Even the shapes of branches and twigs were many and varied. There were words on some of the roots: "Trees have souls. We must protect the trees." No prevailing theory can offer an explanation to account for the children's astounding imaginative power; their drawings have opened my eyes. Since then, whenever I set foot in the Kenyan woods, I have started to appreciate the charm of these ordinary trees. The natural environment where these children were born is also the origin of those magnificent trees they created. Through this project I have come to realize the chemistry between knowledge acquisition and the enlightenment of the soul. Written symbols work wonders when combined with primitive ingredients because they are so closely and intricately connected. The evolvement of alphabets is one of the most fundamental conceptual components in the development of human culture. However, in the eyes of children, words and symbols are just the same as leaves, branches, and flowers. For they all transfer messages and they express our world.

To me, such a bond involves the relationship among human imagery, visual symbols, and diagrams. So what is the connection between

nature and the existence of core symbols in the early ages of history? In fact, when the students first began to draw, it was random and aimless, similar to the emergence and formation of symbols in the early days. The moment they began was the start of a basic concept.

It is also down to the style of drawing and the origin of design. What is the essence of the design? For example, the way the children decorated their trees exhibited an extraordinary sense of style, revered by designers. These children, who were unaware of contemporary design, surprisingly penetrated right through to the core of modern design philosophy. Perhaps the imagination of children is a perpetual fountain of design ideas, for they have their own approach and rationale, exactly what adult's lack.

Children's drawings are mirrors of their thoughts and cognition. They are sensitive, but at the same time vulnerable. Their pictures are reflections of the messages and instructions they receive. I sense that their thoughts, like the two tentacles of a snail, are lively and responsive, though occasionally subject to withdrawal. I often look at these pictures drawn by the children and have no doubt that they offer helpful insights into child psychology, art education and dream realization.

Not long after I returned from Kenya I started to imitate these children's drawings. By incorporating the trees they drew into forest landscape artworks, it was hoped that the students' original works would become more precious and that their values would be potentially increased with a view to promoting

the interests of collectors and the continued cycling of the system. The system's theory of symbiotic-circulation takes root in utilizing the ready-made service functions of the internet, the economic disparity between places (where a hundred trees can be planted in Kenya for US$20) and the principle of shared benefits amongst all participants. The process of this system embodies the transmission of knowledge, artistic creation, love and care, and the mutual benefits of communication. On my first landscape piece I included the caption, "I have imitated the children's drawings like those of a grand master. I dare not make any changes, because once I do it will be like chopping some branches off a tree. The trees are living. They are a part of our natural world." Nowadays, I often make some notes in respect of every tree I imitate as I draw new wisdom and inspiration during the process. It dawned on me that every child possesses their own rhythm, which forms a part of their personality and character. The unique style and stroke employed in their drawings hold some visceral clues. When faced with the object they are about to draw, children often do not know where to begin. By instinct, they know they need to find a motive or reason to get started. Once they find it, the children's persistence, an inborn feature, unfolds. For example, if one leaf of a tree is to be drawn by three strokes, every leaf on that tree has to be done in three strokes. Even when it is impossible to continue – that the leaves are already too densely packed – the three-stroke rule has to be followed, so much so that the three strokes are overlapped and jammed together. It is merely done for the sake of giving oneself a reason to continue. Such temporary reason, a very strange happening in itself, forms a mechanism which is boundless and is not governed by aestheticism. Interestingly, it is very similar to the texture strokes and dotting method used in traditional Chinese paintings which prompts me to ponder how the standardization of Chinese paintings takes shape. This is just an example of one of the many sensational revelations I was made aware of. A lot of children who learn to draw are fascinated by such exhilaration. The interaction between written symbols and primitive elements brings new dimensions while the evolution of alphabets forms the core value of humanity. Naturally, in the world of these artistic children, words are perceived to be exactly the same as leaves, branches and flowers, which are both delicate and expressive.

Every single participant learns something from this project. I have gained tremendous visions from all these children's drawings. Meanwhile, the benefits to the children are not limited to their achievement in art or their understanding towards a certain value. By turning the trees on paper into real trees, they will be able to appreciate how ideals are realized. What is important is that this dream is made real through the socio-economic circulation in real life. It is also the children's reality in the future. In pursuing their dreams, they learn to identify stepping stones to their eventual destinations. We encourage children to have aspirations, but these ideas cannot remain as hollow words and empty talk.

The implementation of the Forest Project in Kenya is gratifying and I have always wanted to bring it to Hong Kong and China. However,

my concern is that children in China are not as imaginative as those living in the Kenyan mountains when it comes to drawing trees. There are not that many nice and colorful trees left in our environment. Will Chinese children come up with "Fuwa-style" trees? The suspense remains. One thing is certain though, this project will generate more discussions in China.

Art alone has not been the major interest of this project but the outcome has led to complex art-related issues. What is the way forward for art and how can art break away from its current predicament? What is the shape and form of art? Where are the sources of inspiration and creation? Art for the good of humanity offers infinite possibilities. With this objective in mind, all complicated concepts can be understood with the greatest of ease. Only by keeping a safe distance from the conventional art philosophy can we inject new life into its very system.

Xu Bing was born in Chongqing, China and currently resides and works in Beijing. He received a Bachelor and a Master degree at the Central Academy of Fine Arts, Beijing and has now returned to serve as the vice president for international relations at the academy. Solo exhibitions of his work have been held at major museums and art institutions throughout the world, and he has won countless prizes and awards including the MacArthur Fellowship in 1999 in recognition of his contribution to the community, particularly in printmaking and calligraphy.

Facing Failure

Winnie So // essay

Creativity and innovation cannot be imported, transplanted, nor taught; there is no master plan or formula, no right or wrong way to be creative and innovative. These fruits are borne only when nurtured by certain values in a warm and open environment. As John W. Gardner explains in his incredibly insightful book, *Self Renewal: The Individual and the Innovative Society*, the difference between a vibrant, thriving society and a rigid and decaying one is simply whether it provides for its own continuous renewal.

How does a society continually innovate and renew itself? The answer lies in its individuals, whether they themselves are self-renewing. Self-renewing people share certain characteristics – a sustained curiosity about themselves and the world around them (they understand that their knowledge of both is limited and continually strive to expand and break limiting patterns of their understanding), courage to fail and be wrong, capacity for compassion, and an internally derived motivation to persevere at an endeavor out of a belief that it is worthwhile or meaningful.

These past few months, I have had the pleasure of teaching a class at Hong Kong Polytechnic University's School of Hospitality and Tourism Management. It has been an enlightening and inspiring experience, where the teacher has been the student. My class of 36 students (final-year Higher Diploma Tourism Management students) has taught me to consider what we need to provide younger generations if we are to expect them to inherit the task of renewing our society.

The first day of class, by way of introductions, I asked the students to share their dreams. For most, it was to become rich one day. To understand why they wanted to be rich, I asked them to draw a picture of their image of "rich." Most drew a free-standing house. In this class about creating and marketing innovative travel products, I also learned that most preferred to travel to new destinations with tour groups rather than explore on their own, because they feared the unknown.

Hong Kong has come a long way in its economic development since Gardner's book was first published nearly half a century ago. In class, I introduced Abraham Maslow's Hierarchy of Needs – at the bottom of the pyramid are survival and safety, at the top, self-actualization. For people to feel free and daring enough to experiment, they must first feel safe and secure. Can an individual feel safe and secure when the notion of a home of one's own seems but a fantasy for most young graduates today?

When asked to share their aspirations, three students replied, "None." Why have they lost the will to dream? Why are they fearful? And how can I (as a teacher) and we (as a society) create a safe and nurturing environment for the younger generation to freely explore, take risks, fail, discover, gain confidence, and learn? While the students have raised these questions in my mind, the most important lesson I have learned from them is faith. Renewal is a process, not an event. The Hong Kong Biennale bears testament to that very truth.

Winnie So is a writer and founder of Little Cream Book and WANLILU Play Ltd, a bespoke travel service. For her, the best stories and travel experiences are filled with the wonder of discovery, possibilities for transformation, and moments of inter-connectedness that underscore our common humanity. Winnie is a committee member of the Hong Kong Ambassadors of Design. She is a graduate of Bryn Mawr College and INSEAD.

Planning for Cultural Districts in Hong Kong and the Pearl River Delta // event

Hong Kong, Macau, and the Pearl River Delta region are seeking for a more sophisticated form of enrichment for cultural urbanism. All cities are challenged to build their districts to serve the public. What are the aesthetics for inspiration? This event, organized by K K Ling and featuring discussion led by Augustine Ng, Jose Chui, Lu Qi, and Luo Min Wang, questions how community building, social integration, humanitarian concerns, and relaxation intersect. Planning experts from Hong Kong, Macau, Shenzhen and Guangzhou share their visions, ideas and experience on the development of cultural districts in a public forum.

Cultural Classroom and CNC Design Lab

ESKYIU // exhibit

A major component of culture is the exchange of creative ideas and design education. Collaborative practices form the basis of cultural enhancement, providing nourishment for creative endeavors. The classroom, in this sense, is not a central, enclosed zone in the Biennale but an outward-reaching and extendable device, connecting the waterfront site with linkages to other academic and cultural institutions.

Computer Numerical Controlled (CNC) machine tools have revolutionized the design process of architecture. The design lab allows exhibitors, students, and collaborators to use these tools in support of their installations. Other media and educational workshops led by various invited architects and designers further enhance the dialogue of making.

BYOB Reading Café

Studio OFF // exhibit

Lately, there have been a series of large-scale urban renewal schemes in the West Kowloon area undertaken by the Urban Renewal Authority (URA) in conjunction with private developers. Whenever a unit in a "target building" is vacated and taken over by the URA, all the windows of that unit are taped in the form of a cross array in order to signify from the outside that the unit is now a government asset. Here, urban renewal is reduced to the notion of symbolic, momentary appropriation of a discrete urban fabric within the city. The design of a cross frame is, thus, the basic, modular unit or partitioning material utilized in the construction of the *BYOB Reading Café*.

城市动员，靠你动员！

BYOB

www.hkszbiennale.org

Bring Your Own Books for the 2009 HKSZ Biennale!

Call for book donations to contribute to the Biennale Public Cultural Library

We are calling for a book donation from YOU.

A book that teaches you to draw
A book that gave birth to your 1st inspiration of architecture
A book that expresses your 'work-done'
A book that moves you to look at buildings
A book that tells you the good and bad of the city
A book that envisions the future
A book that teaches you recycling tips
A book that inspires you to be more 'green'
A book that generates your creativity
A book that sees far beyond your imagination
A book that encourages new thinking
A book that influences you
...... or simply:
A book that blinks!

In addition to your donation, we need also your OWN interpretation of your donated book

Our suggestions include to:

carbon-copy it – paint it — draw it – decorate it – facelift it – sound-record it – digitalise it – cartoon it –
concise it – photograph it – and a lot more to do it on your own ways......

On building up the BYOB Public Cultural Library, we are pledging for your support to promote the
reading culture and your creative reading habits to the general public in the widest extent we can all
imagine! There is no limitation!

RSVP the following details to puiki.sze@hkszbiennale.org:
- Title and author of the book
- Description of how you are going to 're-interpret' the book (or to leave as is)

Delivery deadline:
20 November 2009 (Fri)

Donation to include:
Your donated book (re-interpreted OR left as is)

Delivery by post to HONG KONG:
Attn: The Hong Kong Curatorial Team, 2009 HKSZ Biennale
Address: 16B, Kin Teck Bldg., 26 Wong Chuk Hang Road, Wong Chuk Hang, Hong Kong

THANK YOU VERY MUCH!

facelift it

photograph it

shrink it

paint it

as is

domus

West Kowloon

CITY MOBILI-ZATION

BYOB

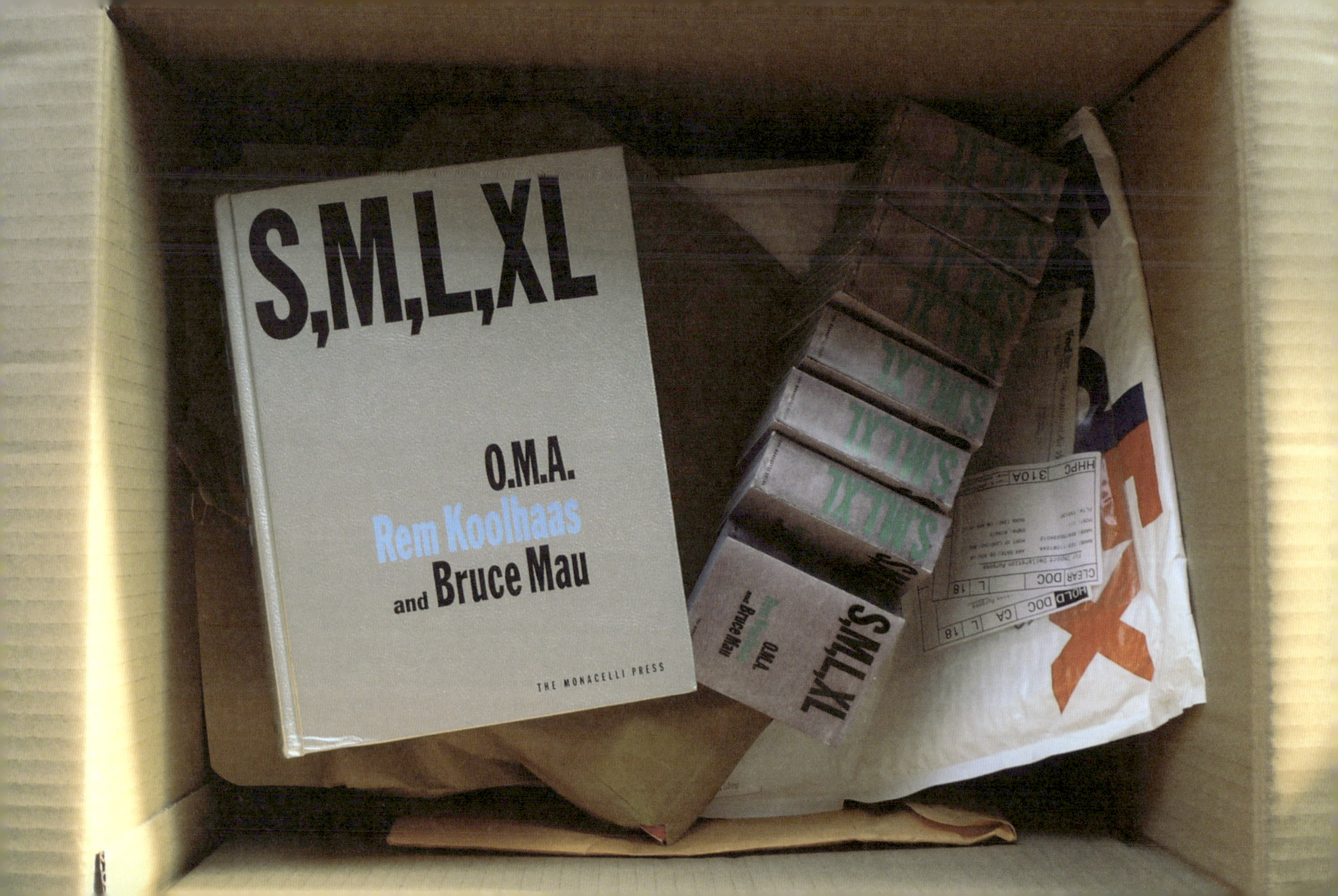
S,M,L,XL
O.M.A.
Rem Koolhaas
and Bruce Mau
THE MONACELLI PRESS

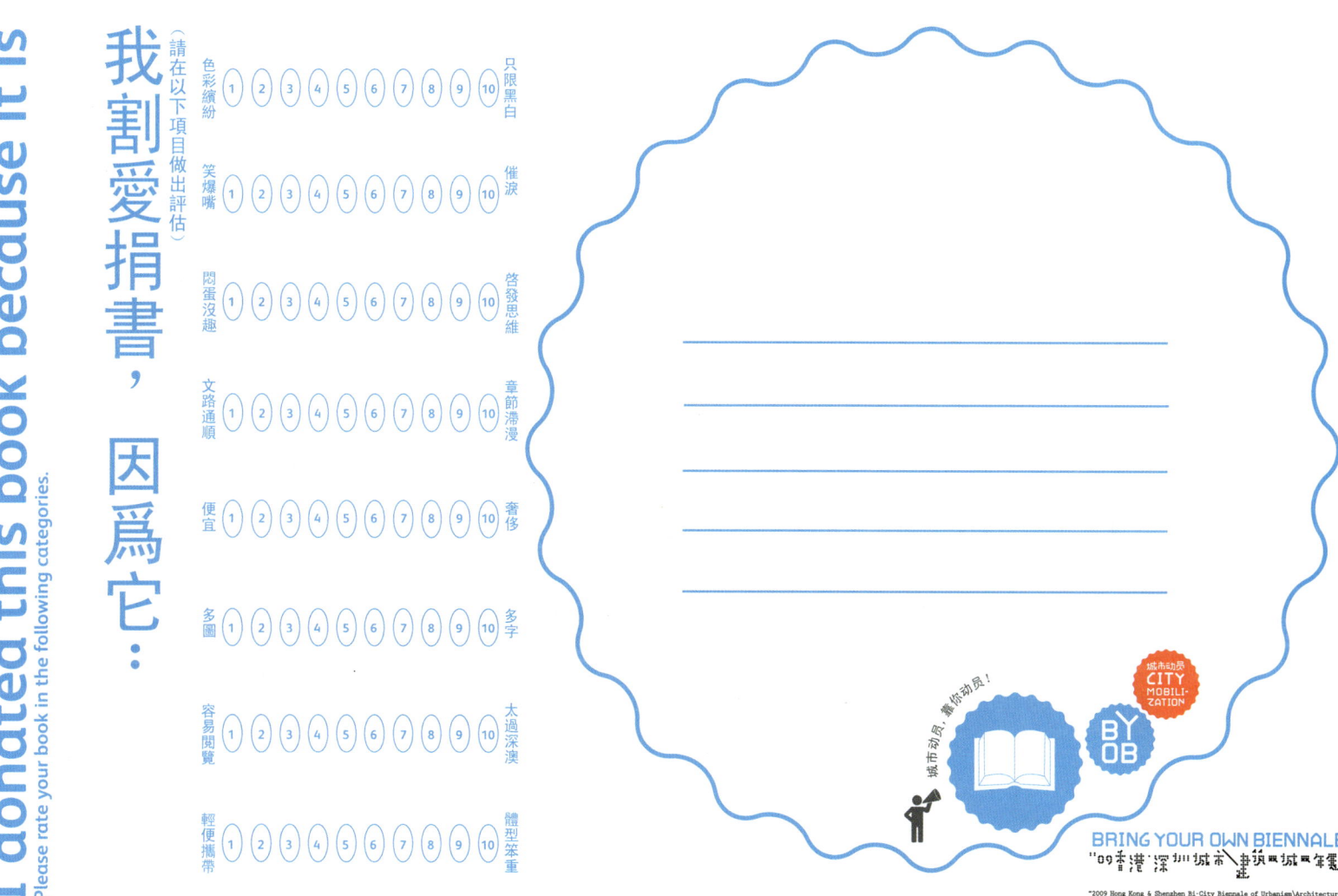

I donated this book because it is

Please rate your book in the following categories.

我割愛捐書，因爲它：

（請在以下項目做出評估）

色彩繽紛	① ② ③ ④ ⑤ ⑥ ⑦ ⑧ ⑨ ⑩	只限黑白
笑爆嘴	① ② ③ ④ ⑤ ⑥ ⑦ ⑧ ⑨ ⑩	催淚
閱蛋沒趣	① ② ③ ④ ⑤ ⑥ ⑦ ⑧ ⑨ ⑩	啓發思維
文路通順	① ② ③ ④ ⑤ ⑥ ⑦ ⑧ ⑨ ⑩	章節滯漫
便宜	① ② ③ ④ ⑤ ⑥ ⑦ ⑧ ⑨ ⑩	奢侈
多圖	① ② ③ ④ ⑤ ⑥ ⑦ ⑧ ⑨ ⑩	多字
容易閱覽	① ② ③ ④ ⑤ ⑥ ⑦ ⑧ ⑨ ⑩	太過深澳
輕便攜帶	① ② ③ ④ ⑤ ⑥ ⑦ ⑧ ⑨ ⑩	體型笨重

城市动员，靠你动员！

城市动员 CITY MOBILIZATION

BYOB

BRING YOUR OWN BIENNALE

"09香港·深圳城市\建筑双城双年展"

"2009 Hong Kong & Shenzhen Bi-City Biennale of Urbanism\Architecture"

134 PAINTINGS IN FULL COLOR

FLOWERS

A GUIDE TO FAMILIAR AMERICAN WILDFLOWERS

THAT ARE STILL HERE

ZIM • MARTIN

FLOWERS

SIMON AND SCHUSTER

A NEW NATURE GUIDE

491

We are now all designers: every square millimeter of the planet has been designed and redesigned by human hands. Post-war planning ideologies, architectural agglomerates, the globalization of oil consumption and global economies driven by resource extraction has resulted in a world that has been completely made and not found. Everyone now is a designer of the environment at large with a different expertise in the world of design.

It is vital to expand architecture beyond "design for us," or beyond a built environment conceived exclusively for our consumption and comfort, to address the wider global ecosystem as a shared space for all species. As "WE design" in the 6th Wave urban design can be recast as a form of new, activist, joint urban and environmental stewardship in order to mange biodiversity and begin to reverse the trajectories of mass extinction on a hot, crowded planet.

-Kate Orff Principal SCAPE Landscape Architecture

BYOBooks:
Flowers That Are Still Here

Kate Orff // exhibit

For BYOBooks the curatorial team invited architects, designers, critics, exhibitors, and professionals from all over the world to alter one book that inspired them, to help build a temporary waterfront library. Kate Orff's contribution, *Flowers That Are Still Here*, examines natural habitats that have been severely disrupted and plants that have nearly gone extinct.

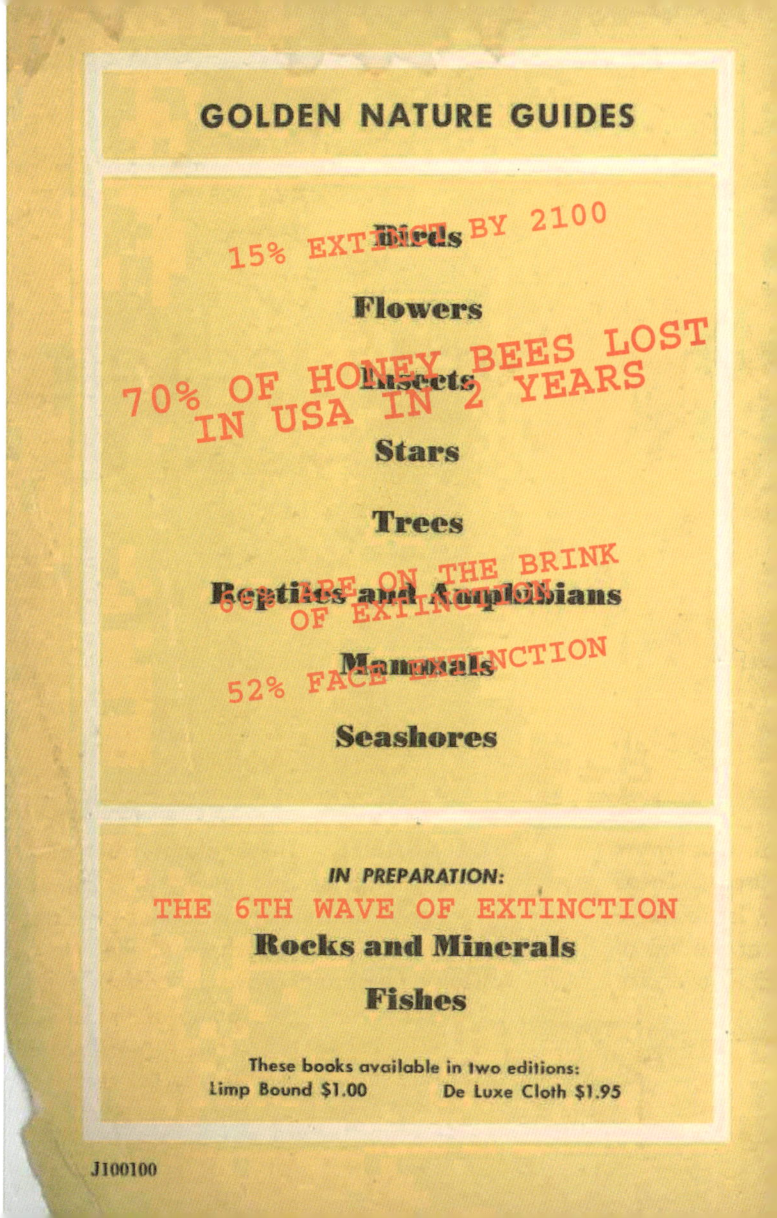

GOLDEN NATURE GUIDES

15% EXTINCT BY 2100

Birds

Flowers

70% OF HONEY BEES LOST IN USA IN 2 YEARS

Insects

Stars

Trees

Reptiles and Amphibians

ON THE BRINK OF EXTINCTION

Mammals

52% FACE EXTINCTION

Seashores

IN PREPARATION:

THE 6TH WAVE OF EXTINCTION

Rocks and Minerals

Fishes

These books available in two editions:
Limp Bound $1.00   De Luxe Cloth $1.95

J100100

th- er species with which we share

l. Ours grow
theast. These
w leaves have
at the top of
ct, Clover-like

50 species

FLEABANES These plants resemble Asters, but their flowerheads usually have 2 or 3 rows of petal-like rays. Magenta and violet Fleabanes provide vivid splashes of color in alpine meadows of the West. The well-known Daisy Fleabane grows in eastern fields and roadsides. Some of the less showy, pale-flow-ered species are common weeds of hayfields and fallow ground — 8 inches to over 2 feet high.—*Summer. Composite Family.*

75 species

SPRING BEAUTIES In masses of thousands on river flood plains or in open woods, the frail Spring Beauties, 6 to 12 inches high, make a striking display. The incon-spicuous, delicate, pink to white flowers, veined with deeper pink, remain open only in the bright light. These succulent plants have starchy bulbs, which the Indians ate. In the West there are several relatives of the Spring Beauties, all small-flowered too.—*Spring. Purslane Family.*

12 species

the planet. Our own species hun- ger

GERARDIAS   The varied species of Gerardias all have dainty, showy flowers on wiry, widely branched stems, 1 to 2 feet high. The funnel-like corollas are red, purple, violet, or—rarely—white. These eastern and midland plants prefer moist habitats; one species grows in salt marshes. The Foxgloves are taller relatives of the Gerardias, with yellow flowers and divided leaves.— *Summer to fall. Figwort Family.*

25 species

JOEPYEWEED   The tiny, lavender, and rarely white flowers of Joepyeweed are borne in fuzzy, flat-topped masses. The coarsely toothed leaves encircle the tall 2- to 12-foot stem. Joepyeweed is widespread in the East, in low ground along roadsides. Of the 50 or so related species, Boneset, with whitish flowers and paired, rough leaves, is most common.— *Late summer and fall. Composite Family.*

50 species

LOOSESTRI
typical of Ea
Several rela
showy Loose
Several nativ

10 species

Urban Picnic

Carlow Architecture and Design // exhibit

Urban Picnic is a flexible furniture system designed as a series of platforms and surfaces that can be reconfigured, flipped, rotated, and reconnected depending on site-specific conditions and programmatic requirements. It explores new combinations of materials and techniques that can visually and socially enhance urban public spaces. In consideration of ecological sustainability, the units are manufactured from a combination of recyclable Corian and green-certified, laminated bamboo plywood.

Dutch Design Chair

Five Spices // exhibit

The Dutch Design Chair was created by Five Spices for BoDW/InnoDesignTech. Using sustainable and reusable materials, the chair showcases the values of Dutch design: open-minded, pragmatic, and resourceful. The chair is made of three different parts and weighs a total of 900 grams. 70% of the material used is recycled cardboard which is 100% recyclable after use. The Dutch Design Chair can take the weight of 200 kilograms.

RESOURCE-FUL

PUSH HERE

Dutch Design

THINKING OUTSIDE OF THE BOX

BYOBench: Sitting Device

The Hong Kong Polytechnic University
// exhibit

These sitting devices are the creation of first-year
students in the Environment and Interior program
at the School of Design, Hong Kong Polytechnic
University. The students were divided into teams of
two, each team limited to using only two pieces of
four-foot by eight-foot plywood as building material.
The students had two weeks to design and build their
furniture, exploring ergonomics, joinery, and form
expression during the design process. The project was
part of the Material and Construction course work
taught by Kacey Wong, Sebastien Saint-Jean, and
Valérie Portefaix.

Bench Design

DESIGNER

VIVIAN CHEUNG
CHAN WENG I

BYOBench: BYOBond

Chris Wai Chi Choy | Ka Hei Chan |
Karn Ka Yin Wan | Kenny Yuen Keung Lau |
Henry Kin Hang Lie | Jeffrey Wing Chiu Lo |
Mantis Wai Ming Hon

// exhibit

A bench is different from a chair, for it allows several people to sit together in order to stimulate interaction. Inspired by the seesaw, BYOBond rethinks the function of the bench and searches for a balancing point through communication, forming new bonds by bringing different people together. Bamboo is widely used as scaffolding, in temporary structures and furniture, but the power of bundling makes bamboo a uniquely resilient material. Here, the bamboo bench creates a bond, so that you can never sit alone.

Bottom Up

Roberto Davolio | **Marc Brulhart**   // exhibit

Bottom Up is the result of a collaborative exploration into the world of performative building skin design. Formal, structural, and environmental expertise is employed in the definition of the rule-driven design process. Each facade module has been programmed to interact and respond to structural as well as environmental constraints. Cladding mullion orientations and structural member sizes are optimized in order increase the performance of the overall building skin assembly. This exercise is driven by the desire to understand and confront the intrinsic properties of Hong Kong's *genius loci*, whereas the resulting form represents the material expression of such an ambition.

Flux

Catherine Ying Xiong // exhibit

Flux is an attempt to design "indefinite" furniture for public space. The idea of "no definition" means that it can be a bench, or a table, or a fusion of different things. It means endless possibilities.

The fluid behavior of the modular timber construction allows the furniture to be changed, demolished, and transported easily. Instead of abandoning inappropriate furniture, it can be reshaped, recycled, and reused.

BYOBall:
West Kowloon
Football Club

Sebastien Saint-Jean in collaboration with Olo Nitka // event

Any city is the physical incarnation and the built outcome of a series of discussions, negotiations, compromises, pacts, and desires.

BYOBall embodies the intricacy of the decision-making process that ultimately shapes our city. A location on the raw open landscape is in opposition to the familiar dense city patterns of Hong Kong and reflects the way informal play spaces are often appropriated by the public to use within the city. This project is a call for collective team work and public participation in the making of recreational spaces.

G.O.A.L.

EFGH // exhibit right

G.O.A.L. is a community-based soccer, education, and health-care facility envisioned for Langa Township in the Western Cape, South Africa, as part of FIFA's 20 Centers for 2010 initiative. The aim of 20 Centers for 2010 is to achieve positive social change through football by building twenty Football for Hope Centers across Africa. The centers will address local social challenges in disadvantaged areas and improve education and health-care services for young people. The design intention for G.O.A.L. is to simultaneously create a clearly defined, inwardly-focused space for soccer as well as an outward-looking, expandable facility that recognizes and interacts with the local landscape and community.

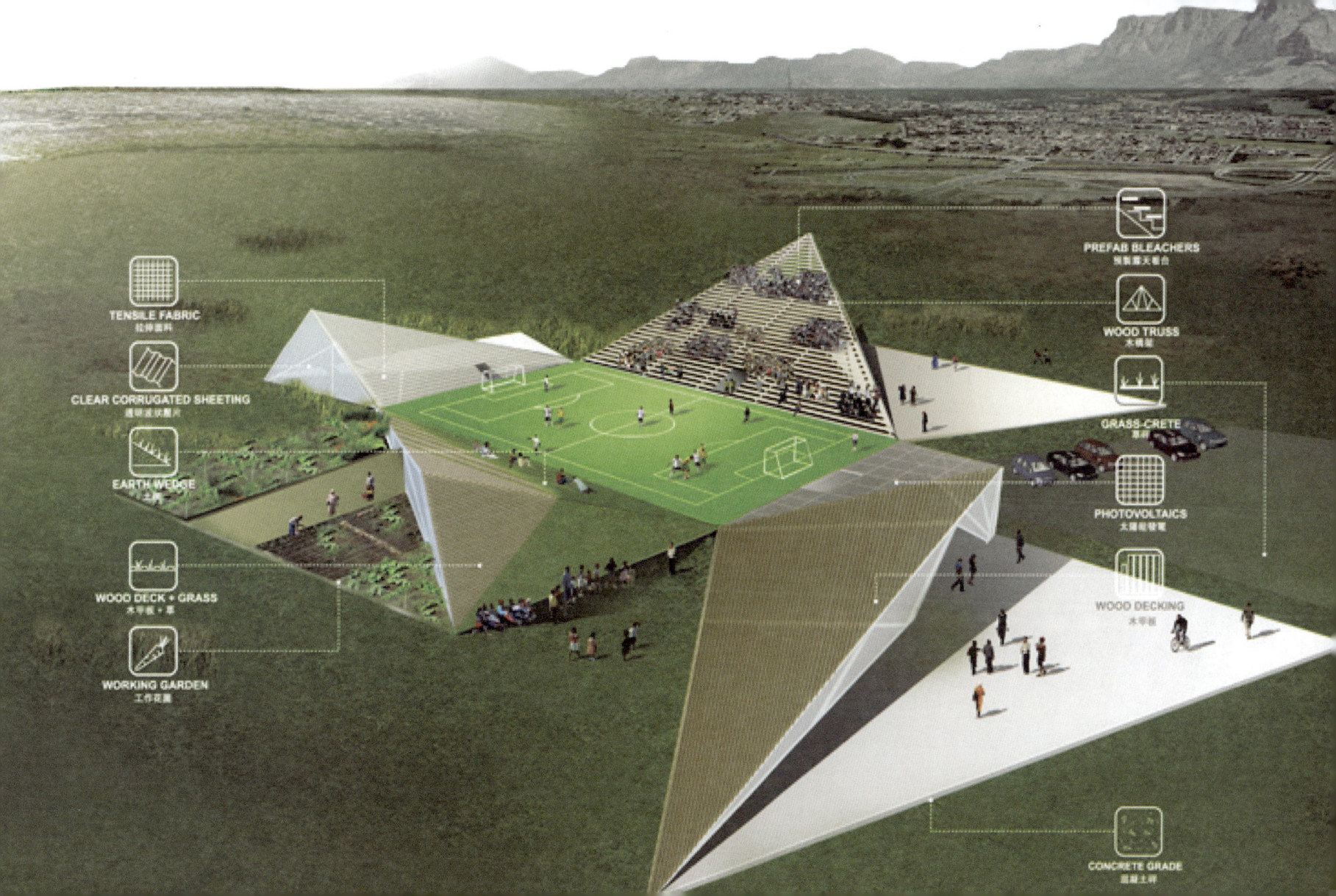

TENSILE FABRIC
拉伸面料

CLEAR CORRUGATED SHEETING
透明波状塑片

EARTH WEDGE
土堤

WOOD DECK + GRASS
木平板 + 草

WORKING GARDEN
工作花園

PREFAB BLEACHERS
預製露天看台

WOOD TRUSS
木桁架

GRASS-CRETE
草格

PHOTOVOLTAICS
太陽能發電

WOOD DECKING
木平板

CONCRETE GRADE
混凝土坪

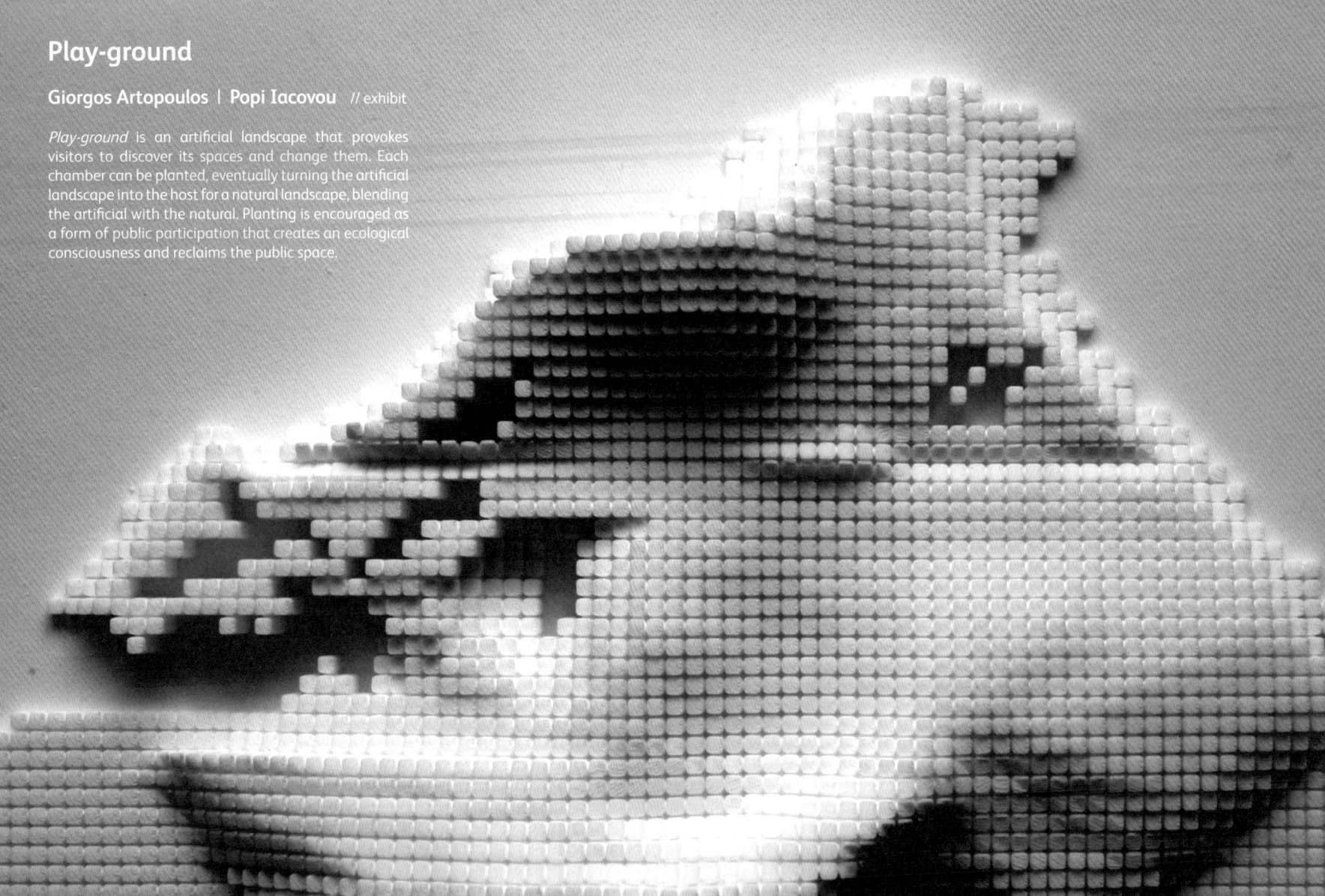

Play-ground

Giorgos Artopoulos | Popi Iacovou // exhibit

Play-ground is an artificial landscape that provokes visitors to discover its spaces and change them. Each chamber can be planted, eventually turning the artificial landscape into the host for a natural landscape, blending the artificial with the natural. Planting is encouraged as a form of public participation that creates an ecological consciousness and reclaims the public space.

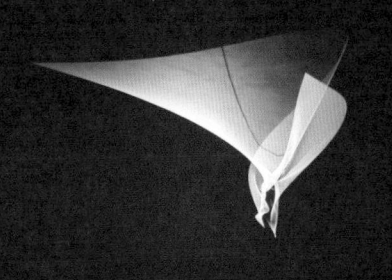

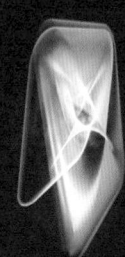

Fossils of Future

Fang Studio // exhibit

In the process of three-dimensional modeling, the computer sometimes does unexpected things. The parameters given sometimes generate outcomes that are unforeseen and undesired.

These mistakes are very similar to genetic mutations in nature. These aberrations either die out on their own accord, or are *de-selected*. Normally, designers discard their mistakes, but I decided to collect them as study objects. They became fossils before they saw life. Through computer experimentation, these fossils are manipulated and transformed, aiding us in our on-going search for a new design language and form.

Glow

davidclovers with C.E.B. Reas   // exhibit

Glow encapsulates two recently designed and completed projects by davidclovers that engage energy in distinct ways – never pure and always bound to material. Using artificial lighting such as LEDs and unique materials, Lunar House (a speculative home in Texas) and Yud Yud (a storefront in Hong Kong) are studies of energy effects. In a preternatural manner, each is an attempt to resituate energy as something to be molded, formed, and synthetically materialized out of that which is essentially immaterial.

"Looking Down" from New York to Hong Kong

Paul Kaiser | **Shelley Eshkar** // essay

Conceived as a public sculpture, Pedestrian's digital projection merges with the sidewalk we walk upon. The tiny denizens wander through this *trompe-l'oeil* illusion, in a city that seems paradoxically upon and within the surface. Their plazas and walkways are texture-mapped with samples of concrete, granite, asphalt, and gravel scanned from the real world. Projected onto the granular surface of the sidewalk, these virtual textures merge with the physical concrete, creating a second order of activity and detail.

The environment under their tiny feet is an abstract and simplified gameboard of dense cities, with strong contours and rhythmic subdivisions. These grids, tiles, and area boundaries echo and emboss the real physical pavestones hit by the projection. Pedestrian's visual logic is strongly oriented toward activating these boundaries in an optical game of figure and ground: a horde of umbrella walkers spirals across concentric cobblestones in a visual rhyme;

a marathon ends when a rink pans into view, bisecting the runners like a sharp white wedge. Rather than depict the density we expect of New York, the Pedestrian environment is mostly shallow and flat, emphasizing the horizontal. We the viewers with our tall dark bodies stand in for the buildings of Manhattan's verticality. In Hong Kong, the original Pedestrian environment of Manhattan is projected and juxtaposed onto the Hong Kong streetscapes.

Pedestrian lies at the intersection of several traditions. One of these comes to us out of the nineteenth century, when the ideal figure of the *flaneur* emerged. This urban wanderer loses himself in his city, reveling in its myriad unexpected juxtapositions and savoring streams of consciousness that jumble inner with outer, daydream with perception. At its start, this was mainly a literary phenomenon, carried out by such writers as Poe and Baudelaire to begin with, and then pushed further in the next century by

Aragon, Benjamin, and Raban, among many others. It had its counterpart in the urban snapshot practices of certain key photographers, most amazingly in Rodchenko's off-angle shots of Moscow, but also in Cartier-Bresson, Frank, and Winograd.

Paul Kaiser is a digital artist and writer. He earned a Bachelor of Arts in film and art history from Wesleyan University in 1978, graduating *summa cum laude*, and his Master of Education in special education from American University.

Shelley Eshkar is a digital artist whose research explores drawing, computer graphics, and human motion. He received his Bachelor of Fine Arts from Cooper Union in 1993.

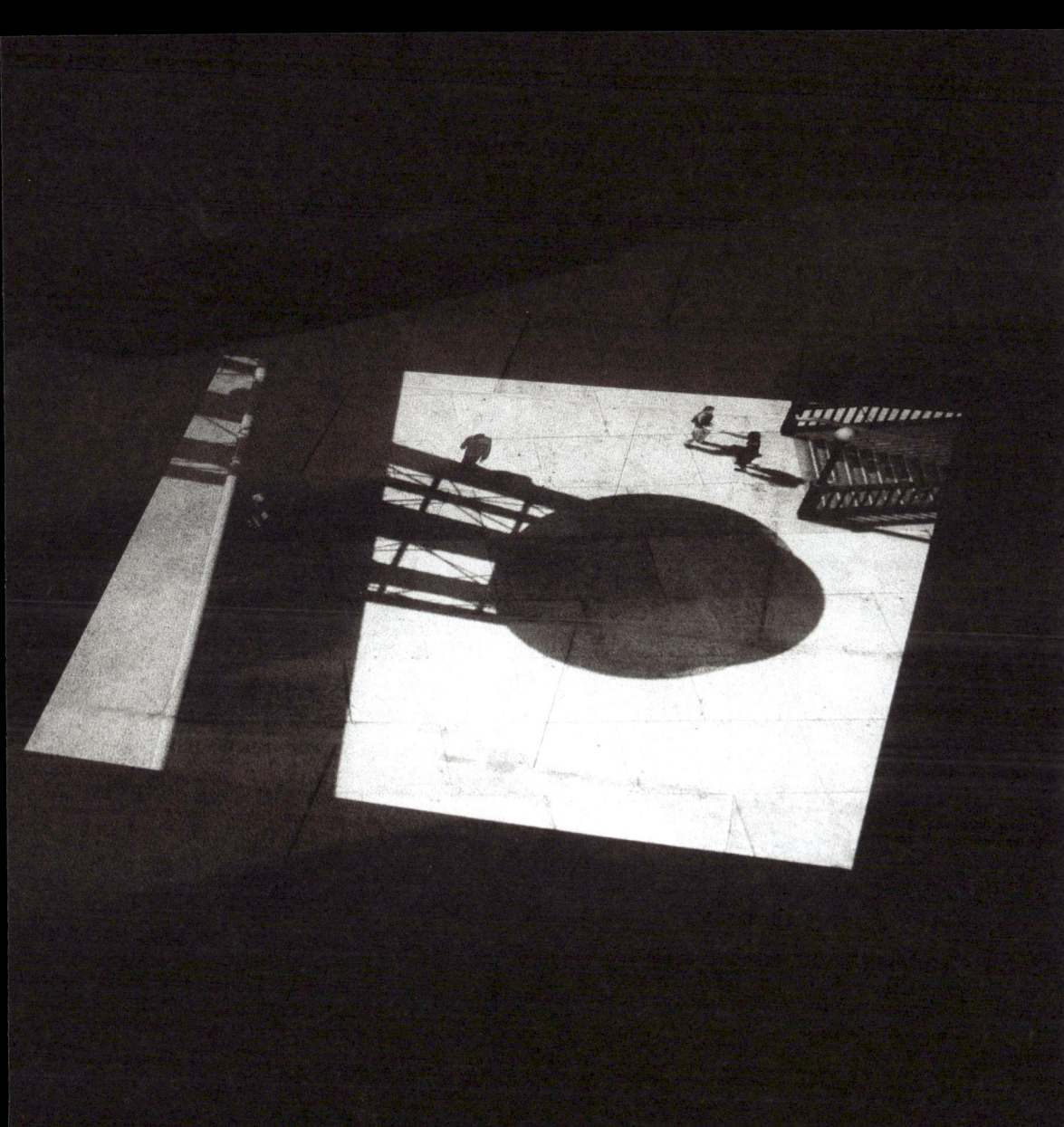

Pedestrian ꓲ Forest

OpenEndedGroup // exhibit

Pedestrian

In this three-dimensional digital animation, the imagery is projected directly onto the rough surfaces of the city sidewalk, where virtual pedestrians, seen from a bird's eye view, wander through the simulated city. The viewers, tall and dark bodies in the projections, stand in for the buildings of Manhattan's verticality. First presented in three public spaces in New York City, Pedestrian has since been exhibited in numerous locations in Asia, Europe, and the United States.

Forest

A multi-screen live installation, Forest is a visual enactment of outdoor childhood games. Virtual children play hide-and-seek among the tree-trunks, while the parallel projections play a similar game as they try to elude and then catch up with each other to create a dynamic disequilibrium. The installation is further bolstered by visual physics embedded in the custom three-dimensional renderings created for the work, which, for example, can conjure up the moving image out of the propagation of its own grain. Forest is on page 388-389.

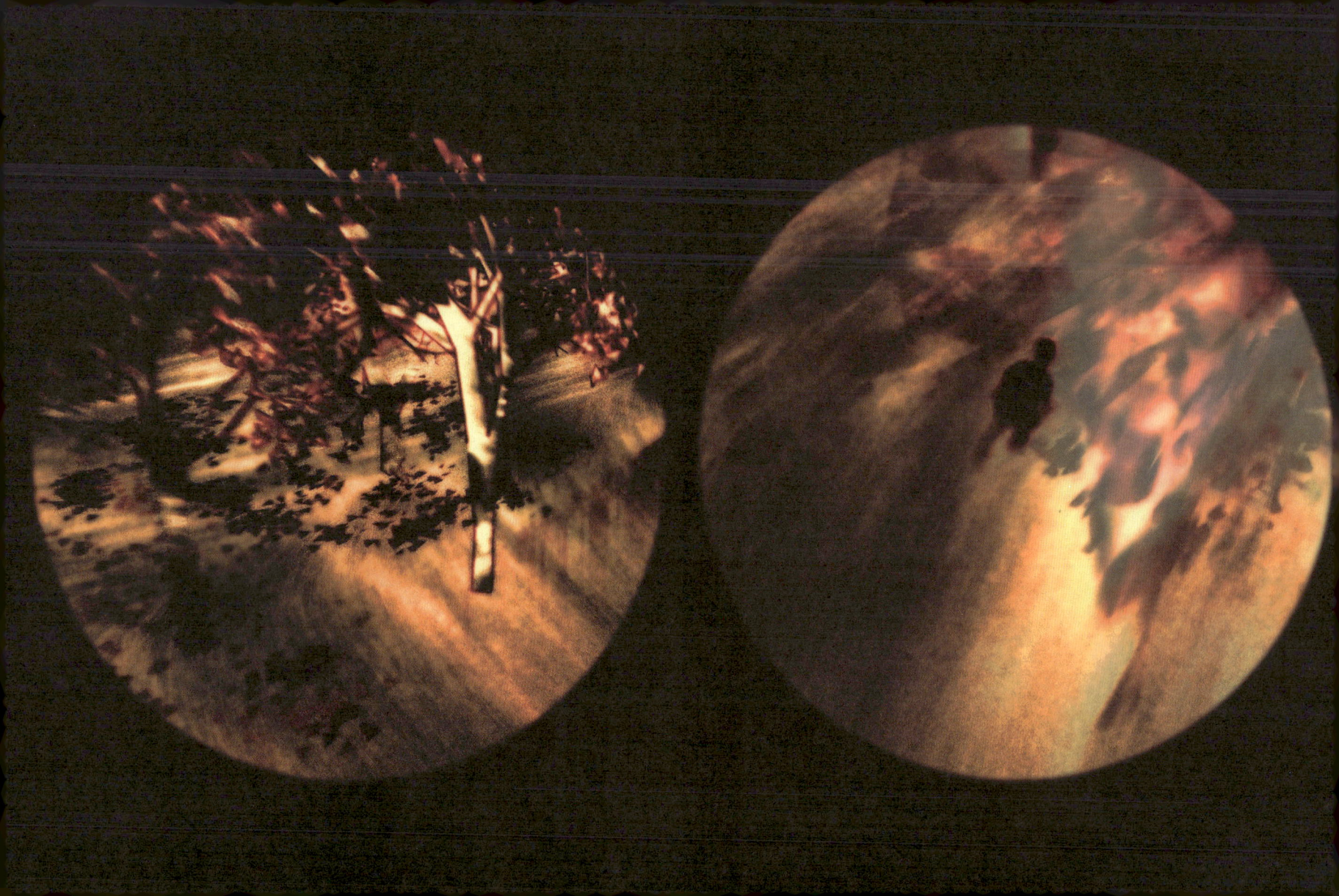

Mediascapes / Narrative Cities

// forum

---

date: 4 December 2009
participants: Cao Fei, Daniel Wu,
David Erdman, Gold Mountain,
Duncan Jepson, Gabu Heindl,
Tao Zhu
moderator: Eric Schuldenfrei

How does the filmic medium translate and construct the city? How do visionary, fictional, and documentary films actively narrate and create a presentation of our social constructs, realities, and city developments? Speakers explore cinematic films, observations, and creations to share their critical position on various architectural and urban processes relating to disappearance, reconstruction, and fabrication.

Gabu Heindl: I am presenting today just eight minutes of our film *Mock-Ups in Close-Up: Architectural Models in Cinemas 1927-2009*. The selected eight minute version features material taken from: Fritz Lang's *Metropolis* (1927); Edmond T. Greville's *Beat Girl* (1960); Francesco Rossi's *Le Mani Sulla Citta* (Hands Over the City) (1963); Nicolas Ribowski's *Cours du soir* (Evening Classes) (1967); Robert Stevenson's *Herbie Rides Again* (1973); Paul Verhoeven's *RoboCop* (1988); Mark Rydell's *Intersection* (1993); Brain Levant's *The Flintstones* (1994); and Ben Stiller's *Zoolander* (2001).

This is just a sample of the 130 films featured in the current, 150-minute version. *Mock-Ups* is a collaboration with my partner, a film scientist, and myself, a practising architect. We started collecting material a couple of years ago and

we keep on collecting. *Mock-Ups* highlights what you do not normally see: that is, it condenses a certain part of film history or filmmaking that is obsessed with architecture. We concentrate on these clips to get at urban issues – and one major theme is destruction and reconstruction. I would say that this comprises maybe half of the scenes. Representations of scale in models typically show the power that the mighty force of urbanism held in the modernist imagination, yet, the models are deceiving and in this sense the models stand for something problematic, even polemical.

Daniel Wu: I chose two films to present: one is Fruit Chan's *Made In Hong Kong,* which is probably his foremost recognizable work; and the other is Ann Hui's *The Way We Were*. Fruit Chan's film is part of the trilogy *Made In Hong Kong, The Longest Summer,* and *Hollywood Hong*

Kong. These three films examine the conditions of Hong Kong pre-handover, post-handover, and post-post-handover; how the changing status of the city reflects what is happening to the people and the collective sense of identity. Ann Hui's *The Way We Were* follows several characters in Tin Shui Wai, a new town in the suburbs. It is a super-realistic film; it captures the feeling of what it is like to be taken out of the city and plugged into a new town and new housing development that has no cultural context or any relationship to the rest of the city.

Representations
of scale in models
typically show
the power that the
mighty force of urban-
ism held in the modernist
imagination – yet the
models are deceiving.
In this sense the
models stand for some-
thing problematic,
even polemical.

— Gabu Heindl

Eric Schuldenfrei: It is quite fascinating that here in Hong Kong 45% of the population at one time lived in public housing provided by the government. The standardized public housing that went up around the city meant that there were roughly eight basic building types for 45% of the population. This idea of constructing such ubiquitous and banal environments should be questioned. How can you foster individuality if each home is identical to all the others? Instead of an ideal future, modernist public housing created uniformity. But it was those social ideals our generation diligently studied in architectural school, even while we acknowledged that many of those modernist dreams had actually failed society.

Duncan Jepson: Recently I have become very interested in how poverty exists in Hong Kong. I started to work with a charity in Sham Shui Po and I was interested in the men and women living in the cages and in children living in some very difficult housing situations. Frankly, some of the places they live in are like cupboards, some are just incredibly small artificial spaces that are created out of planks of woods to break up existing property. These children are five, six and seven years old and live mostly with a single parent. So we started to film there. While doing so, I started to speak to some people in the government, some members of Donald Tsang's policy making group. It was interesting to hear one of the architects speaking at the forum say that Hong Kong has a large middle class. On the contrary, Hong Kong does not have a large middle class at all. If you define the middle class by consumption, which is actually how they are defined, we have a tiny middle class because most people spend the vast majority of their income on rent, subsistence, education for their child, some savings, and then a very small amount on personal expenses, be it going to the cinema or doing something like this. They just do not have that level of income and surplus to spend. And so, without that middle class you end up with what is described by many people as a divided society – rich and poor – and that is what we have in Hong Kong.

If you define the middle
class by consumption,
which is actually how
they are defined, we
have a tiny middle class
because most people
spend the vast majority
of their income on rent,
subsistence, education
for their child, some
savings, and then a very
small amount on
personal expenses.

— Duncan Jepson

Eric Schuldenfrei: Some of these juxtapositions are being addressed and are being changed within the architecture of the city. David

Ann Hui's *The Way We Were* follows several characters in Tin Shui Wai, a kind new town in the suburbs. It is a super-realistic film. It captures the feeling of what it is like to be taken out of the city and plugged into a new town and new housing development that has no cultural context or any relationship to the rest of the city.

— Daniel Wu

Erdman's piece touches upon this as well, with a very ironic juxtaposition created by inserting a new façade into a rather dilapidated building in Wan Chai.

David Erdman: *Urban Course of a Day* is a movie that was made of a project that we just finished. It documents our individual existence on a daily basis in relation to the community around us. There is a lot of discussion these days in the world of architecture about how we use animations and films as tools to design the work that we are making. There is some concern in how the work may have cinematic effects within a neighborhood that already exists. The two projects that we are showing here combine a series of influences together that come from both of those worlds. The storefront is about three meters by three meters. And this area is near Star Street in Wan Chai. It is, in essence, a very old neighborhood. And we kind of imagined the project as a character in the neighborhood, something that you find that is almost preternatural; both of and not of the neighborhood at the same time, given it exists amongst metal fabrication shops and other trade related shops.

I think the film has captured it to some extent – how the material and the way we were working before produces what we call a continuous state of rendering, re-rendering itself and changing throughout the course of the day as the natural light comes up and down. And, of course, there is a series of unforeseen programmatic effects that suggest and comment on ways in which we interact with the neighborhood. Yet, probably one of the weirdest things is we actually find people rubbing it and touching it. And it sounds kind of strange at first, but it actually is a very important condition because in generating the piece we often referred to the difference between making puzzles and producing degrees of mysteriousness. Filmmaking seems to bring this to architecture.

I think the film has captured it to some extent – how the material and the way we were working before produces what we call a continuous state of rendering, re-render-ing itself and changing throughout the course of the day as the natural light comes up and down.

— David Erdman

Gold Mountain: In the beginning, when I first met up with the Biennale curators, they were telling me we had this project, this Biennale, about architecture. I was thinking, they want me to make a song about architecture? Are you

kidding me? So, I thought about architecture; that is an art form. And music; that is an art form as well. Both art forms go back way beyond when civilization began. This is a very, very old thing. You had to build houses, you still have to. By putting those scenes together, where does the inspiration come from? And, I thought about the first beat ever made, the first beat in human civilization had to be the heartbeat. The heartbeat is a bit of a cliché, but it is also a very important concept. There are so many things going on that make you forget your inner voice. So the song I created is really about that. Even the Biennale can be seen in this light. All these different elements and disciplines come together as heartbeats, each person stating in their own way, this is my vision, this is my project. We really have this sense of self in it. And we want you to see it.

> Even the Biennale can be seen in this light.
> All these different elements and disciplines come together as heartbeats, each person stating in their own way, this is my vision, this is my project.
>
> — Gold Mountain

Cao Fei: During the process of shooting the movie, I found out that some of the people interviewed were conscious of their civil rights but only when these rights were violated. Ironically then, when in mainland China environmental rights and civil rights are being violated, more and more people become more and more conscious of these rights. Along with this process of awakening, I believe that civic society will become our common sense.

Eric Schuldenfrei: As I was sitting and watching, I noticed how we are sitting between the police barriers and the "No Entry" on one side and on the opposite side the command post for the East Asian Games, which reminds me that the screen was provided to us by the East Asian Games because we could not afford one within our limited Biennale budget, which talks a little bit about hierarchy and cultural funding – about priorities. But also the funding and the hierarchy that exists within the world of film has the same potential for overlapping concerns, for multitasking, as it were, for borrowing from more substantial or established disciplines. To use the Biennale as a site to voice either critique or visionary potential exists within all of the arts represented here today, but film seems particularly evocative because of its elasticity, its ability to say many things all at once. It is, in many senses, one of architecture's greatest allies, as we have seen in this forum.

I found out that some of the people interviewed were conscious of their civil rights but only when these rights were violated. Ironically then, when in mainland China environmental rights and civil rights are being violated, more and more people become more and more conscious of these rights.

— Cao Fei

Mock-Ups in Close-Up

Gabu Heindl | **Drehli Robnik** // exhibit

Mock-Ups in Close-Up is a video compilation of found footage from nine decades of film history, consisting only of scenes (or single shots) showing architectural models. Scenes are continuously added to the project; presently it is 120 minutes long and comprises clips from roughly 115 different films originally released between 1927 and 2010. This archive of cinematic mock-ups is non-exclusive. It contains obvious classics from the field of architectural cinema, such as *The Fountainhead* (1948) or *The Belly of an Architect* (1987), yet for the most part it consists of films that do not primarily deal with architecture proper. And yet, these films – ranging from German crime drama to Hollywood horror, from James Bond to the X-Men, from Fritz Lang and Sergio Leone to Tim Burton, Ben Stiller and Jia Zhangke – use models or mock-ups for dramatic, symbolic, or humoristic purpose, and sometimes for no discernible purpose at all.

Renouncing any classification or order to the clips other than pure historical chronology, Mock-Ups in Close-Up allows implied meanings to come to the foreground. Impressions of bank heists and military operations merge with a Hollywood freedom fighter (Indiana Jones in his architectural model scene) posing in traditional Arab clothing. The range of power games – games of governing and rendering knowable, calculable, behaviors, perceptions, and developments – tied around cinematic mock-ups, includes sublime moments in which the discursive strategies of the knowledge/power nexus are thwarted. In other words, a new "misreading" emerges from scenes as an unauthorized reading or understanding of the model and its scale.

Double Double

Barry Jacques | David Smith // exhibit

Double Double is a thirty-minute video and music installation focusing on Hong Kong's cinematic qualities. The piece looks at the potential of everyday scenes to become more than what they are, revealing their hidden selves. The video is accompanied by a soundtrack that echoes the sense of drama, intensity, and poetry in the visuals. The work draws on the experiences of the artist-creators, both of whom live in Hong Kong.

401

Nønspace

Nicolas Sauret | Ashley L. Wong
// exhibit

Nønspace is a two-channel video work that probes a puzzling and elusive, essentially non-existent space. In dialogue with Hong Kong, the creators of the film revisit their memories through collected materials of time spent in the city. Through interwoven voice interviews with artists, academics, and architects, Nønspace approaches notions of place to reveal aspects of a city and culture that is difficult to pin down in normative space-time.

Illegal Construction

Zheng Guogu // exhibit

In 2000, Zheng Guogu bought nearly 5,000 square meters of land in the suburbs of his hometown of Yangjiang. It had increased to 20,000 square meters by the time he started to construct his Empire in 2004, expanding to a total of 40,000 square meters today, and it is still growing illegally.

Reflecting the computer game Age of Empires, Zheng Guogu's Empire nevertheless integrates more complicated spatial modalities and social relations. It is not a fixed, viewable work enclosed within an interior space, but a project that extends into an ever truer living space, one that comprises the entire process of dwelling in a spatial location, from conceptual ideal to practical implementation of day-to-day living.

Hong Kong Fantasies

MVRDV | The Why Factory | TU Delft
// exhibit

Hong Kong Fantasies proposes a series of visions for the future of Hong Kong. It suggests that the city's spatial restrictions might prompt inventive new solutions. For instance, the vertical extension of the hills might enlarge the ground space, while a new housing typology could reduce migration to Shenzhen, and a combination of living, working, retail, and cultural facilities along the waterfront might induce attractive marina development. New building guidelines to create canopies and increase shaded areas could also counteract Hong Kong's need for cooling and reduce its high energy consumption.

RMB CITY:
A Second Life City Planning

Cao Fei // exhibit

China Tracy has built a city dubbed RMB City within the web portal Second Life. This is a condensed incarnation of contemporary Chinese cities with most of their characteristics; a series of new Chinese fantasy realms that are highly self-contradictory, laden with irony and suspicion, and extremely entertaining and pan-political. China's current obsession with land development in all its intensity will be extended to Second Life. A rough hybrid of communism, socialism, and capitalism, RMB City realizes, in a globalized digital sphere, the collision of the overabundant symbols of Chinese reality with cursory imaginings of the country's future.

The Changing Room
UNStudio
Music Theatre

UNStudio // exhibit

The Changing Room combines filmed footage of a built structure with animations of the diagrams made during the design process. Displaying spaces where floors, walls, and ceilings flow into each other, the video explores the transformative potential of the material world as a concept behind the "switching on and off" of values inherent in the design of the installation.

The UNStudio documentary features Ben van Berkel and Caroline Bos discussing work ranging from their publications to exhibition design, product design, and building projects as well as providing commentary on the studio and nature of the practice as a whole.

Music Theatre examines the MUMUTH Music Theatre, a faculty building of the University of Music and Performing Arts in Graz designed by UNStudio. The video of the completed building depicts the design solutions incorporated, from daytime when it is used for rehearsal, to the twist structure weaving through the three floors, to the facade in the evenings during performances.

All three videos were produced by A.P. Komen and Karen Murphy.

Culture as Events

Ackbar Abbas // essay

It is possible to distinguish between two ways in which culture becomes event: by noting the difference between a "cultural event" and "culture-as-event."

Cultural events such as biennials and festivals take stock of the existing state of culture. Moreover, when organized by a city, a cultural event is a way of celebrating the achievements of the city, a sign that the city has arrived. Architecture has a privileged place as a cultural event, because it is so public and visible.

By contrast, culture-as-event does something other than take stock of existing culture. It emerges out of the crises and contradictions of culture itself, one outstanding example of which is the new Hong Kong cinema that came into being at a moment when the city was threatened with radical change.

Biennials, festivals, and art centers always seem to have one foot in the cultural event and the other in culture-as-event. The danger comes when these institutions lose sight of culture-as-event, which can be puzzling and provocative, and devote themselves merely to the staging of cultural events, which are more readily understood.

There is also an economic issue: the focus of the cultural event is the spectator, which translates into a member of the paying audience; the focus of culture-as-event is the practitioner, who not only does not pay but requires payment and support.

The sad fate of culture is that it is always being turned into a cultural event – and, therefore, kitsch is not far behind. Can we envision a loopback mechanism where the cultural event can produce culture-as-event?

Ackbar Abbas is Professor of Comparative Literature at the University of California, Irvine. Previously he was Chair of Comparative Literature at the University of Hong Kong and also a codirector of the Centre for the Study of Globalization and Cultures. His research interests include globalization, Hong Kong and Chinese culture, architecture, cinema, postcolonialism, and critical theory. His book *Hong Kong: Culture and the Politics of Disappearance* was published in 1997. He currently serves as a contributing editor to *Public Culture*.

On Action and Repose

Jesse Reiser | Nanako Umemoto // essay

Shenzhen is a manufacturer of components, and thus an exporter of pieces, rather than whole goods. As in the case of many other large, new cities, the compound effects of a global economy have engendered a concept of a piecemeal production. An economy of means has produced an export economy, where workers are often not able to see or use the finished product. This open-ended production process has the potential to mentally alienate workers from the products of their labor and their places of work within the contemporary, developing industrial city.

In order to investigate how to combat the contemporary condition of alienation, we looked at Shenzhen as a poignant example of a phenomenon that exists globally. For the past four years, we have held week-long design charrettes with first-year students in the Department of Architecture at the University of Hong Kong. The classes are comprised of students from Hong Kong, mainland China, and a small number of international students. The design studies explore the relationships in construction between design strategies that involve concepts of continuous variation of mass-produced components (a crucial aspect of contemporary discourse within the international design community) and the use of materials produced in Shenzhen. The first three years of the workshop centered on the creation of furniture. This year's workshop moved up in scale and ambition, exploring the creation of spatial enclosure with the idea that such assemblies would serve as the basis of a future pavilion for one of Shenzhen's public spaces.

Our goal is to return cultural meaning to the process of production, as well as provide a locally finished product that the community can experience and enjoy. The students have realized projects that celebrate the vitality of a new architecture, transcending the everyday functions of the components. Their assemblies return a sense of dynamism to the objects of their constructions and to the community itself.

Jesse Reiser and Nanako Umemoto have practiced as Reiser + Umemoto RUR Architecture P.C. since 1986. In addition to teaching at Princeton University and Columbia University, Reiser and Umemoto have taught and lectured throughout the United States, Europe and Japan.

Design Workshop

University of Hong Kong // exhibit

The Action + Repose Workshop is part of the first-year architecture design studio at the University of Hong Kong. The workshop uses a number of specific and highly regimented design techniques to explore the social, material, structural, and geometrical concepts embodied in a pavilion enclosure. Contrary to the modernist model, where structure and support are typically articulated, this workshop proposes that the two are linked and continuous. Continuity, however, is not achieved through continuous surface models, but rather through the complex repetition of discrete components.

Hyperbolic Rattan Bench

Haewon Shin | Kelly Chow // exhibit

Hyberbolic Rattan Bench is a crossover between a planter and a bench with a circular general form. It offers eight seats with two different positions and a planter at the center. The form comes from a series of studies of hyperbolic geometry. The circular positions of the bench allow various views of the site and the shadows created by the large leaves of the plants provide shade. The entire bench is made of rattan, a traditional and natural material suitable for outdoor use.

BYOB
Graphics

Graphics developed for the Biennale experimented with an obsessive approach to iterative ideograms and visual presentations. The challenge was to develop and produce a legible "B" to describe each event or idea. From event flyers, postcards, education packs, t-shirts, banners and advertisements to the closing finale graphics, the design explored the power of communication between various groups of users. The graphics also aligned with Shenzhen's Biennale logo, exploring ways to further enhance a visual shared identity between Hong Kong and Shenzhen.

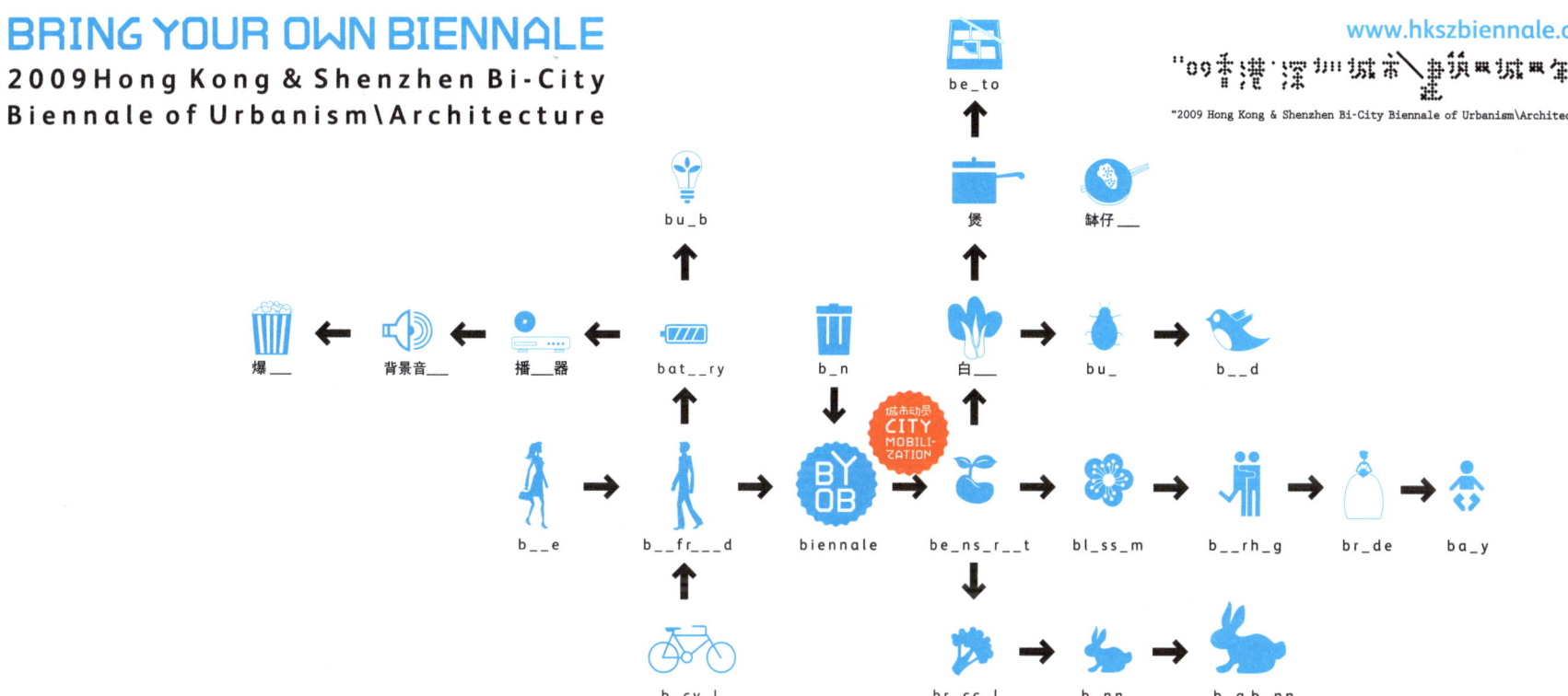

BRING YOUR OWN BIENNALE

2009 Hong Kong & Shenzhen Bi-City
Biennale of Urbanism\Architecture

www.hkszbiennale.org

"2009 Hong Kong & Shenzhen Bi-City Biennale of Urbanism\Architecture"

be_to

bu_b

煲

鉢仔___

爆___

背景音___

播___器

bat__ry

b_n

白___

bu_

b__d

CITY MOBILI-ZATION

b__e

b__fr___d

biennale

be_ns_r__t

bl_ss_m

b__rh_g

br_de

ba_y

b_cy_l_

br_cc_l_

b_nn_

b_g b_nn_

西九龍海濱長廊　　**4/12/2009 - 27/02/2010**

West Kowloon Waterfront Promenade

配料：100％2009年香港深圳城市\建築雙城雙年展內容濃縮

Ingredients: 100% concentrated information from the 2009 Hong Kong & Shenzhen Bi-City Biennale of Urbanism\Architecture

營養資料　　　　　　　每包
Nutrition information　　Per pack

智慧/Intelligence

創意/Creativity

環境認知/Environmental awareness

地點　Venue:
西九龍海濱長廊
West Kowloon Waterfront Promenade

展覽期間　Exhibition period:
04/12/2009 - 27/02/2010

展覽開放時間　Opening Hours:

雙年展公園展場　The Biennale Park
星期二至五　上午十一時至下午七時半
Tuesday – Friday: 11am-7.30pm
星期六及日　上午十時三十分至下午七時半
Saturday & Sunday: 10.30am – 7.30pm
星期一休館
Closed on every Monday

西九龍海濱長廊
The Waterfront Promenade
星期一至日　上午六時至晚上十一時
Monday – Sunday: 6am-11pm

BRING YOUR OWN BIENNALE
2009 香港·深圳城市\建築雙城雙年展
2009 Hong Kong & Shenzhen Bi-City
Biennale of Urbanism\Architecture

用心炮製，不需加防腐劑
No preservatives added

開盒後請即使用
Please consume immediately after opening.

請登入　www.hkszbiennale.org
Visit us at www.hkszbiennale.org

Q:

Does it make a difference knowing that what you are wearing is also art?

當你知道自己穿著一件藝術品，你的感覺

Q:

Can we control nature?

我們能否主宰大自然？

Q:

Do you think Hong Kong needs to bring back more street markets?

你認為香港應復興舊式的街市嗎？

BRING YOUR OWN BIENNALE

2009 Hong Kong & Shenzhen Bi-City Biennale of Urbanism\Architecture

www.hkszbiennale.org

"2009 Hong Kong & Shenzhen Bi-City Biennale of Urbanism\Architecture"

西九龍
West Kowloon
Waterfront Promenade
海濱長廊

城市动员
CITY
MOBILI-
ZATION

BYOB

了解双年展的缔造过程。
find out how the biennale works.

西九龍海濱長廊   4/12/2009 - 27/02/2010
West Kowloon Waterfront Promenade

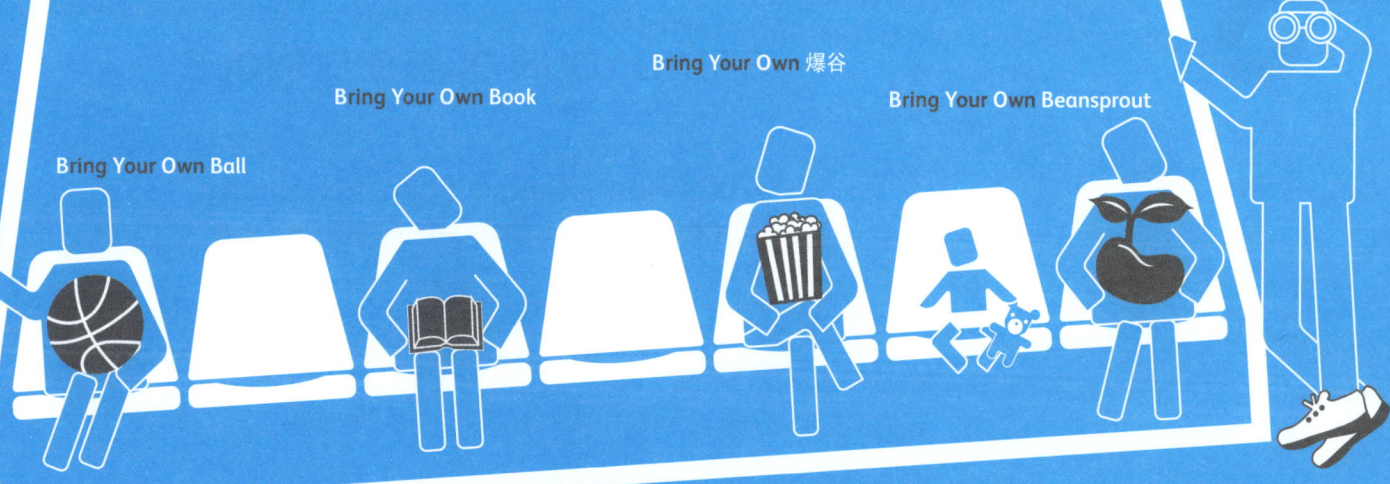

BRING YOUR OWN BIENNALE

2009 Hong Kong & Shenzhen Bi-City
Biennale of Urbanism\Architecture

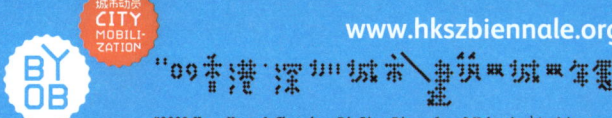

www.hkszbiennale.org

"2009 Hong Kong & Shenzhen Bi-City Biennale of Urbanism\Architecture"

Bring Your Own 波鞋

Bring Your Own 爆谷

Bring Your Own Book

Bring Your Own Beansprout

Get off from Kowloon Station or Austin Station!

Bring Your Own Ball

西九龍海濱長廊

4/12/2009 - 27/02/2010

West Kowloon Waterfront Promenade

BRING YOUR OWN BIENNALE
West Kowloon Waterfront Promenade
西九龍海濱長廊　4/12/2009 - 27/02/2010
2009 Hong Kong & Shenzhen Bi-city Biennale of Urbanism\Architecture

成市动员
CITY
MOBILI-
ZATION

西九龍
West Kowloon
Waterfront Promenade
海濱長廊

www.hkszbiennale.org

4/12/2009
- 27/02/2010

Broccoli
Beetroot
Bokchoy

BYOB

social sustainability 可持續發展 · cultural education 文化教育 · community and heritage 社區及本土遺產

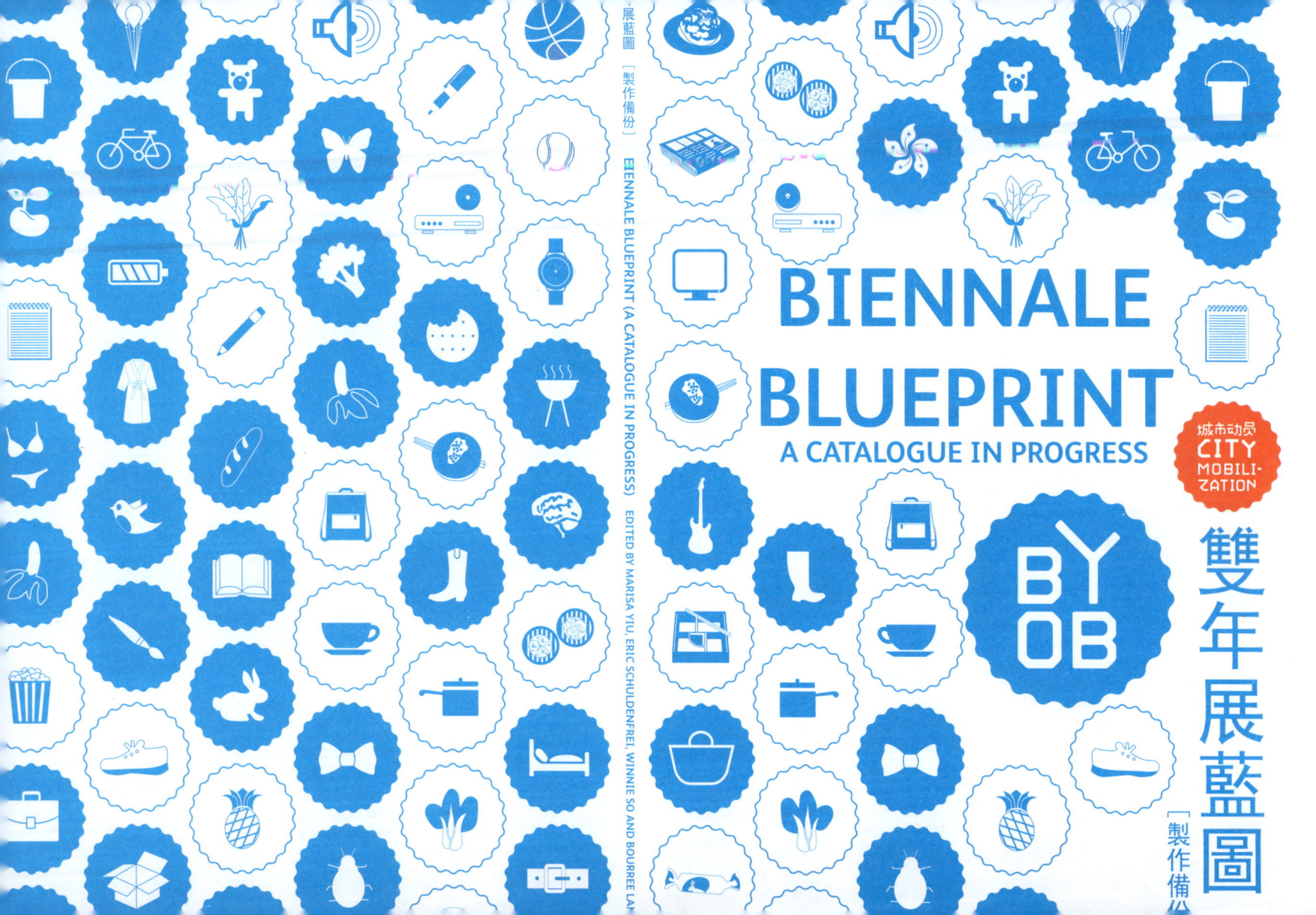

BIENNALE
BLUEPRINT
A CATALOGUE IN PROGRESS

城市动员
CITY
MOBILI-
ZATION

BYOB

雙年展藍圖

BIENNALE BLUEPRINT (A CATALOGUE IN PROGRESS)

EDITED BY MARISA YIU, ERIC SCHULDENFREI, WINNIE SO AND BOURREE LAM

[展藍圖 [製作備份]

[製作備公

Bring Your Own Beansprout

The Hong Kong Biennale of Urbanism\Architecture invites you to join a fun-filled planting event!

Come dressed in bright blue or fire-engine red to farm on our EcoFarm!

Register now!

contact person: Miranda Wong
email address: yse@hkfyg.org.hk
contact number: 3113 7999

find out more on
www.hkszbiennale.org

BYOB

BRING YOUR OWN BIENNALE
"09香港深圳城市\建築城雙展"
"2009 Hong Kong & Shenzhen Bi-City Biennale of Urbanism\Architecture"

When?

15 November 2009, Sunday
1 pm to 4 pm

Where?

West Kowloon Cultural District Lands Area

Who?

- Youths in primary 4 and above who are interested in organic farming

- Parents are absolutely welcomed with their young child in tow!

Biennale Catalogue / Flyer

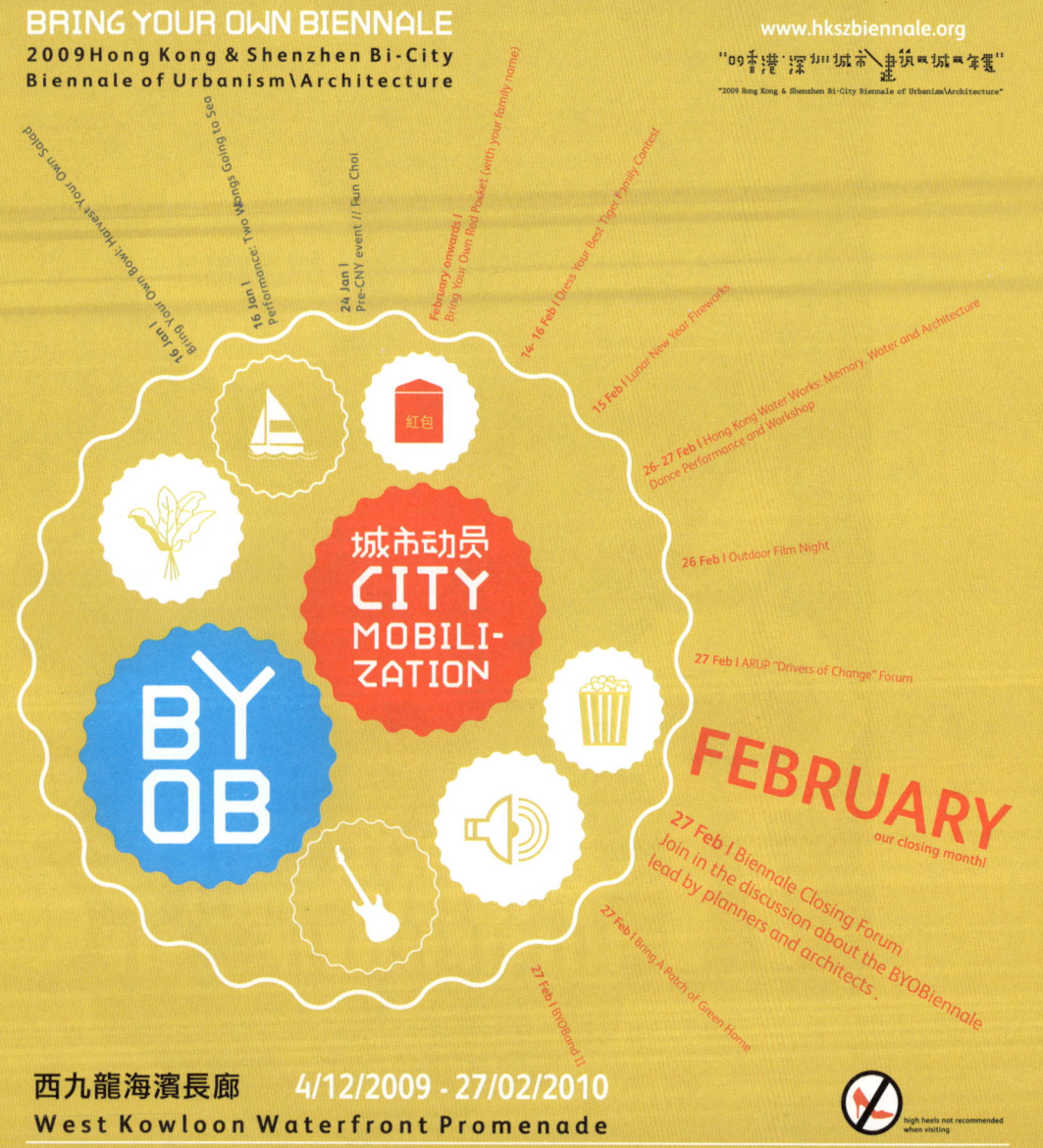

BRING YOUR OWN BIENNALE

2009 Hong Kong & Shenzhen Bi-City Biennale of Urbanism\Architecture

www.hkszbiennale.org

"明香港·深圳城市\建築雙城雙年展"

"2009 Hong Kong & Shenzhen Bi-City Biennale of Urbanism\Architecture"

16 Jan I Performance: Two Wongs Going to Sea

16 Jan I Bring Your Own Bowl: Harvest Your Own Salad

24 Jan I Pre-CNY event // Pun Choi

February onwards I Bring Your Own Red Packet (with your family name)

14-16 Feb I Dress Your Best Tiger Family Contest

15 Feb I Lunar New Year Fireworks

26-27 Feb I Hong Kong Water Works: Memory, Water and Architecture Dance Performance and Workshop

26 Feb I Outdoor Film Night

27 Feb I ARUP "Drivers of Change" Forum

FEBRUARY
our closing month!

27 Feb I Biennale Closing Forum
Join in the discussion about the BYOBiennale
lead by planners and architects.

27 Feb I Bring A Patch of Green Home

27 Feb I BYOBand II

CITY MOBILI-ZATION
城市动员

BYOB

西九龍海濱長廊 **4/12/2009 - 27/02/2010**
West Kowloon Waterfront Promenade

high heels not recommended when visiting

城市动员
CITY MOBILI-ZATION

BYOB

BYOBlanket to the Lunar New Year Fireworks
西九海旁攜席而坐BYOBlanket觀賞維港新春煙花匯演

2月15日 Feb 15th

Snag a coveted spot on the West Kowloon Cultural District waterfront, aptly situated along Kowloon Harbour, as Hong Kong rings in the year of the tiger with its **annual fireworks display** on February 15th.

在雙年展的草地上找一個舒適的位置，觀賞維港新春煙花匯演，陶醉在燦爛的煙花中。

BYORed Pocket
將寫有祝願紅封包掛在展品Pocket Fence上

2月9日至27日 Feb 9th – 27th

BYORed Pocket to celebrate CNY at the Biennale! Enliven the Pocket Fence [E58] by hanging your own **red pockets marked with your surname** on to the exhibit structure and create vibrant red spaces within the three semi-enclosed areas.

帶著印有自己姓氏的利是封，於利是封背後寫下新年願望，並掛在展品Pocket Fence [E58]的欄柵上，洋溢一片艷紅，更添新春朝氣和活力。

BYOBaby Tiger
小朋友老虎裝扮大賽

2月14至16日 Feb 14th – 16th   15:00-17:00

Take your chance at our **photo contest** and doll your little ones up in their finest costumes and head down to West Kowloon Cultural District to have the opportunity to win some fantastic prizes by taking poloarids using FujiFilm instax mini7 camera.

為你的小朋友精心裝扮一番，化身可愛的小老虎或穿上中國傳統服裝，贏取豐富獎品。

西九龍海濱長廊   **4/12/2009 - 27/02/2010**
West Kowloon Waterfront Promenade   www.hkszbiennale.org

BRING YOUR OWN BIENNALE

2009 Hong Kong & Shenzhen Bi-City
Biennale of Urbanism\Architecture

"2009 香港 深圳 城市 建築 城市雙年展"

"2009 Hong Kong & Shenzhen Bi-City Biennale of Urbanism\Architecture"

We warmly invite you to come to our Biennale waterfront - take a stroll in the Biennale park, sit on creatively designed benches, walk through an alley of trees, get lost amidst the overgrown landscape and drift along the waterfront promenade.

Pedal Powered Stage
by Karla Healy Singh

Street Music Event
JAN 9th
curated by Kung Chi Shing

JAN 9th
Bring Your Own Blanket Yoga Event
with Tisha Hartiela

Bring Your Own Ball
Performative Pitch Event
by Sebastien Saint-Jean / UNIT: + Olo Nitka

JAN 3rd
Hong Kong iPhone Orchestra 2010
lead by Samson Young
organised by William Lane/
Hong Kong New Music Ensemble
and Giorgio Biancorosso

JAN 3rd
West Kowloon Palimpsest:
A Soundwalk with Samson Young
lead by Samson Young
Hong Kong New Music Ensemble
and Giorgio Biancorosso
organized by William Lane/Hong Kong New Music Ensemble

城市动员
CITY MOBILI-ZATION

BY OB

JAN 12th & 13th
Organic Farming and
Herbal Tea Workshop
by Kadoorie Farm and Botanical Garden

Lecture:
Bring Your Own green Building
After the Climate Change Conference @Copenhagen

JAN 23rd
Street Culture:
Art+Design+Activism
(partner event)

Workshop:
Xu Bing's 'Forest Project'

JAN 24th
CNY Event//Poon Choi
by St. Johns Organization

Performance:
Two Wongs go to Sea
by Kacey Wong and Stanley Wong

myCity-to-Pattern by ilataaj
presented by Andrew Tirta

Lecture:
The Six Faces of a Socially Responsible Architect
by Koon-Chung Chan

SATURDAYS & SUNDAYS
Cultural & Architecture Tours in West Kowloon
by Samuel Hau and Hong Kong Architecture Centre

Jan 16th
come experience a full day
packed with exciting events
at the biennale !

Feel free to BYOB inter-act and observe outdoor installa-tions from this year's 2009 HK SZ Bi-city Biennale. Come have a drink, pick up a coffee on the waterfront and BYOBook for a relaxed read.

西九龍海濱長廊   4/12/2009 - 27/02/2010
West Kowloon Waterfront Promenade

high heels not recommended when visiting

www.hkszbiennale.org

Poster / Flyer

BIENNALE FINALE: 27th February

城市动员
CITY
MOBILI-
ZATION

BYOB

BRING YOUR OWN BIENNALE

"2009 Hong Kong & Shenzhen Bi-City Biennale of Urbanism\Architecture"

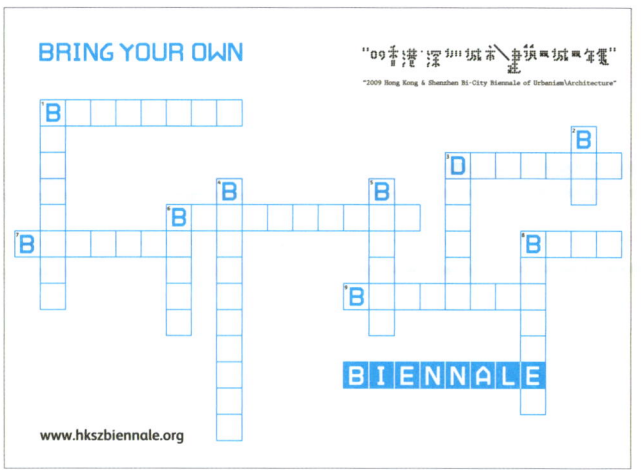

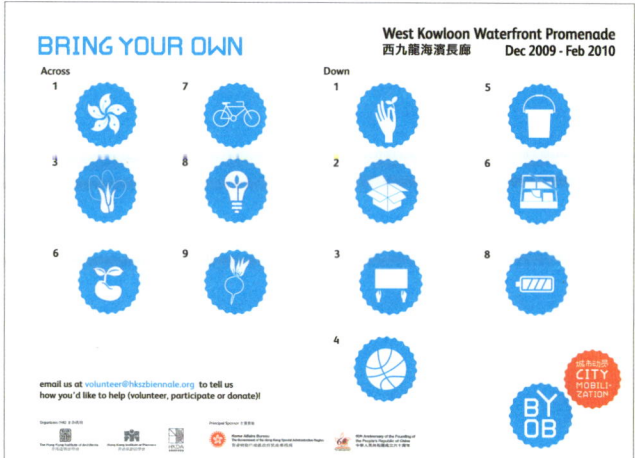

Postcards

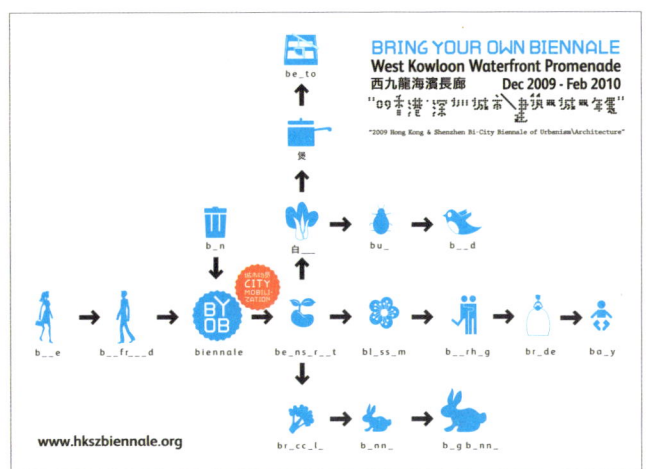

be_to

b_n

白__ bu_ b__d

b_e b_fr___d biennale be_ns_r__t bl_ss_m b__rh_g br_de ba_y

br_cc_l_ b_nn_ b_g b_nn_

www.hkszbiennale.org

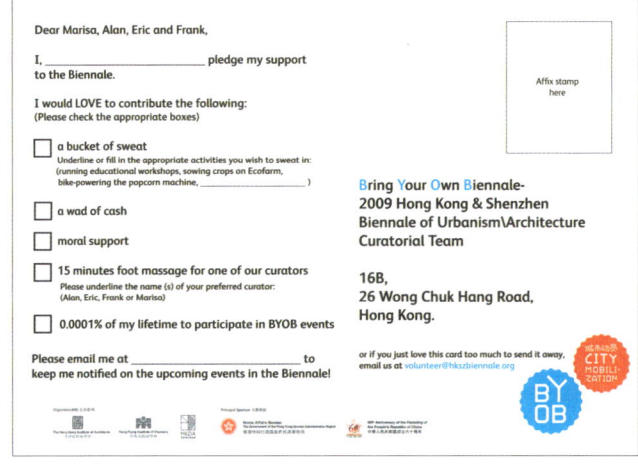

Dear Marisa, Alan, Eric and Frank,

I, _____ pledge my support
to the Biennale.

I would LOVE to contribute the following:
(Please check the appropriate boxes)

☐ a bucket of sweat
Underline or fill in the appropriate activities you wish to sweat in:
(running educational workshops, sowing crops on Ecofarm,
bike-powering the popcorn machine, _____)

☐ a wad of cash

☐ moral support

☐ 15 minutes foot massage for one of our curators
Please underline the name (s) of your preferred curator:
(Alan, Eric, Frank or Marisa)

☐ 0.0001% of my lifetime to participate in BYOB events

Please email me at _____ to
keep me notified on the upcoming events in the Biennale!

Affix stamp
here

Bring Your Own Biennale-
2009 Hong Kong & Shenzhen
Biennale of Urbanism\Architecture
Curatorial Team

16B,
26 Wong Chuk Hang Road,
Hong Kong.

or if you just love this card too much to send it away,
email us at volunteer@hkszbiennale.org

graphics by eskyiu

ATTENTION ALL SNAP-HAPPY PHOTOGRAPHERS!
各位攝影發燒友!

BRING YOUR OWN BIENNALE
West Kowloon Waterfront Promenade
西九龍海濱長廊   Dec 2009 - Feb 2010
"2009香港深圳城市\建築雙城雙年展"
"2009 Hong Kong & Shenzhen Bi-City Biennale of Urbanism\Architecture"

We'd really appreciate it if you'd share your photos with us, we'd love to see a fresh take on the Biennale through your eyes!
SEND YOUR FLICKR LINK TO: info@hkszbiennale.org (with subject heading "Photos")
and/or ADD US AS YOUR FACEBOOK FRIEND at Hkszbiennale.

we want to see what you saw.

Your photos will be added to our website at www.hkszbiennale.org!
And if we really love them, we'll publish your photo in our Biennale book!
Don't worry, we'll seek your permission first and definitely credit you as the rightful photographer!

希望大家可以同我地分享你嘅相!
請將你嘅flickr網址電郵到info@hkszbiennale.org (標題為「相片」), 順便add 我地入你嘅facebook。

等我地睇到你睇過嘅嘢

你嘅相將會上載到 www.hkszbiennale.org
如果我地好喜歡你嘅相, 將有機會將佢地刊登於雙年展刊物!
唔好擔心, 我地一定會得到你嘅同意先及將攝影師嘅名刊登。

www.hkszbiennale.org

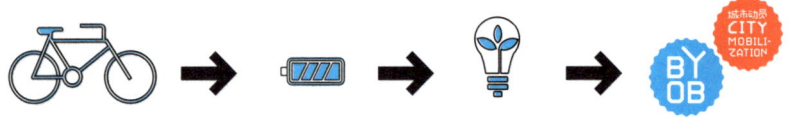

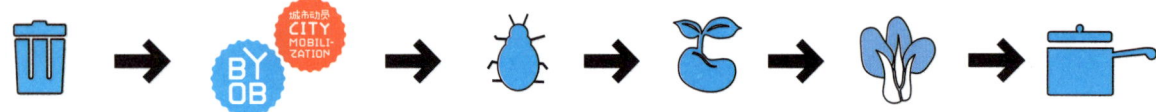

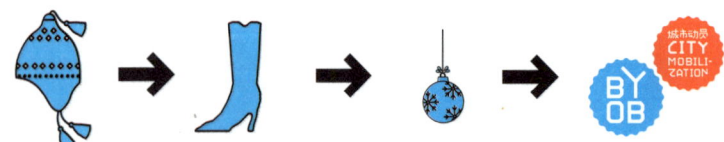

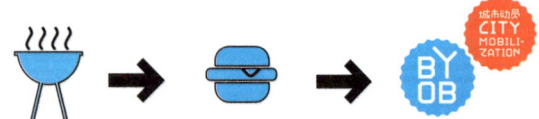

future creative
urban infrastructure

Young Architects at the Crossroad

Raymond Fung // essay

Hong Kong cityscape since reunification with China has undergone substantial changes – super skyscrapers now overwhelm the Victoria Harbor skyline, and at the same time, our older districts are disappearing rapidly. The development policies, with emphasis on market forces, have created a "New Horizon" in Hong Kong. As architects are the key players in mapping the transformation process, the inevitable questions facing us arise: what role should we play in the context of the political changes and what position should we take in the middle of this crossroad?

From a layman's point of view, practicing architecture is sometimes regarded as the most fascinating career amongst the nine professions. There is also sometimes a fictitious impression that architects can pursue their own dream projects at the owners' expense. Many brilliant students have therefore enrolled in architecture as their life-long career and mission with such a perception and impression in mind. However, once stepping into society our graduates immediately realize the hectic life and the immense pressure imposed from real architectural practice. These facts of life, especially after the handover, have tremendous impact on our younger generation. Our young architects find themselves deprived of design opportunities and have to yield to purely commercial constraints. Hong Kong developers, having enjoyed much success over the years with their proven business model, have few initiatives for change. This has rendered Hong Kong architectural design unprogressive.

Moreover, with the economic downturn since the handover, architects are always the first to face adversity. From this, architects have been trained to become sensitive to the overall economic situation and new threats, including globalization, new competition from mainland architects, and politicization in the society. To face these challenges, architects need to equip themselves with new knowledge and technology; to broaden perspectives beyond the border and above all, to have a visionary mindset to face ever growing competition.

Whilst the majority of young architects choose to follow in the footstep of their predecessors by joining commercial architectural practices, some young designers in recent years have sought for greater satisfaction in the field of interior design. There are also an increasing number of architects who venture to explore new platforms in mainland China and there are those who choose to join the Hong Kong Government to search for greater design liberty in the public domain.

Against this background, architectural practices over the past decade have gradually migrated towards diversified profiles, such as project management, interior design, landscape architecture, urban design and architectural specialization like heritage preservation and energy conservation. It is pleasing to note that some of the new generation of architects who represent our future have also reached out to help the needy, are addressing issues of unfair exploitation, and are fully participating within society for the great good of all.

Raymond Fung is an architect, designer, and painter who has won the Ten Outstanding Young Persons' Award and the Ten Outstanding Designers' Award, plus fifty major awards in architecture, visual arts, and interior design. He is the Adjunct Associate Professor of Architecture at The Chinese University of Hong Kong, advisory member of the West Kowloon Cultural District Authority Development Committee, the Advisory Committee on Revitalization of Historic Buildings, the Advisory Committee on the Appearance of Bridges and Associated Structures, the Leisure and Cultural Services Department Museums, and the Hong Kong Designers Association.

Interstitial Spaces

Lars Nittve // essay

A Swedish court will soon decide whether local authorities, sports clubs, and companies were justified in charging skiers a fee this past winter for skiing in the tracks these institutions had laid through the countryside. This issue is not just a legal one. It also cuts deep into the passionately held, age-old right of public access, or *allemansrätten*, "everyman's right," a right that everyone living in Sweden takes for granted. The right of public access is the same for everyone and entitles people to roam freely in the countryside, regardless of private property or zoning. The right of public access itself is not regulated in detail, but it is guaranteed in the Swedish constitution. It strikes me that this is an excellent and concrete example of what Michael Hardt and Antonio Negri call commonwealth – a kind of "third place," neither public nor private but having dimensions of both. Those who want skiers' fees will probably lose the battle against this medieval custom, which has survived the advent of property rights well into the twenty-

first century. But the issue, arising as it has today, obviously holds implications for other areas, too.

The road from the ski track to the art museum is shorter than one might think. Museums of modern art could, in fact, be defined as attempts to establish various forms of intermediary "third spaces." These institutions offer different kinds of freedoms, yet they are always more or less conscious of a context that is actually entirely closed. I could make another sporting comparison here: like Alain Robert, the "human Spider-Man" who scales the empty space between two buildings, there is an impression of considerable freedom. Only the toes and the fingertips need a structure for resistance. But dependence on this support is, of course, absolute. For museums, support from the public sector, the private sector, and the market, as well as from history, expectations, and formal and informal power and influence, is omnipresent. The intermediary spaces of the museum exist in a world that cannot be transcended, that has no "outside."

From the Museum of Modern Art in New York to the Stedelijk Museum, Reina Sofía, the Centre Pompidou, the San Francisco Museum of Modern Art, Tate Modern, and Moderna Museet, we know them well: classic museums of modern art, defined by years of practice. Indeed, they are fundamentally paradoxical creations that have become the dominant model for art museums. Some of these spaces have successfully cultivated the tension between the modern and the museal, between serving as contemporary arenas and as collecting, historicizing institutions. The same tension arises in the symbolic – and often physical – space of these museums, which

is the core (in the broad sense of the word) of all art institutions: a meeting place for artists and works of art on one hand, and for the audience on the other; a place where everything is done to optimize that decisive encounter in which art is activated by contact with viewers, where two entities with diametrically opposite needs meet each other, creating a space where art, people, and ideas can indeed roam freely, as if granted their own right of public access.

The art museum is, quite simply, exposed to pressures coming from many directions today – and I am not referring to the financial pressures experienced by museums, particularly in the US, over the past two years. On the contrary, I am thinking of the pressure from art itself: of the expectations placed on the museum to reshape itself and follow art wherever it may lead – to offer white cubes and black boxes when needed. At the same time, we are coming to realize that the museum is no longer synonymous with a building but depends on an institutional relationship between art and audience. (And this, incidentally, is where the symbolic implications of the institution have grown increasingly and surprisingly important for art.) In other words, a museum needs to be an exceptionally good dancer in order to follow art, in whatever form it takes – materially, conceptually, socially, you name it.

As a consequence, what potential does a museum have today to be meaningful within the structures that support it? Even government-funded institutions which hold privileged positions with respect to various economic interests face complications in providing an external place of

refuge. This is true even in locales where the government has undeniably sought to achieve an open situation that is related to the right of public access, where the director is granted extraordinary executive freedom and, as of the past couple of years, does not have to report to a board of directors. However, not even this hands-off policy will open the secret door to another, more liberated world. The question is which of all the forces influencing the museum's capacity to establish a "third place" is the strongest – and which force is strategically the most effective in creating or maintaining such a place.

Funding is, of course, decisive; but it is relatively manageable (especially if there is a balance between public and private funding), since its influence is so obvious and comparatively transparent. Factors that are infinitely harder to define – such as audience expectations – can be much more difficult to handle. Yet expectations generated by history or media must be adopted by the museum as part of its own identity and self-image, since its entire existence is based on the interface between art and audience – and those museums that forget either party in this equation tend to perish. To the same extent that, say, Tate Modern and Moderna Museet are defined by their collections and events, they are also defined by their millions of visitors. If I think back carefully on my twenty-five years of experience as a curator and museum director, it is here – in the perceptions and expectations of the audience – that the feeling that "there is no outside" is most evident. But it is also here that the potential to create a third space, a "commons," has appeared most strongly.

Events related to creating a public "commons" have occurred at Moderna Museet over the past decade. For example, the museum had to close for two years for technical reasons in 2002-2004, and a nomadic museum was established – "Moderna Museet c/o" – relocating artists' projects to other venues, including a building site (Clay Ketter), a palace (Henrik Håkansson), and a so-called expomobile that toured small communities from south to north (Andrea Zittel); and organizing a suite of "small adventures," thirteen-day exhibitions with twenty-three hours for installation, under the collective name of "Odd Weeks." Thanks to solid public trust, this nomadic existence, in which the museum as a place, a building, was gone and only its activity remained, led to an exchange of ideas and to contact with an astonishingly large new audience.

Public trust is the crucial factor in any museum's quest to succeed in the difficult task of existing in this world, of being defined by it yet able to open up alternative spaces within it as well. Establishing public trust takes time. Ultimately, doing so requires that the public have a solid perception of what the museum is doing and believe that it is doing it with the best of intentions. It involves disclosing the reasons for all major and minor decisions, but also engendering trust in the integrity of the management and staff. Integrity, integrity, integrity, must be the mantra. The slightest suspicion of hidden agendas or ulterior motives must be dispelled. Only then can we open up the possibility of alternatives to prevailing formulas for representation, to "given" hierarchies and working practices. I saw this happen in 1996 at the Louisiana Museum of Modern Art in Humlebiek, Denmark, when the exhibition "NowHere" broke up the exclusionary, monolithic museum policy that had been the norm until then. The entire museum was emptied of its permanent collection; in flowed a cluster of five disparate projects, whose overall name itself signaled a third space. The show aimed to dismantle any idea of a mainstream, of a totalizing truth or art history, by presenting the present through a number of curatorial perspectives. It challenged the traditional way of mounting a large exhibition by, in point of fact, offering clusters of smaller shows; moreover, "NowHere" actually let the space be invaded by outside agents, namely, the curators Laura Cottingham, Bruce W. Ferguson, Ute Meta Bauer and Fareed Armaly, Iwona Blazwick, and Anneli Fuchs and Lars Grambye. Thanks to public trust, this project, which broke all the rules and expectations of its tradition-laden institution, was received with openness and enthusiasm and served as a catalyst for an art discussion of an entirely new caliber, among a much wider set of audiences.

A modern art museum, founded on the principles of twentieth-century modernism, can only challenge itself, its prerequisites, and its existence in this way if it enjoys substantial public trust. A free space exists there – not outside but inside the empire described by Hardt and Negri. Unstable it may be, but it is there, waiting.

Lars Nittve is a Swedish museologist and art critic. Nittve was curator at the art museum Rooseum in Malmö and director of the Louisiana Museum of Modern Art, north of Copenhagen in Denmark. In 1998, he became head of Tate Modern in London and in 2001 was appointed the director of Moderna Museet, the national museum for modern art in Stockholm. Since 2011 he is Executive Director of M+, a new visual culture museum in the West Kowloon Cultural District.

Diagram by Salottobuono

The Paradox of the Cultural Instant

Daniel Chua // essay

Instant culture, like instant coffee, is not real. Culture, by definition, has to be real in as much as it is a cultivation of human practices, beliefs and identities. All the stuff that makes culture authentic takes time – "real" time. Attempts to manufacture culture in powdered form with imported flavor enhancers and even a dash of real milk just will not work no matter how much you stir and add hot water.

Yet in another sense, the test of a vibrant culture is its ability to appear in an instant. And this instant may be highly artificial; after all, cultivation is an intervention on nature; and art, by definition, is artifice. Instant culture, in this authentic sense, is an intervention that artificially frames the real; it is the sudden appearance of what takes time – what philosophers might term the "eternal moment." Take the example of an artist who 'seizes the moment in a mere stroke and frames that creative instant as her masterpiece: the artistic act only takes an instant, but that action is the result of an unseen sedimentation of traditions and long periods of thought, training, accidents, *cul-de-sacs*, and experiments. The authenticity of the instant appears from what is already always there and will never end. You might call this artistic integrity – the integration of doing and being, a fusion of artifice and reality.

In this sense, any cultural program should have already always begun and should never end. Or, to borrow Friedrich Schlegel's definition of artistic creativity, it should "forever be becoming and never perfected." It has to be a coming together of what has already begun in the formation of culture in Hong Kong and an unending work in progress. Only then will a cultural instant have its true moment.

Daniel Chua is the Head of the School of Humanities and the Director of the Advanced Cultural Leadership Programme at the University of Hong Kong. He studied music at Cambridge University, conducted research as a Henry Fellow at Harvard, and served as the Professor of Music Theory and Analysis at King's College London.

On Expectations

Eric Schuldenfrei | Marisa Yiu // essay

To constantly anticipate the unknown is something we experienced in a compressed and reactionary way throughout the five months of preparation time for the Biennale, a process which continued during the three-month long exhibition period. This experience conjures up mixed emotions of defeat, success, failure, and breakthrough as we retroactively evaluate the projects. Yet, we continuously look back at our experience to strategize and propose alternate ways of establishing cultural events at large. For a city like Hong Kong, in the context of China and the world, can events be done in a more seamless way, with improved planning? Is the quick and rapid response the normative practice, where the unplanned is a given and immediacy a fact? Does this ensure quality? If so, then how should one work within this constraint? Do we accept limitations or challenge the system? Where does one find long-term support from the right organizations to secure a forward-thinking and innovative mindset? Can resources be committed and built-in well beforehand, so curators and exhibitors do not need to constantly fight for funding and resources to realize work? By serendipity we were armed with innocence, ambition, and inquiry, with a desire for innovation and support from countless committed individuals who all acknowledged a much-needed reclamation of the cultural landscape of Hong Kong, which in turn transformed the numerous burdens into nimble and effective collaborations. A sensitive and contentious area of reclaimed land with more than ten years of emptiness set the tone for the curatorial theme; for, as a context, the future West Kowloon Cultural District site had its own predilections to contend with. Yet, our challenge was to fill the site with activity, to continually create an ambiance of optimism, excitement, and sheer drive in order to explore its potential.

Many have asked us how we measure success. Is this what you expected? Although we had to count the attendance of visitors and participants in official reports, submit our audit accounts and record the press coverage; for us this was not so important. We believe cultural exhibitions and biennales are ways to touch and impact society, altering preconceptions of what architecture and urbanism is and should be. Events like this must be provocatively meaningful for society. A few highlighted examples of this approach include the curatorial open call for design proposals, which resulted in a large number of submissions where many previously undiscovered designers were selected. Afterward we received a few notes of thanks, since several very young designers at the Biennale had been selected for prestigious awards as a direct result of their work created for the Biennale. One group of young female architects working in various large corporate firms in Hong Kong expressed how their installation, *The Projecting Window*, was an outlet to voice their work alongside the more established local and international architects. *Two Wongs Going to Sea* involved a fearless intervention into the harbor, while simultaneously bringing a sense of humor to the site. Yet, the event was a performative appraisal of the serious problems we face with housing in Hong Kong, questioning both the accessibility of the waterfront and public open space within the city. This added another dimension, becoming a type of social commentary, as well as a way of understanding the laws that govern the legal consequences of the event. Another highlight was the collective day-to-day construction of the Biennale with volunteers and professionals. As we prepared *Eco Farm,* by bringing in youth groups from various districts to jointly build a large farm with organic vegetables, we observed the glistening awe in the eyes of the students, enthusiastically sowing seeds and digging their hands into the fresh soil for the first time ever. They were shocked to discover that this vast, open public space was actually available to them. The same students returned later to harvest the crops and eventually made different types of salad out of the locally grown produce. A majority of the children brought their modular, paper-pulp farm boxes back into their small apartments to continue micro-farming at a domestic scale.

Revealing the predominant priorities of the Hong Kong public in relation to our collective creative culture, the overall program of the Biennale indirectly called attention to human and social behavior. Due to limited resources to properly document the numerous overlapping activities occurring on the site, we decided to create an open call for photographers to freely take pictures and upload them to our social media platforms. Something of note is the culture of vanity in one sense, for people loved to take their own portraits and send in pictures with incessant self-adoration. We optimized this for ourselves, where activities were documented that we could not capture, and as a result we now continuously collaborate with various talented photographers who contribute their time documenting other cultural events across the city. We wonder whether the dense condition of urban living, where severe lack of space is the norm, accounts for the common pleasure in focusing on activities one can efficiently collect in a highly confined space. In Hong Kong creative expression is often via cameras, where photography and film have become the dominant art forms. There is so much skill and talent in the everyday visual culture to work with, offering potential areas for articulating a greater collective experience.

During the Biennale we enjoyed the ability to have access to government land for creating innovative programs. Constant negotiations and forces were at play, where areas once thought available became obsolete and strict regulations forced the removal of certain projects while unexpected funding constraints required the curators to revise our scope and vision for the Biennale. However, the absolute rawness of the site proved that artificial, reclaimed land retains the potential to develop naturally: filled with indigenous cacti, butterflies, flora, birds, and its own ecology – the pastoral landscape of West Kowloon with the harbor beyond provided a calming counterpoint to the extreme density of the metropolis.

Looking back at the exceptional opportunities afforded by the unique site makes us wonder about the critical need for a large urban backyard to improve the quality of life within Hong Kong, for the government to allot far more natural leisure places for children and families. Open space is needed for urban release due to dense living and working conditions; yet, the inaccessibility of large, open spaces has also proved challenging. Most importantly, this urban landscape needs an urgent rethinking of resource availability if it is going to serve as a platform for creative and cultural engagement. So we ask, is this the only site in contention and transition? Other sites to explore in Hong Kong include the old Kai Tak airport, which ceased operation in 1998, and the Frontier Closed Area border zone between Hong Kong and Shenzhen, a 28 sq km uninhabited area since 1951 that will be reduced to 8 sq km as part of a future plan. Do we maintain spaces such as these as vast, open areas with only commerce in mind or do we continue to build them as sites for affordable housing, culture, and the arts? What new architectural solutions could be employed? For decades the grand projects of the Hong Kong Government have achieved success in satisfying housing demand, yet designs are still endlessly repeated to form entire districts of generic towers. This architecture is symptomatic of a bygone era of need, however. What should be explored next? If the domestic environment requirements are so tight, market forces so extreme, and building codes so inflexible – how can we redesign? Public and domestic living spaces need more flexibility for comfort, to provide uniqueness and productive cultural mixing. Can West Kowloon reach out to the larger areas it is surrounded by, such as the Yau Tsim Mong district and Tai Kok Tsui, with an integral vision of a human scale? Can its immediate neighbor, the Express Rail Link station, which connects seamlessly with China, integrate at the scale of the pedestrian? Can large areas within Hong Kong be endowed with special status as an experimental zone, where building codes and plot-ratio calculations are rethought to allow for a truly carbon-free, sustainable, and innovative solution for mixed-use development? The potential for landscape, infrastructure and architecture to be fused and integrated with social behaviors, community life, and vibrancy must take place to allow for a space of socially responsible practices to cultivate sub-economies and small-scaled enterprises. Contemporary Chinese and Asian cultures have an opportunity to work hand in hand to generate new urban fabrics and architectural solutions to create unique aesthetic experiences.

There are future opportunities for our naturalized states where cross-fertilization and interdisciplinary practices are to be productive. It is a collective effort, a collaborative process where knowledge should be transferred seamlessly. Countless forms of cooperation, coordination, and foresight need to run in parallel. We acknowledge that the informal needs the formal; and the formal needs the informal, where grassroots strategies produce their own exceptional cohesion. Throughout the Biennale many exhibitors and supporters of the events poured in much of their own personal resources to achieve this; yet, so much also depends on the social and cultural infrastructure and the networks of influence of the professional institutes. Work must be done to move beyond the effort of committed individuals, so a collective effort from all sectors of industry and governance occurs. We are not afraid to admit this will not be an entirely straightforward and linear process; yet, we have already witnessed the most enlightening and refreshing projects, dedicated architectural solutions and events that are not commercially driven showcases but deep inquiries into our living environment and social behaviors. These provocations, in the context of the future West Kowloon Cultural District, a site that is not yet formulated, allow us to say that it has much potential to offer for the creative communities as a platform to test, share, and exchange ideas. We do wish and desire for more spontaneity and flexibility in all senses, and the approach must support a change of mindset in regard to capacity building, policies, and regulations. We are honored with the opportunity to curate and work with the most committed individuals and friends in Hong Kong, Shenzhen, and around the world. We learned from the respectful members of society who heralded the valuable meaning of participatory interactions: as citizens we all continue to mobilize with instantaneous reflexes to chart a better future. Looking ahead we only wish for more; to see architecture and the city support a socially sustainable ecology that coexists with innovation and respect of our cultural heritages and contemporary aspirations. These are not mutually exclusive, as the culture of architecture and urbanism shapes the values of our society, and the culture of our community shapes the architecture and urbanism that surrounds us. We anticipate further challenges in this instant culture of dynamic exchange and only have even greater expectations for events to come.

index

Marisa Yiu is co-founder of ESKYIU, a design collaborative integrating culture, community, and technology based in Hong Kong. Since 2000 she has been researching issues of production and consumption relating to the cultural landscape of Hong Kong. Her essay "Image Construction: Hong Kong since 1967-8" published in LOG journal examined Hong Kong's relationship to the Pearl River Delta and global networks. In her design practice she examines the ways in which the built environment and constructs of labor shape social relationships by forming connections between civic engagement and sustainable design. Community driven projects include *Brandspider* for Whitney Museum ISP; *Place Markers* with placeMatters, New York. Along with her partner Eric Schuldenfrei of ESKYIU installations include: *Chinatown WORK 2006* an interactive public arts project commissioned by the Lower Manhattan Cultural Council; *SINO* an installation shown at the Brooklyn Museum; *Nutritious: an Aeroponic Facade* exhibited at the Architectural Association, and projects for various international biennales. She has lectured at the China NEXT symposium, UNESCO forum on "Historic Urban Landscapes," and the AsiaGSD "Specific Weights of Architecture: Asian Probes" conference at Harvard University. She has also published in A/D, Log journal, DomusChina, Architectural Record, Metropolis, Journal for Architectural Education, and Routledge. Marisa has taught at the Architectural Association in London, Columbia University, Parsons School of Design, the Cooper Hewitt National Design Museum, and the University of Hong Kong. Currently, she is Assistant Professor of Architecture at the Chinese University of Hong Kong. She received her Bachelor of Arts and Sciences from Columbia University and a Master of Architecture from Princeton University. Marisa is a licensed architect in the state of New York, AIA architect member, an associate member of the Hong Kong Institute Architects. Marisa is chair of the Strategy Committee and a board member of the Hong Kong Ambassadors of Design.

Alan Lo is co-founder and executive director of property at Blake's. He is also co-founder and director of Hong Kong based Press Room Group, owner and operator of food and beverage outlets including The Press Room, Classified, The Pawn, SML and The News Room. He has many years of hospitality project experience, having worked for project management and development teams at a number of international hotel groups including the Mandarin Oriental and Shangri-La. Active in promoting design and creativity in Hong Kong, Alan serves as the board chairman of the Hong Kong Ambassadors of Design, council member of the Hong Kong Arts Development Council as well as advisor to ART HK (Hong Kong International Art Fair), and Para/Site Art Space. He holds a Bachelor of Arts in Architecture from Princeton University.

Eric Schuldenfrei is a designer who focuses on the evolving relationship between architecture and art. Recent projects include an art installation commissioned by Agnes Gund, president emerita of MoMA; multimedia projects for Ferragamo; and computer animations for Diller + Scofidio and the Builders Association's Obie Award winning multimedia theatre work *Jet Lag*. Architectural projects completed in collaboration with Marisa Yiu have been featured in many international biennales: *Urban Pastoral*, an architectural installation created for the 2008 Venice Biennale; *Human Motor: Narratives from the Assembly Line*, in Ljubljana; and *Mediated Labour* for the 2007 Hong Kong-Shenzhen Bi-City Biennale. A video installation *The Measure of All Things*, a collaboration with artist Haluk Akakce, was exhibited at Casino Luxembourg; Kunst Werke, Berlin; The Museum of Modern Art, Frankfurt; and the Centre d'art Contemporain, Geneva. Eric received a Bachelor of Architecture from Cornell University and a Master and Doctor of Philosophy from the University of Cambridge. He has taught at Princeton, Columbia, the University of Hong Kong, and the Architectural Association and has recently presented at the Harvard University AsiaGSD lecture series, the V&A museum in London, and the University of Cambridge.

Frank Yu is design principal of Gravity Partnership Limited. He studied architecture at Pratt Institute, New York, where he received a Bachelor of Architecture. After graduating in 1986, he joined Ellerbe Beckett New York as a design architect in Studio Peter Pran, where he worked on numerous award winning and renowned projects and international design competitions. In 2000 he returned to Hong Kong and founded Gravity Partnership Limited with Claude Wong in 2003. The work of Gravity Partnership has been featured in many exhibitions including the 2004 and 2008 Venice Biennale, and the 2007 Hong Kong–Shenzhen Bi-City Biennale; and won numerous awards including 1st prize in the North Point Harbor Conceptual Design Competition, and 2nd prize in the Concept Design Competition for the Hong Kong Pavilion for Expo 2010. Frank is very involved in community-focused work both through Gravity's development of Intermediate Relief Housing for those affected by the Sichuan earthquake and through his personal involvement with local charities including serving on the board of directors of Tung Wah Group of Hospitals in 2008-2009, and currently a member of the Court of Lingnan University.

Exhibitions

"3:15's Rain Catcher" Let's Celebrate Rain is by Manfred Yuen and Stephen Suen, founders of YS GROUNDWORK along with Alex Jiang, Stephen Ip, Ricky Lee, Alvis Ko, May Ho, Aries Nip, and Lolita Lei. YS GROUNDWORK is a London and Hong Kong based design platform founded in 2007. The work was exhibited in Hong Kong and London with a recent pavilion design and art works exhibited in the 2008 London Biennale. **Acknowledgement** Sponsors include the Department of Electronic and Information Engineering, Hong Kong Polytechnic University; Apex City Financial Consultant, Ulferts Furniture, LWK & Partners Architects, Suen Kwai Ping and Maggie Nip. Special thanks to Prof. Michael Siu, Siew-Chong Tan, S.C. Yip, Derek Li (Dalian), Christy Chan, Rory Leung, and Poonkei Engineering Co.

Abandoned Furniture is by Rosly Mok and Vanessa Chan, both graduated from the Hong Kong Polytechnic University with first class honours, majoring in environmental design. Rosly is now working in an architectural company and Vanessa works in landscape architecture. In their spare time, they create for Apostrophe's Design. **Acknowledgement** Kinlik Decoration Desgin Co., JMB Formula Company Limited, Strata, Tec Architecture.

Action + Repose Workshop is led by Jesse Reiser and Nanako Umemoto, who have practiced as Reiser + Umemoto RUR Architecture P.C. since 1986. RUR Architecture is an internationally recognized architectural firm in New York City. In addition to teaching at Princeton University and Columbia University, Reiser and Umemoto have taught and lectured throughout the United States, Europe and Japan. Workshop tutors from the Faculty of Architecture include John Lin, Yan Chu, Giulia Foscari, Peter Hasdell, Chad McKee, and Thomas Tsang. Works shown are from the first-year architecture design studio sequence. **Acknowledgement** Faculty of Architecture, the University of Hong Kong, and Wheeler Waterproofing (S&C) Ltd.

Andrea is by Mathieu Lehanneur and David Edwards. Mathieu runs his own design studio dedicated to industrial design and interior architecture. In 2008, he received the Talent du Luxe Award and Best Invention Award for ANDREA. David Edwards is a scientist, writer and founder of Le Laboratoire. He is also a faculty member at Harvard University and founder of Pulmatrix and Medicine In Need (MEND). **Acknowledgement** LABOGROUP.

Asia's World City: Hybrid Hong Kong + Shenzhen is curated by Andrew Lam of Museum of Site (MOST) and designed by Elizabeth Sikiaridi and Frans Vogelaar of Hybrid Space Lab Berlin/Amsterdam, an interdisciplinary practice specializing in high-end design and strategic research. MOST is a non-profit organization founded in Hong Kong in 1993 that aims to promote cutting edge art locally and internationally. **Acknowledgement** Sponsors: Hong Kong Arts Development Council. Supported by Leisure and Cultural Services Department.

Black Tee is by Michael Yuen, an Australian artist working across a range of mediums including sound, light and performance. His works investigate the nature of cities and public space through action. He has served on the 2006-7 InterArts panel for the Australia Council of the Arts and received the Ruby Litchfield and AsiaLink awards. **Acknowledgement** Sponsors: Videotage. Produced with the assistance of Wei Zhou and CPU:PRO. This project was developed at reSkin, an ANAT Emerging Technology Lab presented in association with Australian National University and CraftAustralia.

Bloody Haze Inverted Binocular and Maxi Binocular is by MAP Office, a multidisciplinary platform devised by Laurent Gutierrez and Valérie Portefaix. This duo has been based in Hong Kong since 1996, working in drawing, photographs, video, installations, performance and literary and theoretical texts. Laurent Gutierrez is an Associate Professor at the School of Design, the Hong Kong Polytechnic University. Valérie Portefaix is the principal of MAP Office. She is currently a Visiting Assistant Professor at the School of Design, the Hong Kong Polytechnic University. **Acknowledgement** Guillaume Henry, MAP Office assistant.

Bottom Up is designed by Roberto Davolio and Marc Brulhart. Based in Hong Kong, Roberto Davolio is the founder of Form and Structure Consulting Services, an Italian-born architect specializing in building systems. He has worked for Foster and Partners as part of the Specialist Modeling Group and his expertise has been honed on projects such as the Beijing International Airport, the AOL Time Warner Center in New York, and the City of Dreams Casino in Macau. Marc is the founder of Marc & Chantal Design that has over 18 years of experience in crafting unique multi-dimensional brand experiences. Marc studied product and interior design at the European Institute of Design in Milan.

Boundaries is created by Gene Miao and Frederick Wong, who are leaders of an ongoing project to promote and celebrate local establishments that may be or have been threatened by rampant globalisation and gentrification. Gene is a founder of Day Tau Chung, neighborhooding.net, and chief designer of 1:1 Limited, an interior architecture firm. Frederick is director of Architectural Works Ltd. and part-time Lecturer at the Department of Architecture, Chu Hai College, and also at the School of Creative Media, City University of Hong Kong.

BYOB Challenge is sponsored by Time Out Hong Kong.

BYOB Reading Café is designed by Russell Law and Eddy Yip, founders of Studio OFF. They have won two of the most prestigious awards in the industry: Interior Designer of the Year, Residential Interior Designer of the Year and the 2005 idFX / BIDA (British Interior Design Awards). **Acknowledgement** Domus China with the Curatorial team supported the books donation drive.

BYOBall: West Kowloon Football Club is an event organized by Sebastien Saint-Jean in collaboration with Olo Nitka. Sebastien is the founder of UNIT, an architecture firm based in Hong Kong. **Acknowledgement** Equipment Sponsor: Nike.

BYOBench: BYOBond Sharing a diverse educational background, the team includes graduates from Hong Kong, United States, and Australia. Prior to forming this team, the members have individually participated in different architectural competitions and exhibitions. The team came together to explore the profound meaning behind benches and bamboo, with the idea of "bond," which was developed and reflected in their design.

BYOBench: Sitting Device is by the students of the Hong Kong Polytechnic Univeriisty and supervised by Kacey Wong, Sebastien Saint Jean, and Valérie Portefaix. Student participants are Jenny Choi, Cynthia Chang, Vincent Chan, Jinny Mak, Rachel Lok, Dorothy Fong, Zoe Chung, Kyra Tung, Vicky Chan, Silvia Wong, Viki Li, Vivian Cheung, Po Tang, Lorraine Leung, Him Ng, Maggie Chan, Kitty Wong, Ivy Kong, I Chan, Bell Young, Bee Leung, Iris Cheun, Bosco So, Jinny Wu, Nathan Cho, Phoebe Chu, Helen Lai, Jassie Fung, Karine Lam, Pui Wong. **Acknowledgement** The Hong Kong Polytechnic University School of Design.

BYOBotanist: Greenactivities is by Bob Pang and Edith Li. Bob received his Master of Architecture from the University of Hong Kong in 2007. Apart from his professional achievements, Bob was awarded first prize in two photographic competitions organized by Lomography Asia and Cream Magazine. Edith is a practicing architect. Her works aim to integrate art and design into everyday life and to inspire the general public's concern for the community and the environment. **Acknowledgement** Strongly International Limited.

Cabinet of Curiosities is a collaboration between Esther Lorenz, Li Shqiao, and Puay Peng Ho. Esther Lorenz is an Austrian chartered architect currently teaching at the School of Architecture at the Chinese University of Hong Kong (CUHK). Li Shqiao has practiced architecture in Hong Kong, and taught at Architectural Association in London and the National University of Singpapore. Puay Peng Ho is Director of the School of Architecture at CUHK. **Acknowledgement** The School of Architecture, CUHK. Students: Carlos Cho Wa Chan, Janice Hiu Yan Lam, Rachel Shuk Nga Lee, Ivan Yiu Ming Leung, Kar Him Mo, Sarah Shuk Wai Ng, Maud Saget, Jason Yik Wo Tsang, Annie Shuk Man Wong, Doris Shuk Wai Yue, Cherry Cheuk Yee Lam, Hing Ching Lau, Sze Wing Mak, Claire Prinet, Chun Wah Tong, Jamie Ka Chun Tsui, Steven Chi Keung Wong, Jing Zhong.

Cultural Classroom and CNC Design Lab is organized and supported by ESKYIU, a Hong Kong based design practice integrating culture, community and technology. Their interest lies in connections between public engagement, sustainable design and digital media technologies.

Acknowledgement Aedas donation of computers, software support from Adobe and Autodesk, furniture designed by Catherine Ying Xiong, and Jeb Greater China for the donation of materials.

Design for the Anthropocene Era is by Kate Orff, the principal and founder of the landscape architecture studio SCAPE in New York City. Kate is a registered landscape architect and Assistant Professor at the Columbia University. SCAPE strives to redefine the public sector to include natural processes, ecosystems to support life and diversity and wildlife habitat, to cultivate an ethos of civic participation. SCAPE's work connects people to their immediate environment. **Acknowledgement** Ben Abelman, exhibition designer.

Double Double is by Barry Jacques and David Smith, Irish artists living in Hong Kong. Both studied visual arts in Ireland in various art colleges and have exhibited extensively in the last decade. Barry's recent work uses video to explore the many faces of Hong Kong. David creates instrumental music and the soundtrack to this video work.

Draw Your Future with Light and Shadow is a collaboration led by Christopher Mok of Spectrum Design & Associates (Asia) Lighting Design Limited with Frank Leung and Pak King Lam. Christopher attained his professional training in Hong Kong and New York City with experience in both architectural and theatrical space. He has won several awards and has projects in including Hong Kong, Japan, China, and the US. He believes that light can visually and emotionally transform our environment and uses light as a public art form.

dreamgrove.org is by Drifting City, a collaborative based in Athens and Los Angeles founded on the idea that one can be in two places at the same time. Established in 2006 by Petros Babasikas (architect and Adjunct Professor at the Patras School of Architecture), Chrissou Voulgari (visual artist), and Farzad Moré (architect). Drifting City collaborated with Dimitris Doukas a software engineer and web developer, and Lambros Pigounis a composer and interaction designer to create the dreamgrove exhibition and web platform.

Dutch Design Chair is created by Erik Hoebergen and Deborah Meijburg, founders of Five Spices based in The Hague, Netherlands. They work on the cutting edge of graphic design, interactive design, and motion design. Five Spices projects include exhibitions, corporate identities, trade fair presentations, events, brochures, websites, interactive installations, and interiors. **Acknowledgement** Sponsored by the Consulate-General of the Kingdom of the Netherlands.

Eco Farm- Green Pixel is a collaboration between Humphrey Wong and Pad Pui Kwan Chu. Humphrey is a founding partner of Meta4 Design Forum. As well as being a practicing architect, he is involved in education,

exhibition and event design. Pad Pui Kwan Chu returned to Hong Kong in the 1980s and is among the pioneers in the organic movement in Hong Kong. Since 1995 she is the director of The Organic Farm and Simply Organic. **Acknowledgement** The Hong Kong Federation of Youth Groups, students of the University of Hong Kong, Sustainable Ecological Ethical Development Foundation and ESKYIU.

"excavation" is by artist Kingsley Ng, educator Syren Johnstone, and architect Daniel Patzold. They share a common desire to understand the relationship between place, time and community through site-specific works. **Acknowledgement** SPONSOR Oriental Landscapes Limited.

Fa Pai Rides WKCD is created by Lai Chung Wong, a Fa Pai craftsman devoted to promoting the traditional craftsmanship to the next generation. He undertook an artist-in-residence programme at HKICC Lee Shau Kee School of Creativity in 2009. The School of Creativity is the first and unique Direct Subsidy Scheme senior secondary school in Hong Kong devoted to arts, media, and design education established in 2006.

face[GUARD] is by Erik M. Hemingway of hemingway+a/studio and public artist Allison Warren. Erik has been working in installation and architecture for two decades, merging cultural criticism of the commodity culture and special architectural constructs. Awards include a Citation in the 44th Annual Progressive Architecture Awards, 15th Annual Architectural League of New York Young Architects, and Prix de Theatre at the Ecole de Beaux Arts Internationales d'Enseignment. **Acknowledgement** Project team: Erik M Hemingway, Allison Warren, Montana Crady, Aeron Hodges, Chenxi Hu, Mathew Strack, Win-may Au; Graduate student assistants: Stephanie Adamczyk, Romain Béal, Matthew Cho, Yiyuan Zou, Mekram Mohammad, Zaimee Lucca, Philip Dimick, Nicholas Brown, and Donald Ross Smith. Sponsor: University of Illinois.

farmScape is a collaboration between UMAMI-UTILITIES and CL3. UMAMI-UTILITIES is a design studio formed in 2008 by Eddy Man Kim, Edward Yujoong Kim, and Kevin Chin-Kwok Lim, while they were studying architecture at Cornell University. CL3, where William Lim is managing director, is a Hong Kong based architectural firm with a view to explore design forms through the use of local fabrics and materials.

ffformica is by Xu Tiantian, the founding principal of DnA Design and Architecture in Beijing, an interdisciplinary practice of city planning, urban and architectural design. Prior to establishing DnA Beijing, she worked at a number of design firms in the United States and OMA in the Netherlands.

FLUX is by Catherine Ying Xiong. Catherine started her own design firm, CZ, in 2008. CZ's fundamental belief is for *no specified design*, which emphasizes unlimited creativity, explores the unknown, and studies how

design and skill can work together to bring out emotions within people. CZ not only focuses on large-scale designs such as architecture, but also on small-scale industrial and product design. **Acknowledgement** John Wang.

Forest I Pedestrian is by OpenEndedGroup, a collaborative founded by Marc Downie, Shelley Eshkar, and Paul Kaiser. Based in New York and Chicago, OpenEndedGroup creates works for stage, screen, gallery, page, and public space. Among the prizes they have won individually or collectively are the Guggenheim Fellowship, the John Cage Award from the Foundation for Contemporary Arts and a Media Arts Fellowship from the Rockefeller Foundation. **Acknowledgement** Sound Design: Terry Pender of Columbia's Computer Music Center; additional animation: Keith Chamberlain; installation architect: Marco Steinberg; Co-producer: Art Production Fund and Eyebeam; Motion capture was overseen by Lisa Naugle of UC Irvine's Dance Department; software support: Unreal Pictures; technical support: Connecting Point Multi Media; Additional support: Dancing in the Streets, public funds from the New York State Council on the Arts, funds from the UCI Chancellors Distinguished Fellow Grant from the School of the Arts, the University of California: Irvine.

Forest Project is by renowned artist Xu Bing. He was born in Chongqing, China and currently resides and works in Beijing. He received his bachelor degree in the print making department of the Central Academy of Fine Arts, Beijing where he stayed on as an instructor, earning his Master of Fine Arts, and is currently serving as the vice president. Solo exhibitions of his work have been held at major museums and art institutions throughout the world, and has won countless prizes and awards including the MacArthur Fellowship in 1999 in recognition of his capacity to contribute importantly to society, particularly in print making and calligraphy. **Acknowledgement** The Hong Kong Federation of Youth Groups, Hong Kong Ambassadors of Design, Alan Lau, Kai-Yin Lo, and Alan Lo.

Fossils of Future is by Dutch designer Danny Fang. In 2007 he set up the industrial design company Fang Studio Limited in Hong Kong. Fascinated by culture, industrial technologies, crafts and the experimental process, he creates products for mass production as well as unique pieces.

Glaciarium is designed by Jason Kelly Johnson and Nataly Gattegno, design principals of FUTURE CITIES LAB, and Thomas Kelley (lead project assistant), Carrie Norman, Troy Rogers, and Noah Keating. The office has earned second prize in the Seoul Performing Arts International Competition and was a finalist in the History Channel's City of the Future competition. They were the 2009 New York Prize Fellows at the Van Alen Institute in New York City. **Acknowledgement** The Van Alen Institute, Taubman College at the University of Michigan, Graham Foundation for Advanced Studies in the Fine Arts Grant. Fabrication Sponsors: Columbia University's Avery CNC Fabrication Lab; NYC College of Technology, CUNY CityTech; California College of the Arts, San Francisco.

Glow is a collaboration between David Erdman and Clover Lee, directors of davidclovers and C.E.B. Reas. davidclovers' work explores ways in which architectural mass produces distinct sensations. Currently, they are working on projects in the US, Italy, China, and Hong Kong. C.E.B. Reas' work focuses on defining computational processes and translating them into images. He is a Professor of Design Media Arts at UCLA. **Acknowledgement** Design Assistants: Jei Kim, Juliet Hsieh, Laura Goard, Yvette Herrera, Fei Mui and Jason Dembski. Sponsor and Support: DuPont China, SpeedTop Hong Kong. Transportation support of Allied-Pickfords. Cabinetry and installation were made possible by International Engineering Company.

G.O.A.L. is by EFGH, a multi-disciplinary architectural partnership founded in 2007 in New York City by principals Hayley Eber and Frank Gesualdi. Current projects include the design of a public park for the city of Rosario, Argentina, spatial strategies for the New York Jets Stadium, and the design of a new headquarters for CineReach. EFGH was awarded for their submission to Envisioning Gateway: A Public Design Competition for Gateway National Park.

Graham'Super is by Urban Rethink Tank in collaboration with experimental music groups: Re-Records, No One Pulse, Alok, and Edwin Lo. With an impassioned commitment to the city of Hong Kong, Urban Rethink Tank is a cross-disciplinary platform composed of Martin Fung, Stephen Chan, Thomas Chung, Joshua Lau, and Jeff Wong. Their intellectual practice shapes the form and function of urban regeneration by mapping new ways to show the unexplored connections that shape the city and lives in a culturally sustainable way. **Acknowledgement** Manhattan Holdings Limited, Tetra Pak China Ltd., School of Architecture, The Chinese University of Architecture, Jia International Limited.

Green Panel System and Eco-Turf System is manufactured and designed by Strongly International Limited. Strongly is a company specialized in innovative landscape solutions, with a variety of proprietary eco-products for residential, commercial, institutional and industrial facilities owned by both government and private development entities. Being equipped with professionals in marketing, design, engineering, environmental science and horticulture, Strongly provides solutions to customers covering project planning, structural calculation, design, fabrication, installation, and maintenance services. **Acknowledgement** Strongly International Limited.

Green Tapestry is designed by Hay Fung Ip, Kit Wang Choi, Kwan Ho Li, Sing Lam Ng, a team of architecture graduates from the University of Hong Kong who believe that architecture can be a vehicle to explore and solve societal issues. **Acknowledgement** Strongly International Limited.

Greenville Student Design Competition 2009 South China Morning Post's Homes for Hope was set up in the aftermath of the 2008 earthquake in Sichuan, China to provide a thousand homes and essential services for some of the region's hardest hit areas. **Acknowledgement** Co-organizers: Aedas Architects Foundation and South China Morning Post's Homes for Hope. Awards sponsored by HSBC.

Heaven on Earth | Painting by God are by anothermountainman. Stanley Ping Pui Wong, better known as anothermountainman, has a passion for fine arts and photography, often focusing on social issues. His affection for his birthplace is strongly reflected in his art. In recent years, his "redwhiteblue" works, depicting the positive spirit of Hong Kong using the ubiquitous tricolor canvas, have won critical acclaim both locally and internationally and have been collected in museums including the V&A.

Hole in the Wall is by designers Jody Bielun and Pablo Leppe. Their professional work ranges from architecture and interior design. They see architecture as an extension of the human psyche and seek to explore the use of space as a way to awaken the senses. Their work has been exhibited in New York, London, Toronto, Montreal, and Mexico. **Acknowledgement** DeLonghi, Patricia Choi, and Start From Zero.

Hong Kong Fantasies is by MVRDV, a firm founded by Winy Maas, Jacob van Rijs and Nathalie de Vries. MVRDV is a globally operating architecture office with a history of creative solutions for urban issues. The Why Factory is an initiative of Delft University's Faculty of Architecture and MVRDV. Led by Winy Maas, they research urban futures, explore development possibilities for our cities, and deal with pressing issues such as green architecture, food consumption, and post-crisis urbanism. **Acknowledgement** Sponsored by the Consulate-General of the Netherlands.

Hyperbolic Rattan Bench is designed by Haewon Shin with Kelly Chow. Haewon runs her own practice, lokaldesign. She teaches at the Korean National University of Arts and her recent work includes Han River Renaissance Pedestrian Tunnel Design and the UN Village Residence. She has participated in various exhibitions including the Biennale di Venezia in 2006. Kelly founded Shelter as a multi-disciplinary design laboratory in Hong Kong to explore fundamental aspects of architectural design: construction and dwelling. **Acknowledgement** Kyungmi Shin, Hack Seop Shin, and Sanga Kim.

Idea of a Tree is created by mischer'traxler, a design firm founded by Katharina Mischer and Thomas Traxler in Vienna, Austria. Their project The Idea of a Tree won an honorary mention at the 2009 Prix Ars Electronica, the DMY Award 2009 and the Austrian Experimental Design Award. **Acknowledgement** Ricci Cheuk Kin Wong of Art Lab Limited.

Illegal Construction is a film by the Yangjiang Group, founded by Zheng Guogu, Zaiyan Cheng, and Qinglin Sun. **Acknowledgement** William Lim.

Interconnectivity is created by Brian Wing Hang Chow, Louis Hing Wai Law, and Bill Man Piu Or. They are architecture students at the City University of Hong Kong. **Acknowledgement** City University of Hong Kong, Department of Building and Construction, Division of Building Science and Technology.

Jungle Fever is a collaboration between Budi Pradono Architects and Angki Purbandono. Budi Pradono Architects is a research-based architectural studio with a focus on contemporary lifestyle, hospitality, and urban design through an inclusive and rigorous methodology of research, expansive collaboration, and experimentation. Angki is an artist based in Indonesia. **Acknowledgement** Conceptual stage: Budi Pradono with Yuli Sri Hartanto, Ajay Mistry, Ricky Setiawan (BPA) and Angki Purbandono; Design development stage: Yuli Sri Hartanto, Ricky Setiawan; Construction Stage: Ricky S, Daryanto, Hendy, Iskandar, Pak Mien; Pipe specialist: Yogo and Co.; acrylic specialist: safei; BPA team: Reini Mailisa, Shinta Devi, Denaldo Armusadi, Jasmine M.Y. Tsoi.

Live Nature is a project by Ida Ki Shan Sze and Billy Wai Ching Chan. They have been collaborating on competitions and non-profit projects and have been awarded in several competitions including the first prize for the 2010 Shanghai Expo Hong Kong Pavilion Concept Design Competition. The architects have worked for various architectural firms including the Architectural Services Department, Rocco Design, Steven Holl, and Herzog & de Meuron. **Acknowledgement** Construction: Edward Fu Tak Fong, Yuan Ping Tang, Nafour Furniture, Gammon Construction Limited, North Ocean Engineering (HK) Ltd., Ying Wah Construction Group.

Main Pavilion is designed by Shigeru Ban, who was born in Tokyo in 1957 and graduated from Cooper Union School of Architecture in New York. In 1985 he established his private practice, Shigeru Ban Architects, in Tokyo. From 1995 through 1999, he was a consultant of the United Nations High Commissioner for Refugees and at the same time established an NGO, Voluntary Architects' Network (VAN). Renowned for his works such as Curtain Wall House, Japan Pavilion, Hannover EXPO 2000, and Nicolas G. Hayek Center, the Centre Pompidou Metz, France, currently under construction is expected to be completed in early 2010. He has received numerous distinctions, including the Grande Medaille France Academie d'Architecture (2004), Arnold W. Brunner Memorial Prize in Architecture (2005), Thomas Jefferson Foundation Medal in Architecture (2005), and National Order of the Legion of Honor in France (2009). He was a Professor at Keio University in Japan from 2001 to 2008 and has served as a jury for the Pritzker Architecture Prize. **Acknowledgement** Grant Suzuki, Shigeru Ban Architects, Gravity Partnership, Union Construction (Group), Isometrix Lighting + Design, and Berkin Lighting.

m.i.r. is an installation by Lineslab, a venture with a contemporary orientation based in Macau and committed to the design of objects, people and events. Lineslab is founded by Manuel C S, an industrial and urban designer and Clara Brito, a contemporary fashion and product designer. The spaces of Lineslab are laboratories for the synthesis of creation and their work focuses on commercial showcasing and a range of creative services.

Mock-Ups in Close-Up Architectural Models in Cinema 1927-2009 is masterminded by Gabu Heindl and Drehli Robnik, who have been compiling mock-up clips from feature films since 2006. Mock-Ups in Close-Up has been shown in New York, Graz, Munich, and San Sebastian. Gabu is an architect, urbanist and researcher in Vienna where she runs her interdisciplinary office GABU Heindl architecture. Drehli is a historian, film theorist, and researcher at Ludwig Boltzmann-Institute for History and Society in Vienna, focusing on the relationship of film aesthetics with history and politics.

Naked Sunbeam 2017: Cantonese Opera is not North Point's Collective Memory are drawings by George Cheuk Hin Wong. His work negotiates between fiction and reality, constantly seeking the dynamic redefinitions and shifting relationships between architecture, art, and design. George graduated from Central Saint Martins College of Art & Design in 2002, Bartlett School of Architecture, University College London in 2005 and from the Masters of Architecture program at the University of Hong Kong in 2009. George is currently a freelance architectural designer, independent stop-motion animator, and a full-time cross disciplinary creative aberrant.

Night and Day HK-SZ: Crisis Fronts Sampler is by Michael Chen and Jason J. Lee. Michael Chen is an architect and academic based in New York City. He is a partner in Normal Projects, a collaborative design practice encompassing architecture, product and furniture design based in New York and Los Angeles. Jason J. Lee is a partner in tentwenty, a design-research studio that engages in a variety of scales of inquiry. Most recently, he completed a residential building adjacent to the High Line in New York. Together, they codirect Crisis Fronts, a research initiative. **Acknowledgement** Faculty Development Grant, Pratt Institute School of Architecture. Project Team: Cole Reynolds, Tai-Li Lee, Roy Zhuang Crisis Fronts Studio members: Jose Blanco, Joanna Cheung, Andres Correa, Ivan Delgado, Nick Garate, Allison Hoffman, Heidi Jandris, Kamilla Litvinov, Sebastian Misiurek, Jeos Oreamuno, Jun Pak, Anna Perelman, Cole Reynolds, Brad Rothenberg, John Seward, Jintana Tantinirundr.

Nɵnspace is produced by Nicolas Sauret and Ashley Wong who are artists, curators, and facilitator.

Paddling Home is by Kacey Wong, a contemporary visual artist based in Hong Kong. His sculpture and installation art explore architecture and the poetics of space. **Acknowledgement** Ching Man Chan and Kai Yan Tsui.

PLANCH™ | The Grand Resource are designed by Jason Austin and Aleksandr Mergold, founders of AUSTIN + MERGOLD. The duo believe in rethinking and repurposing existing resources rather than tapping new ones. They explore local conditions to discover how an efficient and economical reconfiguration of available materials, forms and methods, using the latest technological advances, can result in an improved quality of life for communities and individuals. This approach to sustainable design is particularly well-suited to the economic and ecological crises that we face today. **Acknowledgement** Cornell University Department of Architecture, Cornell Council for the Arts, University of Pennsylvania Department of Landscape Architecture, the Design Trust for Public Space.

Play-ground is by Giorgos Artopoulos and Popi Iacovou, two London based architects. They both hold a diploma in architecture from Aristotle University of Thessaloniki and Masters of Philosophy in Architecture and the Moving Image from the University of Cambridge. Giorgios has a PhD from the University of Cambridge and Popi is pursing a PhD at the Bartlett School of Architecture. They have received awards in design competitions and participated in many exhibitions such as the 63rd Venice Film Festival, La Biennale di Venezia, amongst others.

Pocket Fence installation is by Eric Bunge and Mimi Hoang, founders of New York based nARCHITECTS. Their recent projects range from buildings to ephemeral environments and include the Switch Building in Manhattan, Windshape in France, Ellicott Park in Buffalo, and Villa-Villa in Ordos, China. Recent awards include AIA Design Honor Awards (2007 and 2005), the Architectural League of New York's Emerging Voices (2006), and the MoMA/P.S.1 Young Architects Program (2004). **Acknowledgement** Dominique Gonfard and Julia Chapman.

Post Generic City – Learning From Shenzhen is by architect Laurence Liauw in research collaboration with URBANUS Architects. Laurence's main area of interest is contemporary Chinese urbanism, typological variation and post-generic cities. For Shenzhen and Beijing based URBANUS Architects, the city has become both a field of study and operation, and architectural practice becomes a projective urban device for effecting critical urban change. **Acknowledgement** Sponsor: School of Architecture, The Chinese University of Hong Kong. Exhibition Team: Judy Nga Ting Lee, Julius Yiu Ming Lee, Alex Li Han, Ryan Yip, Siss Hong Xi Yang, Lok Hin Tsang, URBANUS Architects. Research supported by the Shenzhen Planning Bureau (Guangming Branch).

PPRD / Parametric Pearl River Delta is by Tom Verebes, creative director of OCEAN.CN in collaboration with Gao Yan of Crystal Design and Luis Fraguada of Live Architecture Network OCEAN.CN is a consultancy network composed of Tom Verebes, Ercument Gorgul, Andrew Tirta Atmadjaja, Felix Robbins,Richard Wang, and Stephen Wang and is the coordinating hub of a network of specialist design consultants based in

Hong Kong, Beijing, Shanghai, Jakarta, and London. Tom is the leader of a multi-disciplinary team that includes architects, urbanists, engineers, experts in computational design, manufacturing, visualisation, and information communication. OCEAN.CN strives for innovation across a range of scales and types of design projects. **Acknowledgement** Project assistants: Li Bin, Joyce Chan, Crystal Cheung, Kelvin Cheung, Kenneth Cheung, Man Ho Chu, Ariel Ip, John Tso, Chris Tsui, Middle Wong, Buzz Yip. Sponsors: Crystal Design (Hong Kong, London), E-Grow International Trading Shanghai Ltd. (Shanghai).

RMB CITY: A Second Life City Planning is a film by Cao Fei, a Beijing based Chinese artist known for her multimedia installations and videos. She is one of the key artists of a new generation emerging from mainland China. Her works reflect on the rapid and chaotic changes that are occurring in Chinese society today. **Acknowledgement** 2007 Internet Project, courtesy of Vitamin Creative Space, and William Lim.

Second Skin is created by the AVA Project Group. Formed by a group of teachers and students of the Academy of Visual Arts with interest in the interrelations of space and design. The supervisors are Peter Benz and Tricia Flanagan. Participants are Fanny Kam Kwan Chan, Skye Hiu Tan Lam, Sophy Mengmeng Shi, Yuen-Hing Tam, and Abby Mei Hung Wong. **Acknowledgement** Hong Kong Baptist University Academy of Visual Arts.

SL-Tree Prototype 00 is a collaboration between SLHO & Associates Limited and Motorwave Group (Holdings) Limited. SLHO is an architectural firm based in Hong Kong, whose projects include commercial, residential, nature, and social projects. Always experimenting with technology, techniques, and concepts, while pushing the envelope of design, SLHO received the Special Architectural Award from the Hong Kong Institute of Architects Annual Award. Lucien Gambarota is the inventor and founder of Motorwave, a unique technology that has been created and developed in Hong Kong to tap the power of wave motion in order to make electricity, desalinated water, and produce hydrogen. **Acknowledgement** Ho Sai Leung, Douglas Ho, Zeno Yu, Angela Ng, Lourance Leung, Sunny Yu, Lesley Leung, Denise Tsang.

Street Life installation is by David Benjamin and Soo-in Yang, directors of The Living, an architecture firm that emphasizes open-source research and design that seeks collaboration both within and outside the field of architecture. They have exhibited in museums internationally and won numerous prizes, among them the Architect Magazine R+D Award in 2008. Both David and Soo-in are co-directors of the Living Architecture Lab at the Columbia Graduate School of Architecture, Planning and Preservation. **Acknowledgement** Sponsor in part: Korea Institute of Design Promotion.

Tabula Rasa Reversal is by Anderson Leung Chung Lee, director of Index Architecture Ltd with his team: May Ki Wing Ho, Hover Yang Fei Li, and Sai

Chun Yung. Anderson has won design awards from HKAIA, HKIA, and the Southwest Pacific Regional AIA. He is Assistant Professor of Architecture at the University of Hong Kong and holds a Bachelor of Science from the University of Michigan and a Masters of Architecture from Princeton University. **Acknowledgement** OPTILED lighting international ltd., Ever Green Decoration Works Co. Ltd.

Tetraphobia is by RAD, a planning and architecture design office founded by Aaron Tan in 1994. The office aims to redefine new architecture and urbanism of the emerging cities in Asia and draws on the global nature of its urban architectural experiences to develop new contemporary approaches. RAD has a team of multinational origins and have projects throughout China, Korea, Taiwan and Hong Kong. **Acknowledgement** Aaron Tan, Paolo Dalla Tor, Ewelina Magda Tereszczenko, Alberto Cipriani, Miguel Cormier, Catty Chan, and Stephen Wikeley

The Floating Grassroot Market is a collaboration between Wallace Chang Yin Mo Tse and Marta Bohlmark. Wallace is Associate Professor at the School of Architecture at the Chinese University of Hong Kong. Previously he was a Visiting Scholar at Harvard University. Yin Mo Tse is an art culture practitioner and currently director of Art Products Promotion. Mart Bohlmark lives in Guangzhou, China where she is involved in the planning and exploration of possibilities for new urban development, public education, and green arts along the Kai Tak River. **Acknowledgement** School of Architecture, Chinese University of Hong Kong, UMAG, Art Products Promotion, 1a space.

The High Line is by Diller Scofidio + Renfro and James Corner Field Operations. Diller Scofidio + Renfro is an internationally renowned interdisciplinary studio based in New York City. For three decades, they have realized work of civic and cultural significance through a practice that uniquely straddles all fields of design (urban, landscape, interior, product, exhibition) with media oriented installations including performing art productions. James Corner Field Operations is based in New York City and creates intelligent, high-quality landscape design solutions for cities, landscapes, and public spaces.

The Learning Cloud is designed by Salottobuono. They investigate the urban space by codifying cognitive devices and triggering transformation strategies. Salottobuono's research and design work has been exhibited at the Italian Pavilion during the 11th International Architecture Exhibition in Venice. **Acknowledgement** Assistants: Federica Trevisan, Claire Price, Giorgio Renzi; Tongji University, VIU visiting students: Ying Jie Zhu, Chao Zhi Pan, Li Jun Cao, Qing Xia. Sponsor: DWS Additive Manufacturing.

The Projecting Window installation is by Sophia Ip, Haynie Sze, Edith Li, and Eva Chan. They are practicing architects who graduated from the Chinese University of Hong Kong and have participated in many local

art projects, exhibitions and community projects including the Whistling Aloft outdoor sculpture in Hong Kong Science Museum (Sophia Ip & Haynie Sze) and Smiling Up High, a short-listed sculpture for Sai Kung District Council Public Art Project 2009 (Sophia Ip, Edith Li & Haynie Sze). **Acknowledgement** Hip Hing Construction Company Ltd., Quon Hing Concrete Co., Ltd., ROC Advertising Co.

The Stage is a collaboration between Daniel Wu, Edward Huang, and Teddy Lo. Actor Daniel Wu and architect Edward Huang have known each other since design school and have collaborated on projects as part of DE-sign that includes restaurant, office spaces and Daniel's own home. When not acting, Daniel runs his own management company, Revolution Talent Management and is a co-founder of the creative online social networking platform alivenotdead. Edward's design firm DRIB-DESIGN works on various retail and residential projects in Hong Kong and China. Teddy Lo is the founder and Chief Vision Officer of LEDARTIST, an innovative LED experience design company. Teddy has exhibited in the US, Europe, and Asia. Recognized in international art circles as a pioneering figure in the tech-art scene, Teddy's best known works present a fusion of technological and aesthetic elements. **Acknowledgement** LEDARTIST, Traxon Lighting System and Solutions, Ray On Construction Co. Ltd, Gravity Partnership Ltd.

too much light interactive installation is by Leopold Fiala, Stijn Deferm, and Karta Healy. Leopold was born in Munich and studied graphic design and photography in Darmstadt, Germany. His past installations were exhibited in Germany and New Zealand. Stijn is principally responsible for the design and development of riese und müller bikes. He worked on the Gemini, Frog, and Avenue models. A university-qualified product designer from Belgium, he developed the new Birdy which received the prestigious iF Product Design Award. Stijn took part in World Cup downhilling and has a wealth of experience in suspension technology and aluminum design. Karta is the founder of the brand Two n Fro, where he designs everything one needs for inner city cycling. The intelligently constructed range, covers clothing and accessories, from shoes and shirts to head lamps and helmets, and offers flexible gear for all situations on and off the bike.

UNStudio | The Changing Room | Music Theatre are films by UNStudio, an international architecture studio founded by Ben van Berkel and Caroline Bos in Amsterdam. They work in the fields of urbanism, infrastructure, public, private, and utility buildings on different scale levels. Current projects are the restructuring of the station area in Arnhem, a masterplan for Basauri, and a music theatre for Graz. Past projects include the Mercedes-Benz Museum in Stuttgart, a façade and interior renovation for the Galleria Department store in Seoul and a private villa up-state New York.

Urban Adapter is by Rocker-Lange Architects founded by Christian J.

Lange and Ingeborg M. Rocker. Christian is a German architect and Assistant Professor of Architecture in the Department of Architecture at the University of Hong Kong. In 2006 he cofounded Rocker-Lange Architects with Ingeborg, a research and design practice that currently has projects in Germany and China. His research is focused on conceptual digital design and innovative digital fabrication techniques. **Acknowledgement** Assisted by Yeung Ho Man and Norman Ung.

Urban Picnic is designed by Jason Carlow, director of the Hong Kong based design firm C:A+D, Carlow Architecture and Design, and Assistant Professor of Architecture at the University of Hong Kong. He holds a Bachelors of Art in Visual and Environmental Studies from Harvard University and a Master of Architecture from Yale University. His design work, research and teaching are centered on the relationship between digital and traditional modes of drawing, modeling and fabrication. **Acknowledgement** DuPont™ Corian® Solid Surfaces, Speed Top (Hong Kong) Limited, Ecovision Asia Ltd, Greenback International Ltd, BOAsia Ltd / BAMBOA, and Ricci Wong.

West Kowloon Walled City installation is designed by Douglas Young of G.O.D., a lifestyle brand from Hong Kong. The name means "live better" in Cantonese. Founded in 1996, the company prides itself on finding inspiration from local culture. The long-term vision is to foster pride in the local community by defining a distinct cultural identity. **Acknowledgement** G.O.D. Limited.

World Organization of Transients is by Oval Partnership, a company that designs and executes pleasurable, desirable, and financially-feasible lifestyle projects which embrace the principles of sustainable development. They place great importance on environmental protection, community development and heritage conservation, utilizing digital technologies as key tools for achieving these goals.

xDesign is created by Natalie Jeremijenko, an artist whose background includes biochemistry, physics, neuroscience, and precision engineering. Natalie's projects explore socio-technical change and have been exhibited by several museums and galleries, including the MASSMoCA, the Whitney, Smithsonian Cooper-Hewitt. A 1999 Rockefeller Fellow, she was recently named one of the 40 most influential designers by I.D. Magazine. Natalie is the director of the xDesign Environmental Health Clinic at New York University.

Event Credits

Chief Financial Officer for Bank of America's Asia Region, having worked in San Francisco, Singapore, Tokyo and Hong Kong.

William Yu joined the World Wildlife Fund in 2008 as head of the climate program. He is responsible for leading both public and business engagement programs on climate change including the Climateers Carbon Calculator, Low Carbon Manufacturing Programme, and the Low-Carbon Office Operations Programme. He completed his PhD at the University of Cambridge and holds an Executive MBA degree from Thunderbird, the American Graduate School of International Management. He is a member of the environmental campaign committee under the Environmental Bureau. William is on the sustainability panel of several key business corporations and a committee member of the Eco-village scheme proposed by the Professional Green Building Council.

Official Opening Ceremony Guest of Honour, the Honourable Henry Tang Ying Yen, GBM, GBS, JP, Chief Secretary for Administration; Shenzhen Vice Mayor Tang Jie; Carrie Yau, Permanent Secretary for Home Affairs, Home Affairs Bureau; Anna S Y Kwong (HKIA), Po Yiu Tam (HKIP), Raymond Fung (HKDA), Shigeru Ban, Alan Lo, Eric Schuldenfrei, Frank Yu, Marisa Yiu.

Exhibition School Tours Biennale limited edition educations packets designed by ESKYIU. Education Tours supported by the West Kowloon Cultural District Authority, Education Bureau, Hong Kong Federation of Youth Groups. Assisted by Golin Harris. Tour Guides: Laurent Wong, Flora Ting Fong Lee, Gigi Li (HKFYG) and Youth Ambassadors: Lau Miu Yee, Angie Leung, Lui Kit Yin.

Building Asia Brick by Brick My Cultural City: West Kowloon, a pre-Biennale event. Student workshops, sponsored by LEGO, supported by HKFYG with 400 students. Partners: Peoples Architecture, Federation of Youth Group, Hong Kong University (faculty of architecture), room to read, Sino, G2000, Starbucks, HKDC, Greenery Music Ltd., Sky Magazine, Ketchum and HKAoD.

BYOBackyard, BYOBowl, BYOPatch of Green Home supported by the Hong Kong Federation of Youth Groups, the Organic Farm, Adder Fung, Pad Chu, student volunteers of the University of Hong Kong, Sustainable Ecological Ethical Development Foundation. Guests of Honor: Michael Suen, Secretary for Education, Florence Hui, Under Secretary for Home Affairs.

Chinese New Year Pun Choi Feast is sponsored by HKIA, O.S.J. Funds for the Elderlies, Kowloon Federation of Association, Andrew Lee King Fun & Associates Ltd., T.K. Tsui & Associates Ltd. Supported By Yau Tsim Mong District councilors.

Garden in the City: Towards a Humanistic Architecture lecture by Professor Leo Ou-fan Lee. Panelists: Ou Ning, Chief curator, Shenzhen; Marisa K. S. Yiu, Chief curator, Hong Kong; Pauline J. Yao, Curator, Shenzhen; Eric Schuldenfrei. Co-organizers: School of Humanities, Faculty of Arts; HKU Project for Public Culture, the Journalism and Media Studies Centre, HKU; Sponsors: MUSE magazine; Azalea (1972) Endowment Fund & HKU Culture and Humanities Fund.

Pecha Kucha Night BYOBiennale x DETOUR on the Beach, speakers: Alberto Gobbino Ciszak & Andrea Caruso Dalmas, Alvin Yip, Douglas Young, Gabu Heindl, Haewon Shin, Jason J. Lee & Michael Chen, Karta Healy, Ludovico Centis, Martin Smith, Tom Verebes.

Planning for Cultural Districts in Hong Kong and the Pearl River Delta was organized by K K Ling, the immediate past president of The Hong Kong Institute of Planners. Discussion was led by Augustine Ng, the former project director of the West Kowloon Cultural District Authority; José Sai

Peng Chui, president of the Macao Urban Planning Institute; Professor Lu Qiis of the South China University of Technology; and Luo Min Wang, Professor and Director of Urban Planning and Design Research Institute at the University of Shenzhen.

BYOBands performances by Kung Chi Shing, William Lane, A Roller Control, Poubelle International, The Yours, Unixx, SaxMax, Jing Wong, Mike Yuen, Shadow Kim, Yank Wong, Wilson Tsang, Les Fong, Suitman, Him Lo, Hong Kong New Music Ensemble. Closing band F+B sponsor: Lan Kwai Fong Holdings Ltd.

Kadoorie Workshops pot planting and herbal tea workshops supported by Idy Wong, Wynton Tsui, Sustainable Living and Agriculture Department Kadoorie Farm and Botanic Garden.

Waterfront Bi-City Conversations post-forum event supported by Whotel Living Room.

Xu Bing Forest Project Workshops supported by the Hong Kong Federation of Youth Groups, Hong Kong Ambassadors of Design, Creative YMCArts, Alan Lau.

myCity-to-Pattern workshop by ilataaj (Andrew Tirta).

Invasion and Infringement at the Projecting Window by South Ho, photography artist.

Hong Kong Waterworks: Memory, Water, and Architecture in cooperation with the HKU Summer Institute for the Arts and Humanities; Co-sponsor: the US Embassy: Hong Kong. Director and Choreographer: Kanta Kochhar-Lindgren, PhD, Director of Folded Paper; Dancers: Boniface Ho, Christine Kehr, Courtenay Shivrattan, Keene Chung. Mary Jane Tang, Ming Pak; Singer: Rani Olafsdottir; Saxophonist: Jacky Leung; Composer: Steve Hui; Video Artist: Domting. Photography: John Batten; Research Team: Yang Yeung, John Batten, Rani Olafsdottir; Additional Photography: Xiaoyi Eva Fei, and Students from Indus Valley School of Arts and Architecture, Karachi, Pakistan; Production Manager: Ma Siu Ki; Stage Designer: Bill Cheung; Mixer: Jason Wong; Camera Person: Rex Chan; Production Assistant: Denise Cheuk.

Drivers of Change Forum organized by ARUP. Facilitators of the forum: Dr Colin Clinton (Institution of Civil Engineers president 2004/05, FICE, FIHT, FInstCES), Dr Jack Pappin (FHKIE, MICE), Dr Ricky Tsui (Cantab), Debra Lam (Managing effort in UN Climate Change summit, LEED® AP), Dr Young Wong (MIFireE, MHKIE), Andrew Mole (MIStructE, LEED® AP), Freda Chu (MICE, MHKIE), Paul Lam (MIEAust) and Anita Siu (MHKIE, MICE, MIStructE). Guest facilitators: Eric Schuldenfrei and Lucien Gambarota, MotorWave.

Image Credits

Photographs by Aaron Chow
viii   Biennale Blueprint
p6   Biennale Main Pavilion
p36-41   A People's Biennale of Architecture and Urbanism Forum
p180   Biennale Main Pavilion
p194-199   BYOBands
p236   Fa Pai Rides WKCD exhibit
p256   Hong Kong Skyline
p303   BYOBicycle: Critical Mass
p342   The Future of the Bi-City Biennale Forum
p431   Biennale "B" Signage

Photographs by Alvin Ku
p25   West Kowloon Walled City exhibit
p202   Urban Adapter exhibit
p204   Bring Your Own Biennale Map
p234   m.i.r. exhibit
p277-279   Boundaries exhibit
p367   Dutch Design Chair exhibit
p368-369   BYOBench: Sitting Device exhibit

Photograph by Barry Jacques and David Smith
p400   Double Double exhibit

Photographs by Calvin Tsoi
p56   The Stage exhibit
p304   The Stage exhibit

Photograph by Chris Choy
p370   BYOBench: BYOBond

Photograph by Drifting City
p266   dreamgrove exhibit

Photograph by Eddy Yip
p358   BYOB Reading Café

Photographs by Eric Schuldenfrei
vi   West Kowloon Cultural District Site
x   Eco Farm exhibit
p22   West Kowloon Walled City exhibit
p24   West Kowloon Walled City exhibit
p31   "excavation" exhibit
p42   BYOBands: Suitman
p44   Signage Performance
p47   Cultural Classroom
p48   Eco Farm exhibit
p58-64   Eco Farm exhibit

p70   Green Panel System and Eco-Turf System exhibit
p80-81   The High Line exhibit
p82-83   Idea of a Tree exhibit
p85-86   farmScape exhibit
p88   World Organization of Transients exhibit
p92   West Kowloon site
p95   Painting by God exhibit
p96-99   Live Nature exhibit
p101-105 The Projecting Window exhibit
p119   Heaven on Earth exhibit
p120   Two Wongs Going To Sea
p122-124   Second Skin exhibit
p134   SL-Tree Prototype 00 exhibit
p137   SL-Tree Prototype 00 exhibit
p139   xDesign exhibit
p140   PLANCH™ & The Grand Resource exhibit
p142   Draw Your Future with Light and Shadow exhibit
p155   Bloody Haze exhibit
p178   Biennale Main Pavilion Detail
p184-185   Hong Kong WaterWorks
p202   ffformica exhibit
p206   Graham' Super exhibit
p208   "excavation" exhibit
p212   West Kowloon Walled City exhibit
p226-229   Cabinet of Curiosities exhibit
p238   "3:15's Rain Catcher" exhibit
p240-243   Graham' Super exhibit
p251   "community" event
p252-253   "excavation" exhibit
p260-261   Two Wongs Going to Sea
p264   The Floating Grassroot Market exhibit
p268   Abandoned Furniture exhibit
p280-283   Signage Performance
p306   Pocket Fence exhibit
p309   West Kowloon Cultural District Site
p310   PPRD / Parametric Pearl River Delta exhibit
p320   Pocket Fence exhibit
p322-323   The Learning Cloud exhibit
p324-327   Asia's World City: Hybrid Hong Kong + Shenzhen exhibit
p328   Interconnectivity exhibit
p345   Signage Performance
p366   Urban Picnic exhibit
p372-373   Bottom Up exhibit
p374   Flux exhibit
p376   BYOBall: West Kowloon Football Club
p378   BYOBall: West Kowloon Football Club
p381   Fossils of Future exhibit
p383   Glow exhibit

p385-387   Pedestrian exhibit
p403   film exhibits
p405   Two Wongs Going to Sea
p407   Action and Repose Design Workshop exhibit
p408   Hyperbolic Rattan Bench exhibit
p434   The Stage exhibit
p438-439   West Kowloon Walled City exhibit
p444   Four Curators
p460   farmScape exhibit

Photographs by Evangelo Costadimas
p244   "excavation" exhibit
p246 right   "regeneration" off-site installation
p247   "regeneration"
p248   "excavation" exhibit

Photographs by Future Cities Lab
p158-161   Glaciarium exhibit

Photograph by Giorgos Artopoulos
p380   Play-ground

Photograph by GOD
p33   West Kowloon Walled City exhibit

Photograph by HKIP
p355   Planning for Cultural Districts in Hong Kong Forum

Photograph by Iwan Baan
p73   The High Line

Photographs by Jiaxin Chum
iv   Biennale Main Pavilion Construction
p18   Biennale Main Pavilion and helicopter
p170   Biennale Main Pavilion Construction
p270-271   BYOBlanket: Yoga
p360   BYOBooks
p468   Biennale Main Pavilion Construction

Photograph by John Batten
p217   Here to Tai Kok Tsui

Photographs by Kacey Wong
p111   Paddling Home exhibit
p115-116   Paddling Home exhibit

Photographs by Kate Orff
p362-365   BYOBooks: Flowers That Are Still Here exhibit

456

Endnotes

p27   The Bi-city Biennale: A Catalyst for Change?

[1] Ching Cheong, "Catalyst for change," *South China Morning Post*, June 6, 2008.

p103   Bay Window Boom

[1] Practice Notes for Authorized Persons, Registered Structural Engineers and Registered Geotechnical Engineers, PNAP 68/ APP-19 – Projections in relation to site coverage and plot ratio, Building (Planning) Regulations 20 & 21, paragraph 5.

[2] Criteria of projecting bay window construction for exemption of GFA and plot ratio stated in PNAP 68/ APP-19:
a. the projecting window is from domestic accommodation only;
b. only one such projecting window is located on one external wall and situated in any one room;
c. the total areas of the projecting windows together with the louvres/ open grilles, if any, for the purpose of shielding of air-conditioning plants placed underneath or above the projecting windows, do not exceed 50% of the total areas of the façade of the said floor on the same elevation;
d. the extent of the projection is not more than 500 mm from the face of the main external wall;
e. the base is not less than 500 mm above finished floor level;
f. the top is not less than 500 mm from the underside of the finish ceiling;
g. and the window complies fully with B(P)R 3A. For the purposes of this requirement, the height of 1100 mm protective barrier will be measured from floor level and any part of the window within this dimension should be fixed or otherwise suitably protected in line with clause (2) of the Regulation.

p114   Distant Waters

[1] 2005 report by Jiu.J. Jiao, Chiman Leung, Kouping Chen, Jianmin Huang, Runqiu Huang, "Preliminary Studies on Physical and Chemical Processes in the Subsurface System in the Land Reclaimed from the Sea." Collections of Coastal Geo-Environment and Urban Development, p399-407, China Dadi Publishing House, Beijing, China.

[2] Land Utilization in Hong Kong, Hong Kong Planning Department map, LUM/HK/75, 2007 edition, printed by the Government Logistics Department.

p168   The Crab-Eating Mongoose's Right to the City

[1] Martin Albrow, John Eade, Jörg Dürrschmidt, and Neil Washbourne, "The Impact of Globalization on Sociological Concepts," in John Eade, ed., *Living the Global City: Globalization as a Local Process* (London: Routledge, 1997).

[2] Giorgio Agamben gives a good summary in a chapter devoted to Uexküll in *The Open: Man and Animal*, trans. Kevin Attell (Stanford: Stanford University Press, 1994).

[3] Eric Baratay and Elisabeth Hardouin-Fugier, *Zoo: A History of Zoological Gardens in the West* (London: Reaktion, 2002).

[4] Figure from Agriculture, Fisheries and Conservation Department (AFCD) of the Hong Kong Administrative Region Government.

p314   Landscape Infrastructures

[1] I first used the term "artificial ecology" in an architectural context for an article on the work of MVRDV published in 1997: Stan Allen, *"Artificial Ecology" Assemblage 34*, (December 1997), 107–109. At that time, my understanding of ecology was fairly intuitive; this interest led in turn to the work of Gregory Bateson, which has been the basis for the further elaboration of these early arguments.

[2] Gregory Bateson, *Steps to an Ecology of Mind* (Chicago: Univ. of Chicago Press, 1972) 457.

[3] Charles Waldheim writes: "I coined the term "landscape urbanism" in 1996 based on conversations with James Corner on the notion of "landscape as urbanism." The neologism formed the basis of a conference at the Graham Foundation in Chicago (1997). Cited in " *Center 14: On Landscape Urbanism*, p. 303; see also Grahame Shane, "The Emergence of Landscape Urbanism," *Harvard Design Magazine*, no. 19 (Fall 2003/ Winter 2004); "Landscape Urbanism: A Genealogy," *Praxis*, no. 4, Landscapes (2002); and the two readers: *Recovering Landscape*, ed. James Corner (New York: Princeton Architectural Press, 1999) and *The Landscape Urbanism Reader*, ed. Charles Waldheim (New York, Princeton Architectural Press, 2006).

[4] See Pierre Belanger, "Landscape as Infrastructure" *Landscape Journal*, Spring 2009. Belanger Organized a conference with the same title at the College of Architecture, University of Toronto, Fall, 2008, which could be seen to mark that transition from landscape urbanism to landscape infrastructure.

[5] See Stan Allen, "Infrastructural Urbanism" in *Points + Lines* (New York, Princeton Architectural Press, 1999). This text originally written 1997; Reprinted in *Center 14: On Landscape Urbanism*, Dean Almy, Editor, (Austin, University of Texas at Austin, 2007) pp. 174-181

[6] James Corner, "Terra Fluxus" in *The Landscape Urbanism Reader*, ed. Charles Waldheim (New York, Princeton Architectural Press, 2006) p. 31

[7] Aldo Rossi, *The Architecture of the City*, English translation, (Cambridge MA, MIT Press and the Institute for Architecture and Urban Studies, 1982) p. 29

Sources

p90   C. Y. Jim. "The country parks programme and countryside conservation in Hong Kong." *The Environmentalist*. Volume 6, Number 4, 259-270, DOI: 10.1007/BF02238057.

p91   Interview with Prof. Jim Chi-yung. UPFRONT. *Hong Kong Magazine*. Friday, May 27, 2011: 5.

p106   Housing Authority, Rating and Valuation Department, 2008

p107   Housing – C. Y. Leung. The Market and Public Policy, BRE Advanced Lecture Series, Department of Building and Real Estate, Hong Kong Polytechnic University.

p108   CB Richard Ellis. Market View, Hong Kong Luxury Residential. First Quarter, 2011.

p109   Hong Kong: The Facts. < http://www.gov.hk/en/about/abouthk/ factsheets/docs/population.pdf>, January 2011.

p153   Council for Sustainable Development. <http://www.susdev.gov.hk/ html/en/council/Paper01-11e.pdf>.

p166   *Hong Kong Yearbook* 2009.

p167   HKSAR Government Press Release. <http://www.info.gov.hk/gia/ general/201105/17/P201105170187.htm>. Tuesday, May 17, 2011.

p289-290   UNFPA China, 2006.

Publication Notes

Catching Up with Nature is a condensed version of a profile of Jim Chi-yung that appeared in the April 2010 edition of Muse magazine.

Interstitial Spaces is a version of an essay featured in Artforum magazine © Artforum, Summer, 2010, by Lars Nittve.

As a lover of Hong Kong and culture, it has been a privilege to be part of the Biennale as a member of the Bravo Biennale Committee.

Organizing the Biennale has been a challenging experience, as vision and passion are often understood differently by parties involved. What keeps us going is our belief that Hong Kong deserves better - better cultural education and activities for our people, better definition and recognition as a cultural destination in our own right. Culture is not made on the production floor. It cannot be captured by dollar value and square footage. It is not about getting a job done. Rather, it is an ongoing pursuit of a vision of who we are, as a city and its population.

We are part of the making of the Biennale through our attendance. I urge us all to bring to the Biennale our hearts and our minds. With bravo, we are all makers of the culture and future of Hong Kong.

– Cherry Chan

All arts and design are closely interlinked. This Biennale provides an open platform allowing the arts, design and the environment to cross fertilize and inspire, creating new artistic expressions and giving rise to new design solutions. BYOB is a prime example of out of the box thinking and creative collaboration across the different disciplines. The search for new growth in creativity, requires curiosity and courage to experiment. This is when breakthroughs happen. BYOB Hong Kong also calls to attention that our natural environment as well as built environment must develop hand in hand. Sustainability is a very relevant goal we must pursue as our world faces many an ecological crisis from old patterns of building and development. Design must address this issue and provide solutions. The arts communicates this message by calling our attention to the beauty and fragility of our world. This crossroad provides the many creative and innovative possibilities we have to build a sustainable future.

– Marissa Fung Shaw

As one of the celebration programmes of the 60th Anniversary of the Founding of the Nation, the joint synergies of Hong Kong Bi-City Biennale create the exhibition as a cultural exchange platform between local and mainland professionals. City Mobilization: Bring Your Own Biennale invites everyone to participate in the exhibition, to "re-think" the relationship between architecture and culture and its engagement with Shenzhen, China and the rest of the world. The Bi-City Biennale is a genuine exchange of creativity among professionals, with the local and international exhibitors presenting their creative and innovative works for Hong Kong and overseas audiences.

– Anna Kwong

Hong Kong Curatorial Team

Chief Curator
Marisa Yiu

Curator for Arts, City Integration, and Events
Alan Lo

Curator for Exhibition, Education, Film, and Media
Eric Schuldenfrei

Curator for Architecture, Urbanism and Landscape
Frank Yu

Project Manager
Amber Young

Project Officer
Sam Yu

Curatorial Coordinators
Chow Kayan
Sze Pui Ki
Janice Ho
Celine Chan

Biennale Film
Vanir Chan, Kyna So, Kin Cheong Chan,
Jeff Wong, Janus Li and music by Jonny Falls Over

Architectural and Planning Team

Gravity Partnership Ltd.
Claude Wong
Wang Ho
Solomon Fong

Exhibition, Design, and Fabrication

ESKYIU
Nick Gu
Jiaxin Chum

Site Coordination Support
Woo Sir
Albert Poon
Eva Tiedemann

Quantity Surveyors
Yam Kwan Sum
Daisy Kam Lan Yeung

Structural Engineer
Michael Tai Chun Ting

BYOBlueprint Publication Team

Directors
Marisa Yiu
Eric Schuldenfrei

Editors
Winnie So
Marisa Yiu
Eric Schuldenfrei
Bouree Lam

Graphic Designers
Jiaxin Chum
Sze Pui Ki

Editorial Support
Chow Kayan

Translators
Cecilia Lam
Kriss Wong

Printer
Icicle Group

Biennale Maps
Printed by Card Kingdom

Biennale Education Packets
Designed by ESKYIU
Sponsored by WKCDA

BYOB Steering Committee
The Hong Kong Institute of Architects
Hong Kong Institute of Planners
Hong Kong Designers Association
Alice Yeung (Co-Chairlady)
Alvin Yip (Co-Chairman)
Ivan Fu
Clement Cheng
Raymond Fung
Anna S Y Kwong
Bernard Lim
Kar Kan Ling
Rocco Yim
Weijen Wang
Kam Sing Wong
Stanley Wong

Registrar, HKIA
Rita Cheung

Senior Manager, HKIA
Vivien Sie

Project Officer, 2009 HK-SZ Biennale, HKIA
Tara Chan

International Advisory Group
Shigeru Ban
Wowo Ding
Joseph Grima
Brett Steele
Mark Wigley
Ben van Berkel
Pun Siu-fai

BRAVO Biennale Committee
Allan Zeman
Margaret Brooke
Marissa Fung-Shaw
Nicole Garnaut
Andrew Kinoshita
Kai-Yin Lo
Bryant Lu
Joanne Ooi
William To
Cherry Chan
Christabel Lee
Alan Lau
Monica Chan
Patrick Ma
Dev Suj

Academic Committee
Daniel Chua
Laurent Gutierrez
Puay Peng Ho
Lorraine Justice
Ralph Lerner
Laurence Liauw
Leslie Lu
Valerie Portefaix
Joseph Francis Wong
Paul Chu
Yuen Ying Chan

Principal Sponsors

Home Affairs Bureau
The Government of the Hong Kong
Special Administrative Region

60th Anniversary of the Founding of the
People's Republic of China

Gold Sponsors
Ambassadors of Design
Pacific Coffee Company

Official Hospitality Partner
W Hotels Worldwide

Official Eco Material Sponsor
JEB Group
Infinity

Official Youth Partner
The Hong Kong Federation of Youth Groups

Advertising Sponsors
MTR
megaBOX
The Luk Hoi Tong Co., Ltd.
Sun Hung Kai Properties

Official Green Wall Sponsor
Strongly International Limited

Ecofarm Sponsor
Cheung Ying Wai, Eric

Good Friend
Cargo Services Far East
Duncan Jepson

Best Friends
Consulate General of the Kingdom of the Netherlands

Friends
Chung Chi Ping, Roy
The Annie Wong Leung Kit Wah Art Foundation
Limited
Oscar V. T. Chow
Manhattan Holdings

Lighting Support
traxon
Isometric Lighting Design

Education Partners
Aedas
Kadoorie Farm & Botanic Garden

Symposium Partner
ARUP

Partners
ESKYIU
Gravity Partnership Ltd.
Press Room Group
Blake's Advisors
Domus China

Education Sponsors
Adobe
Autodesk

Events Partners
DETOUR 2009
DIESEL

Media Partners
Asia Tatler Hong Kong Edition
City Magazine
Financial Times
South China Morning Post
Time Out Hong Kong
U Magazine

Official Radio Station
881903.com

Printing Sponsored by
Card Kingdom (Asia) Ltd.
Icicle Group
Standard (Chan's) Corp. Ltd

The Biennale Curatorial Team thanks
Victor Lo
Ronald Arculli
Winifred Engelbrecht-Gresges
William Yiu
Michael Suen
Florence Hui
Cathy Chu
Augustine Ng
Eve M.Y Tam
Edmond Kong-mo Chung

The Pawn, Watermark, Christina Lo, Winnif Pang, Andy Ho, Adder Fung, Matt McGuire, Frendy Wong, James Beeton, Yuen Lup Fun, Louis Kau, Benny Chan, Chau Chun-Wing, CS Koo, Platteen Tsang, Iman Fok, Duncan Jepson, Derek Hung Chiu-wah, Benny Yeung, Vicki Kwok, Grace Cheng, Christina Dean, Carl Ng, Leah Kim, Daniel Wu, Bonnie Chan, Claire Chan, Josephine Cheung, Claire Melwani, Anca Bal, Daniel Molloy, Regina Chan, Velentina Ma, Jane Ram, Idy Wong, Laura Weeks, Robin Leung, William Tang, Randy Kalish, Albert Chong, Tiana Harilela, Chee-may Chow, Florine Tang, Matthew Jung, Gerry Erasme, Charlie Koolhaas, Euphen Wong, Candy Lau, Alex Seno, Desiree Au, Miranda Wong, Andrew Chow, Ricky Tsui, Michele Orlando, Edward Bean, Robert Schuddeboom, Caitlin Lam, Evelien Brinkerink, Anthony Ng, Calvin Tsoi, Sherman Wu, Dr. Jaime Yeung, IR Dr Wong Yuk Lung, Dr. Steven Tsang, Raymond Wan, Alvin Ma, Joshua Roberts, Mei Tam, Yvette Lam, Karen Leung, Steve Mok, Michael Leung, Janet Chan, Benjamin Tsang, Vitalis Wong, Eugenia Yiu, Tina Troester, Larry Tsoi, Maggie Ma, Cheung Hei Wai, Stephen Ip, Keith Chan, Irene Li, Thomas Cheng, Javian Tang, Ricci Wong, Victor Leung, Brooks Yang, Daniel Greteman, Judy Kwok, Chak Tsz Kin Kennith, Fiona Sze, Carla Lung, Albert Chan, Joan Kwong, Vivian Xu, Connie Ng, Ricky Tsui, Andrew Mole, Klas Ehnemark, Linda So, Fanny Sze, Ou Ning, Beatrice Galilee, Kayoko Ota, Wei Wei Shannon, Pauline J. Yao.

Instant Culture
architecture and urbanism as a collective process

Published by MCCM Creations 2011
www.mccmcreations.com
info@mccmcreations.com

Editors
Marisa Yiu, Eric Schuldenfrei

Editorial Consultant
Gavin Keeney

Designer
ESKYIU

Editorial and Graphic Assistant
Wesley Ho, Jiaxin Chum

Translator of Xu Bing essay
Cecilia Lam

Transcription of Forums
Bill Chan, Daniel Greteman, Flora Lee, Sanny Ng

The editors wish to thank the following individuals for text and graphic feedback:
Amber Young, Alexandra Seno, Cherry Chan, Cole Roskam, Diana Ng, Euginie Kwok,
John Batten, Joshua Bolchover, Laurent Gutierrez, Marc Brulhart, Mary Chan,
Thomas Crampton, Thuy-Tien Crampton, Valérie Portefaix, Wing Chan, Winnie So, and
to their family members for their encouragement and support: Eric and Milly Yiu,
Elaine Eskesen, Conrad and Leanne Yiu, John Ackerman, and Robin Schuldenfrei.

Additional support towards the *Instant Culture* publication:
Andrew Lee King Fun
Donald Wun Hing Choi

ISBN 978-988-18584-8-1

Supported by

香港藝術發展局
Hong Kong Arts Development Council

Forum Participants

Ada Wong is a solicitor and Justice of the Peace. She is the supervisor of the HKICC Lee Shau Kee School of Creativity and founder of Hong Kong Institute of Contemporary Culture. Amid her many roles in education and politics, she actively promotes art and culture. Ada is a member of the consultation panel of the West Kowloon Cultural District Authority, a council member of the Academy for Performing Arts, on the Board of Governors of Shue Yan University, and on the steering committee of the Review of Urban Renewal Strategy.

Agnes Ng is the chairman of the board of directors of the Hong Kong Architecture Centre, a charity institution that aims at creating new forms of interaction between the general public and architecture.

Alice Yeung is the co-chairlady of the 2007 and 2009 Hong Kong & Shenzhen Bi-City Biennale Steering Committee and a member of the 2008 Venice Biennale Hong Kong Exhibition Steering Committee. Alice graduated from the Bartlett School of Architecture, University of London. She is a member of the Royal Institute of British Architects and the Hong Kong Institute of Architects.

Anna Kwong is an architect and the immediate past president of the Hong Kong Institute of Architects

Augustine Ng is a town planner and civil servant. He was the former project director of the West Kowloon Cultural District Authority working on a temporary basis. When the Authority recruited its own staff, Augustine returned to the government and now works at the Central Policy Unit.

Cao Fei is a contemporary artist. She lives in Beijing where she made her first film, Imbalance 257, as a student at the Guangzhou Academy of Fine Arts. Since then she has participated in more than 100 biennials and exhibitions. Her work crosses the spectrum of documentary to fiction and has appeared in solo exhibitions at the Serpentine Gallery, London (2008); Orange County Museum of Art, Newport Beach, California (2007); Museum Het Domein, Sittard, Netherlands (2006); and Para Site Art Space, Hong Kong (2006). She has participated in the New Museum Triennial (2009); Carnegie International, Pittsburgh (2008); Prospect.1 New Orleans (2008); Yokohama Triennial (2008); and the Istanbul, Lyon, and Venice Biennials (2007). Her work has appeared at the New Museum, New York (2008); Walker Art Center, Minneapolis (2007); P.S.1 Contemporary Art Center, New York (2006); and Asia Society, New York (2006).

Carol Willis is the founder, director, and curator of The Skyscraper Museum. An architectural and urban historian, she has researched, taught, and written about the history of American city building. She is the author of Form Follows Finance: Skyscrapers and Skylines in New York and Chicago (Princeton Architectural Press, 1995). She is an Adjunct Associate Professor of Urban Studies at Columbia University, where since 1989 she has taught in the program The Shape of Two Cities: New York and Paris in The Graduate School of Architecture, Planning and Preservation.

Christine E. Bruckner is the former president of the AIA Hong Kong in 2009-2010 and a founding member of the American Institute of Architects Hong Kong. Christine is an architect, AIA member, LEED AP sustainability consultant, and a chair of multiple advisory and community boards locally and internationally. She has over 15 years experience practicing in the US, Europe, Japan, and HK . She holds degrees from Rice University, Yale University and a PhD from Tokyo University.

Christopher Law is the founding director of Oval Partnership and director of INTEGER China, an organization which promotes intelligent and green developments in China. Chris studied architecture at the Bartlett School of Architecture, University College London. Chris has received numerous accolades including the Architect of the Year Award. His firm received awards from the Royal Academy of Arts, the HKIA, the HKIP, the AIA, the Sustainable Architecture Award, and the Design for Asia Award. He is the chairman of the Family Welfare Society, member of the Tourism Strategy Group, Women's Commission, and the Social Welfare Advisory Committee.

Claude Wong is the principal of Gravity Partnership Limited, an architecture design practice with 40 professionals. Their projects include prestigious planning and architectural design commissions in Hong Kong and China. He is a registered architect and authorized person in Hong Kong, with the PRC Class 1 Registered Architect Qualification. Claude graduated from the Architectural Association in London.

Colin Ward is a partner at Foster + Partners Hong Kong. He studied at the University of Manchester and joined the Hong Kong office of Foster + Partners in 1994 to work on the Chek Lap Kok airport. Upon completion of the airport in 1998 he returned to the London office to work on the new National Stadium at Wembley. In January 2007 he returned to Hong Kong and is currently overseeing the development of projects in Hong Kong, China, and Singapore.

Daniel Patzold is an architect with extensive experience of the challenges of the built environment to fulfill not only functional needs but also to remain meaningful in a cultural and social sense. Daniel has a wide scope of interest in the fine and applied arts and is continually involved in a number of non-architectural projects.

Daniel Wu is an actor born in Berkeley, California. After graduating from the University of Oregon in architecture, Daniel went to Hong Kong to witness the handover. Art film director Yonfan cast him in his film Bishonen in 1998. Since this film debut, he has been featured in over 40 films.

David Benjamin and Soo-In Yang created The Living in 2004. The architecture firm emphasizes open-source research and design, seeks collaboration both within and outside the field of architecture, and views each project as part of larger threads of experimentation and construction. Works by The Living has been exhibited at the Chicago Museum of Science and Industry, the Innovation Lab in Copenhagen, Southern Exposure in San Francisco, and Eyebeam in New York. Winner of awards and widely published, they currently teach at Columbia Graduate School of Architecture, Planning and Preservation, where they are codirectors of the Living Architecture Lab.

David Erdman is the founding partner of davidclovers with Clover Lee. They are committed to innovative work that merges their design sensibility, material and computational expertise with the intellectual and physical resources of Hong Kong, the Pearl River Delta and China. In 2008 the American Academy in Rome awarded David the prestigious Rome Prize. David received degrees from Ohio State University and Columbia University. He was the co-founder of servo and previously worked with Stanley Saitowitz and Greg Lynn Form.

David Gianotten joined OMA in 2008 and became the partner in charge of OMA Asia in 2010, overseeing OMA Hong Kong and Beijing. Selected projects under his supervision include the Shenzhen Stock Exchange, the Taipei Performing Arts Centre, and Chu Hai College in Hong Kong. In 2010 he delivered the OMA conceptual masterplan for the West Kowloon Cultural District. He studied Architecture and Construction Technology at the Eindhoven University of Technology. Before joining OMA he was the managing director and architect of SeARCH.

Debra Lam is a policy and sustainability consultant at ARUP. She recently undertook a two year assignment for Arup in Hong Kong after joining Arup in London in 2007. She specializes in climate change, sustainability, and low-carbon issues. She advised the Vietnamese Government on water and climate resilience, and has been involved in Arup's partnership work with the C40, a group of 40 of the world's largest cities committed to tackling climate change. She also contributed to a report for the World Economic Forum presented at Davos in 2011.

Donald Choi is the managing director of Nan Fung Development Limited with projects in Hong Kong, China, Singapore, and Vietnam, as well as property funds in China. He studied architecture at the Rhode Island School of Design and was the authorized person – architect for the Hong Kong International Airport at Chek Lap Kok. He coedited the book One Hundred Years of Hong Kong Architecture and is the chairman of the Hong Kong Architects Registration Board.

Duncan Jepson is a lawyer by profession and has been involved in a wide range of film and television work. He has produced feature films and received awards from the Newport Beach Film Festival, the Houston Film Festival, the Hong Kong Film awards, Hong Kong Asian Film Festival, and the Best Film Awards (both jury and public awards) at the Lyon Asian Festival 2006. He has made documentaries for Discovery Channel Asia and National Geographic Channel. In 2004 he launched the Asia Literary Review with Nury Vittachi, and organized China's first youth street writing competition in 2005. He runs a charity which funds a school in Kabul and is an advisor to the Child Welfare Scheme.

Duncan Pescod is Justice of the Peace, Permanent Secretary for Transport and Housing, and Director of Housing. He joined the Administrative Service of the Hong Kong Government in 1981. Since then he has served in various bureau and departments, including the former Home Affairs Branch, the former Security Branch, Lands Department, the former Urban Services Department, the former City and New Territories Administration, and the former Civil Service Branch. He was Deputy Commissioner for Tourism from June 2001 to November 2004, Head of the Efficiency Unit, from November 2004 to February 2006, and Special Representative for Hong Kong Economic and Trade Affairs to the European Communities from March 2006 to August 2008. Duncan was the Permanent Secretary for Commerce and Economic Development from August 2008 to May 2010.

Edward Ng is an architect and Professor at the Chinese University of Hong Kong (CUHK), where his specialty is in Environmental and Sustainable Design. He is director of the Sustainable and Environmental Design Programme at CUHK. As an environmental consultant to the Hong Kong SAR Government, he developed the performance based daylight design building regulations and the Air Ventilation Assessment Guidelines. Edward is a daylight and solar energy expert advisor to the Chinese Government. As Visiting Professor of Xian Jiaotong University, China, he is designing ecological schools and building sustainable projects in China. He has twice been the recipient of the International Awards of the Royal Institute of British Architects.

Elizabeth Diller is Professor of Architecture at Princeton University and a founding principal of Diller Scofidio + Renfro, a 50 person interdisciplinary design studio that integrates architecture, the visual arts, and the performing arts. With her partner Ricardo Scofidio they received the MacArthur Foundation "genius" award in 1999-2004, in recognition of their commitment to integrating architecture with issues of contemporary culture. She was made a Fellow of the Royal Institute of British Architects and inducted into the American Academy of Arts and Sciences in 2008. The Guardian named Blur as one of the top 10 buildings of the decade while The New York Times, Los Angeles Times, and The New Yorker named Alice Tully Hall and The High Line among the most culturally significant projects of 2009.

452   **Eugene Tan** is an art historian, critic, and curator. Eugene holds a PhD

in Art History from the University of Manchester. He was previously the director of the Institute of Contemporary Arts Singapore, curator for the Singapore Pavilion at the 2005 Venice Biennale, and co-curator of the inaugural Singapore Biennale in 2006, and former exhibitions director of Osage Gallery, Hong Kong. He is coauthor of the publication Contemporary Art in Singapore and has written for exhibition catalogues, publications, and art magazines such as Art Asia Pacific, Art Review, C-Arts, Contemporary, Flash Art, Metropolis M, and Modern Painters.

Gabu Heindl is an architect, urbanist and garbologist based in Vienna. She studied architecture in Vienna, Tokyo, and at Princeton University and previously worked for de Architekten Cie. in Amsterdam and Diller+Scofidio in New York. Since 2007 she founded GABU Heindl Architektur in Vienna, designing public, cultural, and social buildings as well as urban research projects and publications. Projects include the design of the Austrian Film Museum in Vienna, exhibitions for the European Cultural Capital Linz, and the Art Biennale in Venice 2009.

Gregory Yager is director of the urban design and master planning studio at RTKL Shanghai after serving as director of RTKL's urban design in the London office. An architect andurban planner he brings to RTKL over 25 years of experience in urban design and master planning of mixed-use, new community, urban and suburban development projects. He became the senior vice president in 2007.

Hendrik Tieben is a registered architect in Germany, urban designer, and Assistant Professor at the School of Architecture of The Chinese University of Hong Kong. He received his architectural education in Germany, Italy, and Switzerland. In his doctoral dissertation at ETH Zurich he studied the relationship of architecture, history, memory, and identity in context of the German reunification. Hendrik is a founding member and academic advisor of the Hong Kong Institute of Urban Design.

Ian Hau joined Woods Bagot in 2007 as the Urban Design Practice Leader of Asia, responsible for master planning and urban design projects in Asia. Ian's experience includes mixed-use master planning, exhibition, convention centers, sports, cultural, waterfront, and lifestyle projects in Australia, China, and the Middle East. Ian was educated at the University of Technology Sydney and worked for Australian architect Philip Cox from 1995 to 2003. Practicing architectural and urban design over 12 years, Ian is one of the founding members of the Hong Kong Institute of Urban Design and an International Committee member of the Planning institute of Australia.

Jason J. Lee is a partner in tentwenty, a design-research studio that engages in a variety of scales of inquiry. Their investigations include installations to architecture; interiors to brand strategies; and landscapes to urbanism. He is currently Visiting Assistant Professor at Pratt Institute,

and codirects Crisis Fronts, a research initiative, with Michael Chen.

Jay Forster is in the fields of graphic design and event production. Jay has developed a host of self-initiated projects that focus on underdeveloped forms of expression. These include magazine production, underground music events, Clockenflap Multimedia Arts and Music Festival, and various exhibitions in favor of urban and cultural preservation.

Jeffrey Johnson is founding director of China Lab an experimental research unit at the Graduate School of Architecture, Planning and Preservation at Columbia University, where he also teaches. He is a cofounding principal of SLAB architecture based in New York City. Jeffrey's previously worked at OMA in Rotterdam and New York. His research focuses on China's rapid urbanization over the past 30 years that include research on China's large-scale superblock development.

John Batten comments, broadcasts, and writes on art, culture, heritage, and policy issues for Hong Kong newspapers and overseas magazines and regularly writes art reviews for Hong Kong's South China Morning Post. He has lived in Hong Kong since 1992 and ran his own gallery since 1997. He is the Organizer of the yearly charity art event, Hong Kong ArtWalk. He is a member of the International Art Critics' Association and coeditor of their web-magazine Art Forum. He is also an advisor to the non-profit 1a space at the Cattle Depot Artists' Village in Hong Kong; member of the Editorial Advisory Board of Australian Broadsheet magazine; and a contributing editor for the Asian Literary Review.

Joshua Bolchover is an urban researcher, academic and architectural designer. He is currently Assistant Professor at the University of Hong Kong and is designing buildings in rural China. He has exhibited his work, Rural Urban Ecology, at the Venice Biennale 2010, and Utopia Now: Opening the Closed Area at the Venice Biennale 2008. He has curated, designed, and contributed to several international exhibitions including Get it Louder; Airspace: What Skyline Does London Want; Hydan; Can Buildings Curate; and has exhibited at the HK-SZ Biennale. Joshua was a local curator for the Manchester-Liverpool section of Shrinking Cities between 2003 and 2005. He was educated at Cambridge University and at the Bartlett School of Architecture.

K K Ling is the immediate past president of The Hong Kong Institute of Planners.

K S Wong, an architect with over twenty years of architectural practice and recognized by both local and international awards, is director of Ronald Lu & Partners and leads the in-house Sustainability Steering Committee. His current projects range from building design, master planning, urban regeneration to research studies, and include the first zero carbon building in Hong Kong. He also served as the Professional

Green Building council chairman and HKIA vice president in 2009-2010. He currently chairs the Green Labelling Committee of the Hong Kong Green Building Council.

Kacey Wong is a contemporary visual artist using sculpture and installation art to explore architecture and the poetics of space. Kacey was born in Hong Kong in 1970, and studied architecture at Cornell University, received a Master of Fine Arts from Chelsea School of Art and Design, and his PhD in Fine Arts from the Royal Melbourne Institute of Technology. He is now an Assistant Professor at the Hong Kong Polytechnic University. Kacey received the Rising Artist Award and the Outstanding Arts Education Award given by the Hong Kong Arts Development Council in 2003 and has curated many exhibitions exploring issues of space and city.

Kai Yin Lo is a scholar of Chinese culture and a recipient of the Hong Kong Design Centre's prestigious award, World's Leading Chinese Designer 2007. Her latest book, *House Home Family: Living and Being Chinese* was named as one of Fifteen Great Books for Understanding China by the Association of Museum Curators, USA.

Kathy Ng is the Head of Greening and Landscape Office and Tree Management Section of the Development Bureau of Hong Kong. She received her education in geography, landscape architecture, project and business management from universities in Hong Kong and the UK. Kathy is a registered landscape architect in Hong Kong, a UK Chartered Landscape Architect, a Certified Arborist, a proctor of the International Society of Arboriculture, the Chair of the Architectural Services Department Landscape Architects Association, and a director of the Professional Green Building Council.

Katty Law is a neighborhood activist, convenor of the Central and Western Concern Group and convenor of the Government Hill Concern Group. As a resident of Central District for 40 years, she is passionate in working for better urban planning and heritage conservation in Central, Hong Kong's most historic neighborhood. Her latest project involves campaigning against the government's sale of part of Government Hill.

Kingsley Ng is a multimedia artist who has exhibited his works internationally and has received numerous awards for his achievements. His work reflects a profound interest for the type of interaction which connects art with the community.

Lam Chiu Ying is a Hong Kong meteorologist, bird-watcher, environmental activist, and blogger. He was the director of the Hong Kong Observatory from 2003 to 2009. He is an honorary Fellow of the Royal Meteorological Society of the United Kingdom and the honorary president of the Hong Kong Bird Watching Society.

Laurence Liauw is an architect and academic in Hong Kong currently teaching at the University of Hong Kong as an Associate Professor. He has practiced in the UK, Malaysia, and China after graduating from the Architectural Association in London. His interest is in contemporary Chinese urbanism, typological variation, and post generic cities. He has published in Architectural Record, A+U, Domus, and AA Files, as well as served as the guest editor of AD: New Urban China. His past research, produced with the BBC, examined the rapid urbanization of the Pearl River Delta in 1997. Laurence has exhibited in the 2006 Venice Biennale, 2007 Shenzhen Hong Kong Bi-City Biennale, the 2008 New York Skyscraper Museum, and the 2009 Rotterdam Biennale.

Liu Xiaodu is the founding partner of URBANUS, one of the leading architecture firms in China. Born in Beijing, Xiaodu is a member of the 2009 Shenzhen Hong Kong Bi City Biennale Academic Committee. He received his Bachelor of Architecture from Tsinghua University and Master of Architecture from Miami University. Xiaodu has taught in Tsinghua University and worked in US design firms as a project architect. He has been invited to lecture by both domestic and international academic institutions.

Mathias Woo is the executive director and co-artistic director of Zuni Icosahedron, a Hong Kong arts organization. Mathias engages in theatre and multi media creative works, architectural designs, and is well versed in cultural policies and arts education. He was appointed by the government of the HKSAR as a member of the Public Service Broadcasting Review Committee, a member of the Advisory Groups (Performing Arts and Tourism) of the Consultative Committee on the Core Arts and Cultural Facilities of the West Kowloon Cultural District. In 2009 he was appointed as a member of the Task Force on Economic Challenges by the Chief Executive of Hong Kong.

Michael Chen is an architect and academic based in New York City. He is a partner in Normal Projects, a collaborative design practice encompassing architecture, product and furniture design based in New York and Los Angeles. He is currently Visiting Assistant Professor at Pratt Institute School of Architecture and codirects Crisis Fronts, a research initiative, with Jason J. Lee.

Michael Ng is a partner of Foster + Partners Hong Kong and has worked extensively in Hong Kong, Asia, and Europe. He studied architecture at the Architectural Association in London and at the University of Cambridge, and joined Foster + Partners upon graduation. In 1990 Michael returned to Hong Kong where he established an architectural consultancy and became Visiting Professor and Lecturer at the Chinese University of Hong Kong and the University of Hong Kong. Since rejoining Foster + Partners in 2006, he has coordinated many high profile projects in Hong Kong, Shanghai, and Beijing.

Patrick Sau Shing Lau is Justice of Peace, an architect, Hong Kong LegCo member, and Fellow member and past president of the Hong Kong Institute of Architects. He was the Head of the Department of Architecture at the University of Hong Kong and Honorary Professor of Architecture. He serves as a member of the Housing Authority, founding director of the Hong Kong Architecture Centre, founding chairman of the Professional Green Building Council, past vice chairman of the Town Planning Board and past member of the Antiquities Advisory Board.

Paul Zimmerman is the executive director for Jebsen Travel, BCD Travel (Greater China) and Pacific Aviation Marketing. Amongst other things, Paul is also the founding member of Designing Hong Kong, an organization aimed at sustainable planning and building a better city.

Peter Cookson Smith is an architect, planner, and urban designer. He has been a resident in Hong Kong since 1977, when he founded Urbis Limited one of the first specialist planning, urban design, and landscape consultancies in South East Asia. The firm has carried out more than 2000 projects in Hong Kong, China, and the Asia Pacific area. He has won more than 100 local and international awards, including the Urban Land Institute's Global Award for Excellence and the American Waterfront Centre's Top Honor Award in 2008. He is the Convener of Hong Kong's Urban Design Alliance and vice president of the Hong Kong Institute of Planners.

Platteen Tsang has been actively involved in organizing cultural tours and social events for members of the general public. Platteen studied architecture, town planning, and construction project management, is a part time graphic novelist, and occasionally acts as a cultural tour guide

Puay Peng Ho is Director of the School of Architecture, Professor of Architecture, Honorary Professor of Fine Art of the Chinese University of Hong Kong, and director of the Centre for Architectural Heritage Research. He is a honorary adviser of the Hong Kong Museum of History and the Hong Kong Heritage Museum. He received his Master of Arts and Diploma in Architecture from the University of Edinburgh and a PhD degree in Art and Architectural History from the School of Oriental and African Studies at the University of London. His research and major publications are in Chinese architectural history, vernacular architecture, Buddhist art and architecture, architectural theory, and Chinese art history.

Raymond Cole is Professor of the School of Architecture and Landscape Architecture at the University of British Columbia. Ray has been teaching environmental issues in building design in the Architecture program for the past 30 years. He was co-founder of the Green Building Challenge, an international collaborative effort to benchmark progress in green building performance and environmental assessment. He serves on numerous national and international committees related to buildings and the environment. He is the recipient of the Architectural Institute of British Columbia Barbara Dalrymple Memorial Award for Community Service and the US Green Building Council's Green Public Service Leadership Award. He is currently a director of the Canada Solar Buildings Research Network, a past director of the Canadian Green Building Council, and holds the UBC designation of Distinguished University Scholar.

Raymond Fung is an architect, designer, and painter. Raymond has won the Ten Outstanding Young Persons' Award and the Ten Outstanding Designers' Award, plus 50 major awards in architecture, visual arts, and interior design. He is Adjunct Associate Professor of Architecture at the Chinese University of Hong Kong, board member of the West Kowloon Cultural District Authority, honorary advisor to museums under the Leisure and Cultural Services Department, member of the Advisory Committee on Revitalization of Historic Buildings, and member of the Advisory Committee on the Appearance of Bridges and Associated Structures

Rem Koolhaas founded OMA in 1975 together with Elia and Zoe Zenghelis and Madelon Vriesendorp. He graduated from the Architectural Association in London and in 1978 published *Delirious New York: A Retroactive Manifesto for Manhattan*. He heads both OMA and the research branch AMO, operating in areas beyond the realm of architecture such as media, politics, renewable energy, and fashion. Koolhaas has won several international awards including the Pritzker Architecture Prize in 2000 and the Golden Lion for Lifetime Achievement at the 2010 Venice Biennale. Koolhaas is a Professor at Harvard University where he conducts the Project on the City.

Rocco Yim was born and educated in Hong Kong, and is currently Executive Director of Rocco Design Architects Limited. Since winning a First Prize Award for the Opera de la Bastilla international competition in 1983, his works have consistently been awarded both in Hong Kong and internationally. Rocco is a regular invited speaker to academic institutions and international symposia. He is a director of the Hong Kong Design Centre and Honorary Professor of Architecture at the University of Hong Kong.

Sada Lam is a director of Oval Partnership and is the research director of INTEGER China. Sada graduated from the University of Cambridge and the Chinese University of Hong Kong. At Oval Partnership Sada's projects include the Kunming eco-town, and a number of museums and large scale developments in China.

Stefan Al is a Dutch architect and urban planner. He is the director of the Urban Design Program and Assistant Professor at the Department of Urban Planning and Design at the University of Hong Kong.

Sujata Govada is the managing director of Urban Design & Planning Consultants Limited and teaches part time at the Chinese University of

Hong Kong and the University of Hong Kong. Sujata has been an AIA member since 1992 and a member of the Hong Kong chapter since 2002. As urban design committee chair since 2007, she organized symposia and community charrettes to raise member and public awareness on critical urban issues. She is an award winning designer and certified professional urban planner with over 24 years of international experience in Hong Kong, PRC, India, and USA.

Sylvester Wong is a LEED AP and certified planner of the American Institute of Certified Planners. He is the design leader of the global urban studio at Woods Bagot, Hong Kong. His interest lies in enabling communities to responsibly use land and water to protect resources and heritage. The focus of his team is sustainable development, mixed-use, waterfronts, cultural and natural heritage, regional planning, policy, transport and aviation. He holds a Bachelor of Arts in Architecture and a Master of City Planning from the University of California, Berkeley.

Syren Johnstone has been involved in the relationship between art and society through several paths, including theatre, film, and working with a variety of performers including the Hong Kong Ballet and Cirque du Soleil. He is an Honorary Fellow at the University of Hong Kong.

Tao Zhu is Assistant Professor of Architecture at the University of Hong Kong, a PhD candidate in Architecture History and Theory at Columbia University, and a co-founder of the design firm ZL Architecture. He received his Bachelor of Engineering in Architecture at Chongqing Architecture and Engineering Institute in 1990, a Master of Architecture at Columbia University in 2001, and a Master of Philosophy in Architecture History and Theory at Columbia University in 2007. While actively practicing in China, he writes extensively on contemporary Chinese architecture and urbanism.

Thomas Traxler and Katharina Mischler are founding partners of mischer'traxler based in Vienna, Austria. Since finishing the Masters programe for Conceptual Design in Context at the Eindhoven Design Academy in Netherlands, mischer'traxler have been jointly developing and creating products, furniture, and exhibitions, with the main focus on experimentation and conceptualization. Their projects are shown at international exhibitions, art, and design festivals. Their shelf called Limited Fungi is part of the Droog collection and their project The Idea of a Tree won a honorary mention at Prix Ars Electronica, the DMY Award 2009, and the Austrian Experimental Design Award.

Tom Verebes is the creative director of OCEAN.CN, a Hong Kong based design consultancy network. He co founded the OCEAN design network in 1995, subsequently directing OCEAN UK within OCEAN D. Tom is Associate Professor of Architecture at the University of Hong Kong. Formerly he was the codirector of the Design Research Lab at the Architectural Association,

where he has taught for a decade. Tom worked in the offices of Rick Mather, Munkenbeck+Marshall, and Stanton-Williams. Tom studied architecture at McGill University, LoPSiA in France, and the Architectural Association in London.

Trevor Ng is a sustainable building design consultant of Ove Arup and Partners and a member of the Sustainable Design Team of Arup.

Valerie Doran is an independent art curator based in Hong Kong. Valerie is also an art critic and translator specializing in the field of Chinese art, with a special interest in cross-cultural currents and comparative art theory.

Vincent Cheng is director of Building Sustainability at Ove Arup & Partners Hong Kong and the leader of the Building Sustainability Group in East Asia. Vincent is an industry-known expert, specializing in green code formulation, LEED certification, life-cycle analysis, and green technology applications. He has extensive experience in designing and managing large-scale sustainable master planning and infrastructure projects and is involved in the design of Zero Carbon Buildings in China, Hong Kong, and Korea. He is a council member of the Hong Kong Professional Green Building Council.

Weijen Wang is Associate Professor of Architecture at the University of Hong Kong. He received his Masters of Architecture from Berkeley, as well as degrees from Taiwan University. Weijen has won several AIA Design Awards, the Far Eastern Architectural Award, and HKIA awards. He has exhibited at the Venice Architecture Biennale of 2008, Beijing Architecture Biennale, Taipei Museum of Modern Art, Shenzhen Biennale of Architecture and Urbanism, as well as the Hong Kong Biennale of Architecture and Urbanism. He was the lead curator of the 2007 Hong Kong & Shenzhen Bi-City Biennale of Architecture/Urbanism and his research mainly focuses on Chinese architecture and cities.

William Lim is a Hong Kong architect and visual artist. William is the founder and managing director of the design firm CL3 Architects with studios in Hong Kong, Beijing, and Shanghai. They specialize in architecture, installation, hospitality, corporate retail, and interior design works. William graduated from Cornell University with Bachelor and Master Degrees in Architecture. He worked in Boston for five years before returning to Hong Kong in 1987. William has a great passion for art, especially Chinese artifacts and contemporary art, and his works are mixed with Asian elements. Recent projects involve traditional Chinese craftsmanship, such as one which utilized bamboo scaffolding shown at the Venice Architecture Biennale in 2006.

William Y Yiu is the former executive director of charities at the Hong Kong Jockey Club. He joined the Jockey Club in 2001 and was responsible for its portfolio of charitable projects until 2010. Previously, William was